THE CASE FOR UFO CRASHES

FROM URBAN LEGEND TO REALITY

Timothy Green Beckley

THE CASE FOR UFO CRASH SECRETS
From Urban Legend To Reality

Timothy Green Beckley

With Sean Casteel

This edition greatly expanded and © 2003 and revised and copyrighted 2013 by Timothy Green Beckley. All Rights Reserved.

ISBN 13: 9781606111505
ISBN: 1606111507

GLOBAL COMMUNICATIONS

P. O. Box 753

New Brunswick, NJ 08903

Copyright@ 1981, 1983, 1985, 1988, 1989, 2003 and 2013

by Timothy Green Beckley.

Early pen and ink illustrations by Carol Ann Rodriguez

Portions of this book appeared in slightly different form in issues of the newspaper-magazine UFO REVIEW. The author acknowledges the kind assistance of those many individuals who have made this book possible and hopefully has properly credited these researchers throughout the pages of this book.

PUBLISHER'S NOTE: Interviews and materials obtained from other researchers do not imply their endorsement of this work, or our personal conclusions regarding these purported government documents.

CONTENTS

WHAT IS HIDDEN IN THE MYSTERIOUS "BLUE ROOM" AT WRIGHT-PATTERSON AIR FORCE BASE?

DOES "HANGAR 18" CONTAIN WRECKAGE OF A CRASHED UFO AND PRESERVED BODIES OF ALIENS FROM OUTER SPACE?

Access has been denied for over 50 years to even the likes of the late Senator Barry Goldwater, who has said: *"I have never gained access to the so-called Blue Room at Wright-Patterson, so I have no idea what is in it. I have no idea who controls the flow of need-to-know information because, frankly, I was told in such an emphatic way that it was none of my business that I've never tried to make it my business since."*

EVERY PRESIDENT SINCE TRUMAN

HAS BEEN PART OF THE "GRAND DECEPTION" –

NOW IS THE TIME TO EXPOSE THE "COSMIC WATERGATE!"

Learn the significance of the MAJESTIC 12 and Presidential Briefing Papers and view previously classified CIA, FBI and State Department documents pertaining to this explosive subject – a subject that calls for high-level Congressional hearings. A possible connection has been uncovered in newly declassified documents sent to researchers by "unknown sources" within the Shadow Government. Is there proof that an organization known as the Interplanetary Phenomena Unit is involved in the recovery of extra-terrestrial spacecraft and their occupants?

OR IS THIS ALL AN URBAN LEGEND?

OR PART OF A DISINFORMATION PROGRAM?

Here are dozens of unpublished Crashed Saucer stories uncovered by the author including . . .

* The night a UFO came crashing down over an Ohio shopping mall.

* A bizarre tale of an "alien artifact" uncovered by a jogger and displayed in the lobby of a Florida movie theater before it was mysteriously removed and vanished completely.

* An unbelievable eye witness account of a UFO that fell inside New York City's bustling Central Park after being shot at by the military.

* The astounding tale of a UFO pilot who was taken alive from a downed spaceship   while resting at the end of a military runway in New Jersey. The being later died, but not before the incident was witnessed.

* Controversial "alien body" photos of an entity known as "Tomato Man," photos which have never been satisfactorily explained.

* A seemingly documented account of a UFO that came tumbling out of the sky inside the former USSR, an event that was observed by so many that it could not   be satisfactorily hushed up.

* A mysterious professor who seemed to have the "inside track" on a real alien autopsy long before a British movie studio faked a similar happening.

ALSO INCLUDED HERE ARE NUMEROUS DOCUMENTS WHICH APPEAR TO VERIFY THESE ACCOUNTS OF NUTS AND BOLTS SPACE SHIPS FROM OTHER PLANETS.

THIS BOOK MAY CONTAIN THE MOST IMPORTANT WEAPONS OF INFORMATION IN THE ARSENAL OF THOSE WHO ARE NOW DEMANDING DISCLOSURE WORLDWIDE!

Potentially deadly encounter! UFO embeds itself into arcade smack dab behind author Tim Beckley. "Narrow miss, but one has to take changes!" he was heard to comment as he proceeded to take cover. (Photo by Angelia and Sandra Buck, Ole Town, Florida)

CRASHED DISCS – FACT OR FICTION?

It remains one of the most fascinating aspects of UFOlogy.

Have UFOs fallen from the sky and been confiscated by the armed forces or some group whose status is way above Top Secret?

Moreover, have the occupants of these craft – i.e. the aliens! – been taken away either dead or ALIVE???

If so, is this purported wreckage being stored – not to mention crew members who might have been – or still are – kept in either friendly or hostile captivity?

The late Cincinnati researcher Leonard Stringfield filed a half dozen reports on numerous and highly classified occasions in which the military apparently arrived at the scene of one of these crashes and picked up all the wreckage that may have been lying about and rode off into the sunset to an unknown destination.

Of all these cases, of course, the crash outside of Roswell, New Mexico, in July of 1947, is the tale that has been told – in various ways – many, many times. The government has proclaimed the crash a product of a downed weather (later changed to Mogul) balloon struck by lightning. The witnesses, including Jesse Marcel Sr., attest to the "fact" that they handled pieces of something not manufactured on this Earth.

The incident at Roswell has become part of a large cottage industry including books, T-shirts, a TV series, a Showtime special, annual parades and concerts, and even a museum in the center of town.

The late Colonel Philip Corso's *"The Day After Roswell"* made it to the top of the New York Times best seller list with its sensational rumors about bodies strewn across the desert and parts of a destroyed vehicle from outer space that was carted off to various locations to be reverse-engineered. Possibly, some of the large boomerang and triangle-shaped craft that have been seen by thousands over various towns and cities, including Phoenix, have resulted from the government's retrieval efforts, although the question remains, why would we be flying them so openly and in such close proximity to large population areas? That idea is almost as bizarre as the credibility of all those who have supposedly been involved in hushed up UFO crash episodes.

To complicate matters even more is the theoretical existence of a super sensitive organization known as Majestic 12, or MJ-12 for short, which has kept track of such crashes since Roswell and maintains a broader organization whose task it is to quash each and every UFO crash incident and keep the very existence of ET life forms hidden from the unassuming public.

Said to have been formed in 1947, MJ-12 remains a hard core matter of major controversy inside the UFO field itself among some of its most major players. By now, hundreds of supporting documents have been added to the surreptitiously released President Briefing Papers originally signed by President Harry Truman. The FBI claims they are bogus, while such researchers as nuclear physicist Stanton Friedman, Linda Moulton Howe, and the father and son team of James and Ryan Wood maintain that at least some of the papers in their possession are legitimate.

I have followed the subject of UFO crashes and MJ-12 pretty much since their inception. I remain noncommittal about the reality of such crashes or the MJ-12 papers themselves, though I currently lean toward believing that the Majestic papers are part of a disinformation program. But whether or not to believe in such a program is impossible for me to say. Thousands of hours have obviously been put into the creation of these highly official-looking documents.

Personally, I am fascinated by some of the stories I have uncovered myself, which are detailed in the pages of this volume. For example, the story told by Ms. Barbara Hudson about a vehicle she saw in the middle of Central Park after it had been shot at and clipped by the military, as well as the story of the alien glove that seems to have been made for someone with a very tiny hand. Yet there is a printed marking inside the glove (in English no less) that says LARGE. Made for a chimp perhaps? Not so, say the experts, who point out that the thumbs and fingers of the glove are not separated and positioned properly for a primate to wear.

Whether you believe in the reality of crashed UFOs or tend to put them in the category of Urban Legends, I think this book will keep the reader enthralled with tales that are difficult to believe but fascinating and perplexing just the same.

So let us venture forth with an open mind and cast aside our lingering doubts as we speculate and investigate the mystery of the crashed flying saucers.

Timothy Green Beckley

March, 2013

Updated. Originally published as "MJ-12 and the Riddle of Hangar 18."

"First Responder" Tim Beckley arrives at the scene of a mock UFO crash in the middle of Sedona, AZ. No doubt the slightly mangled occupant appreciated Beckley's heroic efforts. (Photo by Charla Gene)

1

CRASHED SAUCERS—A "COSMIC WATERGATE"

"Next call please..." With these words talk show host Jamie Jamison hit one of the blinking lights on the telephone in front of us. The format of the program allowed for listeners to call the station and ask questions of the guest on the air.

The woman's voice boomed over the WDBO loudspeakers so that Jamie and I, as well as his large audience in Orlando, Florida, could hear what was on the minds of those hearing the broadcast throughout thousands of homes in the area.

Many of the listeners not only had questions to ask, but apparently had had a number of experiences themselves. Though it was pushing 1 A.M. and the station was supposed to have signed off an hour ago, Jamie had gotten the okay to stay on the air for an additional while, since the response to my appearance had been so positive.

"I want to tell you something," the female caller started to say, and then there was a short pause. "I've kept quiet about this a long time, and I have been listening to the program and just had to let someone know about an experience that involved my son."

The caller's voice cracked at this point, and it was obvious that she was under a great deal of stress. She seemed hardly able to control her emotions, and it appeared as if she were about to break out in sobs at any moment.

"My son was a patient in a military hospital while in the service." According to the woman, her son had been wandering about the hospital corridors late at night, having had trouble sleeping. "He walked into a room where apparently he wasn't supposed to be," the caller went on, "and there stretched out on a mortuary slab was the charred body of a strange looking creature." The woman was now at the point of near hysteria, unable to restrain herself any longer. It was obvious she was getting ready to hang up. Realizing that the woman wasn't a crackpot or a kook, I tried as best as possible to calm her down. Before she finally did end the

1

conversation, she revealed how her son had been discovered by his superiors wandering around the hospital "where he shouldn't have been." He was told that if he ever told anyone what he'd seen, he would be immediately court martialed and drummed right out of the service. He told only his mother, who would not give us her name, and finally she hung up when she was pressed too closely for additional details.

Rumors have long been circulated to the effect that the U S. Government has in its possession the remains of space ships which have crashed, as well as the bodies of alien beings who died in these mishaps, most of which—but not all—are said to have transpired in the southwestern region of America during the late 1940s and early 1950s. According to these same sources, the crafts were dismantled and taken to several locations. A number of the dead aliens are supposed to have made their way to Wright-Patterson Air Force Base in Dayton, Ohio, where they were put in deep freeze compartments. Security guards were placed around the building—stated by most individuals "in the know" to be Hangar 18— and prevented anyone outside of the highest of military brass from entering the hangar.

Even Senator Barry Goldwater, who was in the Reserves and obviously has many contacts in the government, was refused entry to this specific building. The syndicated radio news broadcast, "Earth News" for Thursday, Oct. 24, 1974, confirmed that a press spokesperson for Senator Goldwater "says that the Senator was once denied permission to the Wright-Patterson Air Force Base's Hangar 18."

The stories, the rumors, and the speculation continues to this day. Over the last few years I have done my best to research these accounts, and have tried to formulate some opinions as to the validity of the crashed saucer and dead alien reports. Are they truth or fiction?

Now with the release of several previously classified government documents (from the CIA, the FBI and the State Department), it becomes quite obvious that Uncle Sam does have some knowledge of such events and may have been trying to pull the wool over our eyes for more than four decades.

As news of these fantastic events leaks out little by little, it appears that more and more individuals are willing to come forward to tell of their involvement in the cover-up of the century. A recently published book, *"THE ROSWELL INCIDENT"* (Charles Berlitz and William Moore) discusses—and documents—only one of what apparently are many such incidents. Even former military personnel are willing to admit that they were instructed to remain silent, and the mysterious pieces of an interplanetary craft were later switched for a wrecked sky-hook balloon when it was time for the military to go before the press.

TIMOTHY GREEN BECKLEY

Many independent sources have confirmed that Hangar 18 hides a dark secret. There are those who maintain that the bodies of the alien beings have been preserved in liquid nitrogen after being examined by top military physicians.

Robert D. Barry has had as extensive career as a news commentator and reporter. He started out in 1957 as a correspondent for the Buffalo Evening News and news director for a radio station in Olean, N.Y. Today his syndicated "UFO Monitor" show is heard in Canada as well as the United States. Barry has spent considerable time and effort to confirm the crashed saucer stories.

Says Robert Barry about one such case he personally investigated: "I have a taped interview with a Civil Air Patrol cadet from Florida who, along with 20 other such cadets, was on special training at Wright-Patterson during 1965. From the outside, they witnessed the famous hangar with the tall wire fence around it... completely around it...and all windows knocked out and replaced with concrete.

"My contact source within CIA/NASA confirmed this, and he should know. He's been inside Hangar 18 on several occasions and is involved currently with a former Project Blue Book counterintelligence man who has spent a lot of time in Hangar 18. My source spent three months there on one occasion. His past work has involved him in crashed craft cases in the U.S. and other countries."

In "**THE CASE FOR UFO CRASH SECRETS**" I'm finally able to lay all my cards upon the table. In addition to my own findings, we've called upon several topnotch UFO researchers and writers to help us uncover what has definitely got to be a "Cosmic Watergate."

COSMIC WATERGATE

It will probably anger you, as it did me, to find out that: Some years ago a disc-shaped flying saucer landed in full view of an Air Force film crew, who took some startling motion picture footage of this historic event. The film was viewed by a commanding officer at the base (a man later to become a highly respected astronaut), who in turn sent the reel on to his superiors in Washington, only to have it vanish like so many planes that fly into the eye of the Bermuda Triangle—mysteriously and without a trace.

There are those of a high rank in the military who swear that our government has long possessed the remains of a spaceship that crashed on Earth, as well as the alien occupants who died on board the craft at the time of the fatal mishap.

Certain NASA officials have admitted "off the record" that they have actually communicated, not by long distance radio signals, but face-to-face, with beings from other planets.

On the surface these may appear to be extravagant claims, but little by little the public—as well as the usually hard-nosed academic community—are beginning to awaken to the fact that everything is not exactly as our appointed officials would have us believe when it comes to unidentified flying objects, known more simply as UFOs.

In recent times an accusing finger has increasingly been pointed in the direction of the U.S. Government for trying to "coverup" a host of sins. There are even those, for example, who insist that the "powers that be" were involved in a conspiracy—perhaps even directed the plans—to assassinate President Kennedy, as well as murder Martin Luther King. Serious charges brought against tax-supported agencies, such as the CIA and FBI, have become rather commonplace since Watergate, with more and more people seemingly losing faith in our country's appointed leadership, and subscribing to the theory that the public is not being told what's going on within our own boundaries—and most certainly not on an international scale.

The latest conspiracy making the rounds (one that is gaining in popularity each day) is definitely "further out" than all other coverups, and is positively universal in scope; the contention being that Uncle Sam is hiding the fact that vehicles from other planets have been arriving here on a regular basis over the last four decades, and that aliens from some distant world (or worlds) are on the verge of establishing contact with mankind.

Lee Spiegel, a bearded man in his late thirties, sees himself as the "Woodward and Bernstein" of UFology. For the past several years he has spent out-of-pocket cash trucking back and forth between coasts, trying to pin down anyone who will talk—but shouldn't—on the matter of extraterrestrial voyagers.

"It's been a constant battle to get people in any way connected with the military or government to commit themselves," quotes the ever-energetic New Yorker, who has had a varied career as producer of records, radio talk shows and various TV news specials. "The UFO subject is like a poisonous snake—they don't want to get too near it," he declares. Off the record, Spiegel has been told some absolutely incredible things, "but for the most part, when it comes to making a public statement, their lips remain tightly sealed."

AN ASTRONAUT SPEAKS OUT

One of the few individuals whose prominence is beyond question has, however, over the past few months, dared to open his mouth and challenge the status quo.

Gordon Cooper was one of America's original astronauts. He helped pioneer this country's space exploration efforts when, aboard a tiny space capsule known as Mercury 7, Cooper orbited the earth for 34 hours, proving that man could live outside our atmosphere for prolonged periods. His patriotism, bravery and respectability go without saying. Until his death, Cooper was privately employed as vice President of Research and Development for Walter E. Disney Enterprises, and made several public pronouncements concerning his strong belief in UFOs. While a guest on the Merv Griffin Show, Cooper shocked the viewing audience by speaking for over five minutes on a topic that was only within the past few years often considered too bizarre for polite conversation.

But there were some things that Cooper wouldn't even discuss on the air in front of the curious multitudes.

Mercury/Gemini astronaut Leroy Gordon Cooper was one of the few to make positive public statements about the existence of UFOs. He believed that the crashed saucer theory was worthy of serious study. Some years before his death at age 77, October 4th 2004, in Ventura, California, he even addressed the United Nations on the UFO topic.

Luckily Lee Spiegel was a personal friend of Gordon Cooper. They conferred on several occasions, and while in the company of the man who is bound and determined to crack the "Cosmic Watergate" which he is convinced exists within the higher echelon of government, the former space traveler is more than happy to talk about his UFO experiences—and they are many.

In the early 1950s, Cooper was assigned to a jet fighter group in Germany. While stationed there, he remembers very vividly the week an entire formation of circular objects passed over the Air Base on almost a daily routine.

"'The first day, a weatherman spotted some strange objects flying at high altitude and, before long, the entire fighter group was out looking at these groups of objects coming over," Cooper recalls, telling details of what was to turn out to be an eye-opening episode for him. "But, unlike jet fighters, they would stop in their forward velocity and change 90-degrees, sometimes in the middle of their flight path."

THE CASE FOR UFO CRASH SECRETS — From Urban Legend To Reality

Within the next few days, Cooper and his men were climbing higher and higher in their jets, trying in vain to get close to these strange, other-worldly craft.

"We never could get close enough to pin them down, but they were round in shape and very metallic looking," Cooper points out. UFOs were to continue to haunt him when the Air Force Colonel was transferred several years later to Edwards Air Force Base Flight Test Center in the California desert. What happened one afternoon while he was on duty at this military base is evidence enough that the government definitely does keep a hell of a lot of secrets when it comes to UFOs!

The incident took place in the late 1950s, either 1957 or 1958 as Cooper can best recall, and, to this day, the photographic evidence of an actual UFO touching down upon the earth is being kept under wraps.

During this period, Cooper was a Project Manager at Edwards Air Force Base, just three or four years before entering America's space program. After lunch this particular day, Cooper had assigned a team of photographers to an area of the vast dry lake beds near Edwards.

In a taped interview with UFOlogist Lee Spiegel, the former Astronaut disclosed that while the crew was out there, they spotted a strange-looking craft above the lake bed, and they began taking films of it. Cooper says the object was very definitely "hovering above the ground. And then it slowly came down and sat on the lake bed for a few minutes." All during this time the motion picture cameras were filming away.

"There were varied estimates by the cameramen on what the actual size of the object was," Cooper confesses, "but they all agreed that it was at least the size of a vehicle that would carry normal-sized people in it."

Col. Cooper was not fortunate enough to be outside at the time of this incredible encounter, but he did see the films as soon as they were rushed through the development process.

"It was a typical circular-shaped UFO," he recollects. "Not too many people saw it, because it took off at quite a sharp angle and just climbed straight on out of sight!"

Cooper admits he didn't take any kind of poll to determine who had seen the craft, "because there were always strange things flying around in the air over Edwards." This is a statement Lee Spiegel was able to verify through his own research efforts, having obtained closely guarded tapes of conversations between military pilots circling the base and their commanding officers in the flight tower, tracking the presence of unknown objects.

"People just didn't ask a lot of questions about things they saw and couldn't understand," notes Cooper, who adds that it was a lot simpler to look the other way, shrug one's shoulders, and chalk up what had been seen to "just another experimental aircraft that must have been developed at another area of the air base."

But what about the photographic proof—the motion picture footage—that was taken? "I think it was definitely a UFO," Cooper states, as he makes no bones about it. "However, where it (the object) came from and who was in it is hard to determine, because it didn't stay around long enough to discuss the matter—there wasn't even time to send out a welcoming committee!"

After he had reviewed the film at least a dozen times, the footage was quickly forwarded to Washington. Cooper no doubt expected to get a reply in a few weeks' time as to what his men had seen and photographed, but there was no word, and the movie vanished—never to surface again.

"I'm sure that there's a great deal of information up in Washington if only somebody could just find it," Cooper so diplomatically puts it, offering his theory that "I don't think a great deal of UFO information was ever classified. As a rule, if you really want to keep something a secret, you don't classify it! I'm sure that a lot of that stuff was probably just thrown into a file someplace in Washington and forgotten. I'm certain that there are roomfuls of such films that have things in them that people don't even know about. As soon as you classify something, every Congressman in the U.S. tries to get a hold of it, and broadcasts it all over the country. Our classification system isn't always the best way to keep something a secret."

On coast-to-coast television, Cooper once made a blockbuster statement that had the telephone lines tied up the next day, as viewers telephoned the stations which carry the syndicated Merv Griffin Show, anxious to find out if their ears had been playing tricks on them the night before.

Toward the end of the talk show host's interview with the former astronaut, Merv broke into a secretive tone of voice right on the air, and aimed a hundred thousand dollar question at his guest: "There is a story going around, Gordon, that a spaceship did land in middle America and there were occupants, and members of our government were able to keep one of the occupants alive for a period of time. They've seen the metal of the aircraft and they know what the people look like—is that a credible story?"

For all intents and purposes Cooper should have laughed, for assuredly such a speculative story belongs in the category of science fiction or space fantasy. But Gordon Cooper kept a straight face when he replied: "I think it's fairly credible. I would like to see the time when all qualified people could really work together to

7

properly investigate these stories and either refute or prove them."

The bombshell had been dropped. Cooper went on to say that from the various reports of UFO contacts and abductions he had been privy to, he was convinced that the occupants of this crashed UFO were "probably not that different from what we are," that they are almost totally humanoid (i.e., have two arms, two legs, a torso and readily identifiable facial features) in appearance.

Taken aback by what Cooper had said over the national airwaves, Lee Spiegel telephoned Cooper's office the following morning and managed to get past his private secretary, though others in the media were getting the cold shoulder.

"Cooper admitted to me that he could have revealed more on the air, but he decided not to play his entire hand because he felt certain that some 'official eyebrows were going to get raised."

OTHER EVIDENCE

In actuality, Cooper is not the first person to confirm that parts of a crashed UFO, as well as the remains of its crew are being kept under lock and key at some top-secret military installation. For several decades rumors have circulated that the top brass in the Pentagon have had their asses collectively parked on their hands, not willing to release any of the data that remains in their possession. Slowly but surely the truth is being exposed to the light of day, as dedicated individuals try to rip aside the veil of secrecy surrounding these highly classified reports.

Movie producer Peter Kares says he first heard the stories when he was in California several years back looking for new properties to film. And while he was unable to track down the rumors at the time, since then he has, as head of Scotia American Productions, established contact with several individuals "who have a reputation for being solid types with military backgrounds," who have willingly verified these reports for him, as long as they were able to remain anonymous.

"One of my contacts is an ex-Air Force pilot," Kares states. "He was there at the scene when the UFO was carted away. Later he was harassed, sent to a psychiatrist and nearly drummed out of the service, because he refused to sign a pledge that he would never talk about what he had inadvertently seen." The highly articulate producer hopes to eventually film a dramatized version of what he has learned, and believes the government definitely likes to "play games" when it comes to UFOs. "We were even able to get to talk with a full colonel who claims he saw with his own eyes a UFO that was being kept in storage," Kares continued. "We know for a fact that the government isn't being entirely truthful. In one case we investigated, motion picture footage was taken of several UFOs traveling along at speeds upwards of 10,000 miles per hour. The film was actually taken at a missile tracking range in the Southwest, with the most sophisticated equipment available at the time. It showed these disc-shaped devices streaking along at 16,000 feet." An analysis by the Cambridge Research Laboratory showed that they were at least twenty feet in diameter. The government denied that such a film even existed, until we were able to show them a copy of the shipping receipt showing that the film had been returned to them by Cambridge. Then they said it was sent to the National Archives. In Washington we were told that they never had such a film, that it was probably sent to a warehouse outside of Baltimore where eventually all military property that no one has any use for anymore is sent before it is finally destroyed.

It is Kares' belief that this warehouse probably contains much physical hardware. "We've been invited to go through the building which is the size of a giant airport hangar, but nothing is catalogued, and there's no way to tell where anything is."

It is also the producer's feeling that 'technological information gleaned from this crashed UFO was used in our own space program,' and that the reason all this is so hush-hush is "because the government thinks that they are withholding information for the good of the public so that people won't panic in the streets. Even the top brass admit that they don't know how to deal with the situation."

AN EXTENSIVE ACCOUNT

There are others who seem to have a good inkling of the situation. Charles Wilhelm, executive director of the highly respected Ohio UFO Investigators League, said he recently conversed with a radar electronics expert who was in the Army in the mid 1950s and who claims he was flown to Ft. Monmouth, New Jersey, to observe a special film. As Wilhelm recounted the story:

His [the electronics expert] job was to analyze from the film anything that he could define from his experience in radar technology. After arriving at the base, he was escorted to a guarded building where the film was going to be shown. There were already nine others present, plus a major who was setting up the projector. Before the film was shown, all those in attendance were told to take notes and when the film was over, never to discuss what they had seen with each other or with anybody else. He even signed papers to that effect afterwards,

The film started out showing a strange, disc-shaped object with two guards, one on each side of the craft. The ship was sitting on two large blocks, and the technician estimated the craft to be 15 to 18 feet in diameter. Its surface was smooth, except for some tool marks around the door entrance. A ramp extended to the ground. The UFO was either silver or light gray in color.

Next the interior of the craft was slowly shown. There were no meters, radar screens, buttons, or windows of any kind. The only things he was able to see were some type of levers that looked like sticks. The interior was decorated with light pastel colors.

Then the camera panned outside and off to the right. According to Wilhelm's informant, "There was a table with three small bodies laid out. The film showed the bodies up close for about five minutes. They were approximately five feet tall. Their heads were larger than ours, their fingers were longer than a human's, their noses were sharper, ears longer, their eyes were closed but looked oriental, and their body color was ash-looking. They were dressed alike in uniforms of yellow with black trimming. Their skin looked quite wrinkled, as if they were very old.

The Ohio UFO researcher maintains that the man who told him this story was being sincere. "He wasn't making anything up—he had no reason to. He wasn't looking to profit in anyway from this story; it was just something you could tell he wanted to get off his chest after all these years. He said the people at the screening had many questions, but when the film was over the major wouldn't discuss what they had seen any further, except to say that the craft was found in New Mexico. The Army technician concluded that the technology of the people who built this craft was at least 1,000 years more advanced than our own primitive propulsion system.

NASA KNOWS!

In an interview in the National Enquirer, astronaut Gordon Cooper revealed that there are those connected with our space agency—NASA—who "have had contact with the creatures on board UFOs," apparently right here on earth.

Researcher Robert Barry confirmed this when he wrote an article *"The Surviving Aliens"* for the UFO Review. In this exclusive story he reveals how a space agency official told him "off the record" that the U.S. Government has tried on several occasions to communicate with UFOnauts who were alive when removed from the wreckage of flying saucers.

Another veteran investigator, Ricky Hilberg, of the Northern Ohio UFO Group recently met a NASA employee who let his guard down and disclosed some startling information about NASA's secret involvement with UFO's. Tending to confirm what astronaut Cooper will only hint at, Hilberg quotes:

Several weeks ago I received a call at the Report Center from a man I'll call Jerry. Jerry had seen our listing in the phone book, and wanted to talk to someone about things that had been bothering him for a long time. He claims he has been receiving impressions or something that someone connected with UFOs might be trying to make mental contact with him. This has led Jerry, a man in his late twenties to early thirties, to purchase a van and begin to fill it with various electronic instruments in an effort to go to places where UFOs are being seen and make contact with them.

Well, after hearing this I was ready to politely end the phone conversation, thinking that he was either someone pulling my leg or else a little on the strange side. I changed my mind, however, when I learned that Jerry was an engineer at NASA's Lewis Research Center!

The equipment for his van, he explained to me, he was able to purchase from NASA as surplus for literally pennies on the dollar. Jerry also said that while there were several others with an interest in UFOs at Lewis, he was interested in making contact with an organized UFO group that might supply him with some volunteers for his UFO contact project.

I told him about our group, and also mentioned to him some of what I knew relating to other such attempts at making contact with the UFOs. I briefly ran through the John Otto story from the 1950s, the work done in Ohio by a group known as NSAPRO back in the 1960s and what Project Starlight International in Texas was doing at the present time.

It was at about this point in our conversation that I asked him what the official NASA position was regarding UFOs. He seemed to hesitate for a moment, and then said: 'NASA has been looking into the UFO thing for a long time. There's a lot going on that even people with access to some of the really secret stuff can't get the whole story on. But I do know one thing—that NASA has at least one UFO in its possession, and has been able to find out a lot about them.'

I asked Jerry if he was really sure about this, and related to him the many similar stories that have come up recently, and how they always seem to lead to dead ends when investigators try to substantiate them.

Jerry's response was 'No, I'm sure about this. I've talked with too many people who've had something to do with this business for it all to be some sort of crap. There's even talk going around that NASA is selectively leaking word on UFOs out to the public; and that sometime in the near future some kind of announcement on UFOs will be made. I've heard this same thing from more and more people around here lately.'

This really had me going and I asked Jerry if there was any soft of documentation to all this that he might produce to lend credence to his claims, but he told me that all the leaks on the NASA UFO project were verbal in nature, and that no documents had ever filtered down on the subject.

CONFIRMATION FROM THE ACADEMIC COMMUNITY

Retired Prof. Robert Carr of the University of South Florida was living in southern New Mexico when a UFO crashed near Aztec, New Mexico in 1948. Prof. Carr, through high level academic contacts, insists that the military recovered the bodies of 12 crew members who died during a decompression accident. Carr says that autopsies were performed on the humanlike beings. He maintains that the aliens were from 3 to 4 feet tall, had yellow to whitish short hair, and were whitish-tan in color with blue eyes. Although Prof. Carr is reluctant to discuss these matters with those he feels are not open-minded enough to seriously consider his claims, he has struck up a close personal friendship with UFO investigator Gray Barker who has spoken to Carr on many occasions.

Prof. Carr recently told Barker how his initial interest was piqued: "The first confirmation I got was from a biologist who (this was already in 1952 and the autopsy had already been performed) had a biological section of a larger report which had been torn out forcibly from the binding with jagged edges. It was a carbon copy—they didn't make Xeroxes in those days. At that time I was the public relations director for a scientific research foundation at Fort Meyers Beach, and we would have visiting scientists from all over the nation. This was the James Foundation, headed by the distinguished scientist, Dr. Robert L. James.

"He had the official report, although he had not been present at the autopsy. But he had been allowed to see the report and he simply tore the biological section out. He wasn't interested in anything else-for example, aeronautical engineering. To my great sorrow, he didn't take the whole report! That would have been priceless. It no doubt still exists."

Carr further states that the UFO alien bodies were removed from the first crash and were taken under guard to Muroc Dry Lake (later called Edwards Air Force Base) in the California desert. From there they made their way to Hangar 18 at Wright-Patterson.

"By the time the remains went up to Wright-Patterson they went into deep-freeze. They didn't have the preservation facilities at Muroc and the temperatures were too high; and besides, the security wasn't good."

According to the information Prof. Carr has gathered, the beings found on board the crashed UFOs are very much human and not monsters like you might see in a science fiction movie.

"They have Type "0" blood. They could give you or me a transfusion tonight! The organs were all in the right places. The occupant was in excellent health. The only physical characteristic which produced shock and amazement was when the brain surgeon cut open the skull and looked at the brain. Now the head was a little bit large for the body. He was just a little bit megacephalic. But after all, we see megacephalic little people ourselves.

Many little people have heads a little too big. If these occupants were given children's clothing, they could pass undetected on the streets of any large city like New York. Maybe they would be noticed in a small town where everybody knows everybody else, but in New York they wouldn't draw a passing glance.

"Well, when they opened the skull they found themselves looking at the brain of a man several hundred years old! Yet he appeared to be a vigorous young man which we, in human terms, would estimate to be between 20 and 30. An Olympic athlete, only small. "But the brain! The brain of Charles Darwin is preserved in the British Medical Museum in London. It is the most deeply convoluted brain known (the brains of idiots are smooth). The brain of the alien was more deeply convoluted than any brain they had ever seen and the entire staff bent down to see it and drew back with a shock of amazement. Their life spans must be longer than ours. That's how they can achieve interstellar travel."

A COMMERCIAL PILOT TELLS HIS STORY

Perhaps one of the most fascinating stories related to UFO crashes is told by a former commercial airlines pilot, who, himself, had a near brush with an extraterrestrial craft almost three decades ago. Retired Pan American pilot William B. Nash remembers the hours of intensive grilling the Air Force put him through following his July 14, 1952 sighting of six orange-red discs that glowed like "hot metal." Nash and co-pilot, William Fortenberry were above Norfolk, Virginia when they saw parading 2,000 feet below them, a half-dozen unidentified craft, each over 100 feet in diameter. They were performing aerial acrobatics, which included making sharp 90-degree right-angle turns, and stopping on a dime— performances that would have crushed any human being on board.

According to Nash, (who still insists that what he saw 25 years back were interplanetary craft piloted by super intelligent beings), during the cross-examination he and his co-pilot were put into separate rooms and individually grilled to see how closely their stories agreed.

"Before the interview," Nash explains, "both Fortenberry and I agreed to ask the Air Force men if there was any truth behind the rumor that the Air Force had one or more crashed saucers. Bill remembered to ask, and one of the investigators told him, 'Yes, it is true!' Nash regrets to this day that he forgot to ask the same question, but later on, when he brought up the question in the presence of a Major and several other officers, before any of the other men could speak, the Major answered with a loud "NO!"

To Nash it appeared as though the Major was telling his men to shut up, rather than answering the question specifically put to him. Nash, like so many others, is positive the military is withholding a great deal of information and he is very upset about it. "What right," he asks, "does the Air Force have to put our civilization behind the times by keeping it in ignorance? It's too big an issue, and it belongs to the world, not the Air Force alone!"

There are so many reports of crashed saucers that we can no longer ignore them; to do so would be unscientific and could well prevent us from taking giant leaps forward in our own technological development and advancement. Researcher Len Stringfield has compiled over 20 UFO crash cases which he says he has tried to carefully check out and document. Perhaps those reading this, who have been in the military will be able to verify much of what has been written.

As Gordon Cooper has said without any sign of hesitation, "UFOs are, I believe, very likely travelers from some other planet; visitors from some other world that is hundreds of thousands of years more advanced than we are, and they certainly have a far more efficient system of propulsion than we have."

His only regret is the fact that the UFO which landed at Edwards Air Force Base while he was stationed there didn't "stay on the ground long enough for us to make contact with it."

As Cooper so aptly puts it, "It comes down to the same old thing—we need to find a friendly one who's not afraid of us, and who's willing to interchange information."

But how can that ever happen when our own government tells us such things as UFOs just don't exist?

2

INSIDE THE FLYING SAUCERS

"I first became interested in UFOs after reading an item in Dorothy Kilgallen's column pertaining to the crash of a flying saucer in Mexico in 1948. Due to my scientific background and my friendship with Einstein, I was naturally skeptical, but the fact that this report had been carried in a serious tone in her nationally syndicated feature opened my mind to the intriguing possibility that our planet was being surveyed by extraterrestrial intelligence."

Harold Salkin is one of the few remaining pioneers still active in UFO research. "Around 1950 I started subscribing to every newsletter and publication, both here and abroad, which pertained to this fascinating topic." A former correspondent for the Associated Press, Salkin went to work for publisher Lyle Stuart and seriously considered doing a book that would expose the truth about UFOs. Although never completed, Salkin later penned a most definitive piece for the then prestigious *Argosy* magazine in collaboration with Major Donald E. Keyhoe on government secrecy.

Taking up residence in the nation's capital, Salkin met the retired Marine Major and became one of the charter organizers of the National Investigations Committee on Aerial Phenomena. Later, feeling that NICAP was limited in scope, content to investigate reports of lights in the sky, Salkin joined forces with Clara John, a well-known researcher into all aspects of the paranormal, and together, published for many years a scientific newsletter called the *Little Listening Post*. This publication was aimed primarily at the media, providing capital correspondents with important UFO-oriented data.

Among his credits, Salkin collaborated with Albert Johnson of the *Voice of America* in producing a serious documentary on UFOs that was broadcast worldwide to three hundred million listeners. He also contributed to such books as *"UFOs—Top Secret"* by journalist Mort Young, and is the only full-time publicist who has specialized in putting the press in touch with important figures in the field during peak flap periods.

Currently he is Managing Editor of *UFO Review* and General Manager of the New York based public relations firm, World Media Group.

THE FBI LETTERS

In the spring of 1950, three years after the start of what has been called the "modern flying saucer era," the well-known and highly respected publishing firm of Henry Holt and Company (New York, N.Y.) brought forth a smallish hard-cover book which shook up the American literary scene with tremors that have not ceased to be felt even in 1981.

Written by a man who was not among the foremost authors of the time, it nonetheless attracted a huge audience by virtue of its material—it purported to give the first look into the government's handling of several ships of unknown origin which had allegedly landed in the Southwest portion of the United States.

Through the Freedom of Information Act, two startling documents written on official stationery seem to testify to the legitimacy of the information published in a highly controversial book titled *"Behind the Flying Saucers,"* by the late Frank Scully. Long pooh-poohed by conservative elements in UFOlogy as being a fanciful tale, as it turns out the volume was the subject of inter-office communiques between the head of the FBI and several special agent chiefs. These classified memoranda prove that the U.S. Government was totally aware of the facts laid down in the Scully book and verified that the military indeed did possess wreckage from a crashed UFO as well as the alien occupants of the ship who apparently died entering the earth's atmosphere.

The first memorandum is dated March 22,1950 and was sent by agent Guy Hottel of the Washington division to J. Edgar Hoover. This memo is reproduced in its entirety in the chapter "Crashed Saucers in U.S. Government Documents."

Nine days later, yet another detailed memo was sent to Hoover concerning this same subject. On March 31, 1950 special agent chief of the New Orleans branch, "JML", wrote to the director of the FBI regarding Scully and Dr. G. The letter contains certain names and addresses that have been blanked out in the original text released under the Freedom of Information Act in order to protect certain confidential sources.

OFFICE MEMORANDUM * UNITED STATES GOVERNMENT

To Director, FBI

From SAC, New Orleans

Subject Flying Discs

Special agent—, of the New Orleans Division, has a brother—, of the advertising agency,—, Denver, Colorado. —has advised Special Agent that an employee of the—, has been contacted by one—, Street, telephone—, Denver, Colorado, regarding Flying Discs.

— is alleged to have told in January, 1950, that he,—, knows a prominent Denver oilman named—, also known as "Mysterious Mr. X", and an official of the—, — Denver, Colorado. —is claiming that he leased land in the Mojave Desert in California and that on this land a flying disk had been found intact, with eighteen three-foot tall human-like occupants, all dead in it but not burned. Further, that the disk was alleged to be of very hard metal and near indestructible. — is said to have exhibited a radio set to —, purported to be a souvenir of the space disk.

According to —, — has been telling of the story off and on for the three month period prior to January, 1950, and is said to have notified —of it weeks prior to the publication of a flying disc article published in the *True* magazine, and one by Frank Scully published in the *Variety* magazine in January, 1950. — claimed to have been visited by Donald Keyhoe, author of the article in the *True* magazine.

Further data was furnished that — had been telling the tale so prolifically in Denver that he claims to have had telephone calls from Washington, D.C. and from the Federal Bureau of Investigation in which he was requested to keep the information to himself and that, thereafter, he became mysterious about the entire matter.

It is noted that considerable publicity regarding these discs has been found in Denver and other papers.

This information is being furnished to the Bureau and the designated offices for informational purposes.

AN AMAZING BOOK

Behind the Flying Saucers was written in a straightforward style, which somehow had the unmistakable ring of truth to it. The details were related very carefully, as if the author felt it necessary to be overly meticulous in order to fend off his critics. What's more, all the material contained in the book was to some degree corroborated in later years by subsequent events on the UFO scene.

For example, the theory put forth that the UFOs fly by magnetic propulsion was picked up a half decade later by the French engineer Jean Plantier, who wrote a highly technical book describing in the most complicated mathematical terms exactly how the UFOs propel themselves magnetically. This book was to lead to further studies by the French equivalent of NASA, which gives strong credence to the existence of interplanetary UFO's. And everything in Plantier's book agrees in principle with everything in the book we are about to examine.

How did Frank Scully come to get involved in this subject? After all, he was a nontechnical writer most of his life. When flying saucers hit the headlines in the forties, he was living in Los Angeles, doing Hollywood-type articles for newspapers and magazines, plus an occasional book, and was best known for his urbane column in the show business newspaper, *Variety*, where he wrote under the heading *"Literati,"* covering the world of books, authors, etc.

He got into the saucer scene by virtue of being an old and dear friend of Silas Newton, the millionaire oilman who broke the weird story to the world. If not for this one fortuitous contact, the book would never have been born, and the facts—which are among the most important ever written on this monumental subject—would probably never have reached a mass audience. In this book, Scully attacks the UFO problem with a rapier wit, flailing away at his adversaries (in and out of the Pentagon) like a latter-day D'Artagnan, thrusting his two-edged sword of cynicism and good humor as he cuts down the false facade of governmental denials of flying saucers. Even if one had not the slightest interest in the subject, the book would be a joy to read. In part, that explains why it leaped to the best-seller lists when it appeared in 1950. It was one of the first flying saucer hardcover tomes, and it caused a stir of excitement across America, opening the way for writers like Keyhoe and Gerald Heard, and leading to the formation of "saucer clubs" by the hundreds in every section of the country.

The story unfolded in this 230-page book is one of intrigue, and the two main characters are nothing if not "intriguing." The first is Silas Mason Newton, president of the Newton Oil Company of Denver, Colorado. Scully introduces him as a graduate of Baylor University and Yale, who did postgraduate work at the University of Berlin, a self-made multimillionaire, discoverer of the vast Rangely oil field, patron of the arts, and formerly amateur golf champion of Colorado—in brief, "a man of substance as well as science."

He was one of the great geophysicists of the oil industry, with a record of successful exploratory operations unmatched in the field. He hunted for oil with instruments that cost a fortune and were a closely guarded secret; it was known, however, that they involved the broadcasting of magnetic microwaves by the petroleum deposits deep in the earth. The microwaves were picked up on the delicate instrumentation.

"DR. GEE"

Our second "character" in this story is a top-rated magnetic engineer whom Scully refers to only as "Dr. Gee." This was obviously his way of covering up the man's real name, beginning with the letter "G." In the years of controversial investigation by other writers who tried to learn the identity of this source, no one ever came up with the answer. As we shall see later in this chapter, a false "discovery" was made in a national magazine article, but it fell far short of matching the facts. Whoever the magnetic scientist was, his identity to this day has remained a well-kept secret.

Scully first met Dr. Gee in the Mojave Desert in the summer of 1949 while Scully was with a group of scientists engaged in magnetic research. He describes the doctor as having "more degrees than a thermometer, from such institutions as Armour Institute, Creighton University and the University of Berlin." During World War II, he was head of a scientific team whose task it was to knock submarines out of the seven seas and guided missiles out of the skies. They conducted 35,000 experiments on land, sea and air on this defense project. They worked out of two laboratories and had a budget of one billion dollars at their secret command.

Though this very crucial research was profoundly successful—and helped in our victory over the Axis forces—it was never publicized because it was part of an on-going project that is still being followed up, and is rated "Top Secret" to this day. Dr. Gee was released from the government project after seven years of difficult work. When he met Silas Newton, he told him that the instruments Newton had developed worked not merely on microwaves, but on magnetic waves. He believed that a magnetron, such as was invented during the war, might be able to detect the volume of oil underground. This was possible, he said, because magnetic waves will not go through oil. They move over and under the petroleum, and thus indicate the size of the deposit. This was the answer Newton was looking for and he assigned Dr. Gee to check on the Mojave Desert field. It was not long afterward that the subject of flying saucers came up, and Dr. Gee related his experience. The first UFO that Dr. Gee was called in to examine landed near Aztec, New Mexico, in April, 1948. He said this was the earliest known landing of such a craft in the United States; one had landed in the Sahara Desert in Africa before this, but was a total wreck, whereas this one had gently pancaked to earth and was in good shape.

The ship was detected as it came into earth's atmosphere. They were able to estimate its trajectory and probable landing point. Within a few hours after it landed, Air Force officers reached the flying field at Durango, Colorado, and took off in search of the object. When they found it, it was on a very high, rocky plateau east of Aztec. They arrived in jeeps, stationed a military guard around the UFO, and sent out word to get Dr. Gee and his magnetic scientists to the location as soon as possible, as they had deduced by the flying motion of the UFO that magnetic power was probably involved here.

The first thing Dr. Gee and seven of his group did on arrival was to order a "hands-off" policy of discreet observation. For two days they studied the strange disc-shaped object from a safe distance, bombing it with Geiger counters, cosmic rays and other probing devices. Finally, deciding it was apparently free from harmful radiation, they agreed to proceed and attempt to get inside. Nothing had happened to indicate there was life in the ship; it gave off no sounds, vibrations or radio signals. The scientists moved in close to the UFO, circled it warily looking for some sign of a door, but none could be found.

THE STRICKEN CRAFT

The craft looked like a huge saucer, measuring just a fraction short of 100 feet in diameter. From the outer tip of the rim to the surface of the ground, it measured 27 inches. There was a large, cup-shaped projection, set in an insert in the bottom of the saucer, which the men assumed to be a cabin. It was entirely round, 18 feet across and 6 feet high. There were six round portholes, evenly spaced around this cabin, with glass-like windows.

The only marking of any sort on the exterior of the ship was a small crack in one of the portholes, which had apparently been caused by a collision with some object in our atmosphere. It seemed to offer the only chance of obtaining entrance in to the craft. One of the men located a strong metallic pole with a sharp point at one end and, with the help of the others, began probing and pushing into the damaged porthole. After a few minutes of pressure, they managed to ram a hole through the defect.

Now able to peer inside, they could make out the shadowy shapes of 16 small bodies, apparently lifeless. By prodding around with the long pole, they were able to locate a knob-like protrusion along the wall opposite the broken porthole. It was actually a double knob, which yielded to the pole's pressure and, to the surprise of the scientists, caused a door to fly open. Now they could enter.

THE ALIENS

The little bodies were taken out on the ground for a thorough evaluation. Ranging in height from 36 to 42 inches, they seemed to be normal from every standpoint, as compared to humans. They were not like midgets on this planet; that is, they had heads that were much smaller than ours, and in perfect proportion to their miniature bodies. Their skin seemed to be charred a very dark brown, leading the examiners to deduce that they had been burned as a result of air rushing through the broken porthole at a tremendous rate heating the interior through friction.

The UFOnauts appeared to be about 35 to 40 years old, by our standards of age. Later studies by medical scientists revealed they were in all respects perfectly normal human beings, except for their teeth. There wasn't a cavity or filling in any mouth and their teeth were 100% perfect.

As to clothes, they all wore the same type of uniform, a dark blue garment with metal buttons. There was no insignia of any kind on the collars, sleeves or caps-simple caps with a plain visor.

They began an examination of the ship itself. The metal body was similar in appearance to aluminum, though it was apparently impervious to any of our cutting tools. In the curved interior of the cabin was what appeared to be an instrument panel with an array of push-buttons. The scientists were driven by a desire to solve the mystery of how the ship was propelled, and Dr. Gee was the first to suggest it probably flew on magnetic lines of force. Some of his staff suggested experimenting by pushing the buttons on the panel but after a brief discussion it was decided this could be dangerous—if the ship started, nobody would know which button to push to stop it again!

There were two "bucket seats," as the doctor called them, in front of the instrument board, and two of the little creatures were sitting there slumped forward on the instrument board. It appeared that this ship, if flying on magnetic lines of force, must have had an automatic type of control, so that when it came into danger, or when its occupants were not in a position to operate the ship, it simply settled automatically to earth.

The investigators could not determine when or how the port window had been cracked, or at what possible point in space the occupants had died. But the fact remained that they were dead; either from burns or from the bends (from atmospheric pressure changes).

MYSTERIES OF THE SPACESHIP

On further examination of the interior of the UFO, the earthmen were elated to find a number of booklets, which they believed probably dealt with navigation problems. Then they realized that the writing, "a pictorial type of script, not unlike ancient Egyptian hieroglyphics, "would be very difficult, if not impossible, to decipher." All of these booklets were turned over to certain officials of the Air Force, who in turn reported they were going to have them placed in the hands of cryptographic experts. As far as the scientists on the project could learn later on, no progress was made in deciphering the strange language.

They found no maps of any sort. As far as they could make out, there were no instruments of destruction, nor any firearms or other weapons. The doctor pointed out to his staff that weapons would hardly be necessary to these beings because if the ship had been operated magnetically, it unquestionably had the means to demagnetize any object, from an asteroid that crossed its path to an F-80 fighter plane that might attack it. The demagnetization would completely disintegrate the obstacle. This of course would apply to human beings on earth, or any form of matter with which they came into contact on this planet.

As for the construction of the UFO, the outer skin looked like our aluminum, but on all tests later made, it did not match any form of aluminum we have on earth. It was so light that two or three men could lift one side of it off the ground. On the other hand, it was so strong that as many as a dozen of them had crawled up on top of the wing and made no impression on it whatsoever.

Then came a major decision: how to move it out of there. The Air Force officers finally decided to try to dismantle it, as it was far too big to move otherwise. But how to break it apart? There were no rivets, no bolts, no screws; nothing on the outer skin to indicate how the ship was put together.

After a long study, however, it was found that the ship was assembled in segments; the segments fitted in grooves and were pinned together, internally, around the base. The engineers were able to lift the cabin section out through the bottom of the saucer, and were amazed to find a huge gear completely encircling the bottom of the ship. This gear neatly fitted into another large gear that was on the cabin. The whole thing was very ingeniously put together, and it had to be taken down very carefully.

After breaking the UFO apart, it was moved to a government testing laboratory where it remained for a considerable period of time while the parts were being tested. When Dr. Gee next saw it, he was greatly upset to find that the entire instrument panel had been broken up and all the inner elements of it had been torn apart. This, he said, prevented any further study by them as to the magnetic operation of the ship itself.

The doctor said that had they been able to keep it intact long enough, there might have come a time when they could work out a plan to analyze the different push-buttons on the panel. These, he was certain, held the clues to the magnetic form of combustion developed when the ship was in flight.

As to the question of what became of the little men on the craft, Dr. Gee said that some of them had been dissected and studied by the medical division of the Air Force, and that from the meager reports he had received, they had found that these little fellows were like earthmen in every respect, except for their tiny dimensions.

Dr. Gee described some small objects found on the bodies of the UFOnauts. He had seen three pieces which he thought might be the equivalent of our watches. These "timepieces" were about the size of a silver dollar in diameter, and slightly thicker. They had four markings-one at the top, one at what would be 3 o'clock, another at 6 o'clock, and a fourth at 9 o'clock. It was discovered that the inside part of this artifact actually moved, but it took a full magnetic month to complete its cycle.

Dr. Gee explained, "You know, of course, that a magnetic day is 23 hours and 58 minutes. We found that the time it took for the timepiece to make this complete circumference was 29 days. In hours and minutes, that totalled exactly the number of magnetic days in a magnetic month." All this lent further credence to the belief that magnetism was the central element in all the UFO's functions.

He said there also appeared to be a sort of "food" on this ship resembling little wafers. They fed them to guinea pigs who thrived on the morsels. On one occasion, one wafer was put into a gallon container of boiling water, and it very quickly boiled over the sides of the container.

There were two containers of water on board, and they found it to be normal in all respects to our water, except that its weight was about twice that of earth water. The doctor pointed out that there was a water in Norway that was about the weight of this water.

MORE CRASHED SAUCERS

One day Dr. Gee took Silas Newton aside and told him that he was trying to get clearance for Newton to inspect the craft, and he let slip that there was more than one UFO in captivity now. Newton was amazed.

"Yes," said Dr. Gee, "we have had three and we saw a fourth but that one got away. The second one landed near one of the proving grounds in Arizona, as opposed to the first which settled down near a proving ground in New Mexico. When we got to the second one, we found almost the same conditions as the first, except that the door was open, and the sixteen dead little men on board were not burned. In fact, medical opinion was that they had not been dead more than two or three hours. Our conclusion was that they had died in our atmosphere when the double knob of the door was opened and our air rushed into their cabin, which was probably pressurized for their atmosphere but not for ours."

Newton asked, "How do you determine the presence of these ships? Do you stumble on them, or do you know the moment they come into our atmosphere?"

Dr. Gee replied, "In the laboratories, and also at Alamagordo and Los Alamos, and at different parts of the country, we have telescope observers who spend 24 hours a day watching for evidence of any non-earthly objects in the sky. Everything that comes within the range of these instruments is noted. If it is unfamiliar and lands, the Air Force is aware of it almost immediately, and if it presents scientific problems, we or other groups are consulted."

He said that the second UFO was smaller, 72 feet in diameter, but otherwise similar to the 100-foot ship. He and his fellow scientists had decided that the mathematical system of the space creatures was in all probability the same as ours, "because mathematical law should follow for all the planets in this solar system."

The third UFO he and his staff examined landed a short distance north of Phoenix, in Paradise Valley. At the moment it touched down on earth, Dr. Gee and his staff happened to be in Phoenix, so they were able to arrive on the scene in short order. When they drove up to the landing area, they saw that one of the UFOnauts was half out of the escape door—he was dead. The other little fellow (there were only two on board this craft) was sitting in his seat at the control board—also dead. This ship was 35 feet in diameter, and the size of the cabin and all the rest of the dimensions were proportionate to those of the other two spacecraft.

Asked if they had any sleeping quarters or toilet facilities, the doctor explained that the 72-foot ship had a very ingenious device which, when they analyzed it, turned out to be a collapsible screen; as it was pulled out, accordion-fashion, it moved around in a half circle, and when it reached the wall of the cabin, little hammocks had dropped down from this screen. These were the sleeping quarters!

He said there were what appeared to be toilet facilities inside the sleeping quarters. However, the smallest ship had no such conveniences, from which the doctor deduced that they were making round trips so fast, they didn't feel the need for such facilities any longer. Newton asked, "Where is the little ship?"

"We have that one in the laboratories at the present time," replied Dr. Gee. "As soon as I get your clearance through, you will be able to inspect it." In time Newton's appointment came through, but by then the ship had been dismantled and reportedly shipped to Dayton, Ohio, and all comment thereafter was denied or turned aside.

STRANGE ARTIFACTS

All the doctor had to show for his labors was what appeared to be a tubeless radio, some gears, some small discs and several other items that were small enough to be carried in one's pocket. He was allowed to take these things for research.

Author Scully declares in this book that he saw and was allowed to examine these artifacts, which to him were hard evidence that could not be explained away. He writes that "more than 150 tests failed to break down the metal of the gears." The gears themselves were of a ratio unfamiliar to engineers on this earth. They had no play, no lubrication.

As for the radio, it was not much bigger than a pack of cigarettes. It had been torn from a corner of the cabin, which in all likelihood served as its antenna. It had no tubes, no wires and only one dial. Dr. Gee built a special antenna for it, about 4 inches high, and was able to catch a high-pitched tone at 15 minutes past every hour. Says Scully, "It wasn't radio as we know it, but it was a means of communication with somewhere!"

Asked what possible reason there could be for keeping all this secret, Dr. Gee surmised, "Fear of panic or the upsetting of certain religious beliefs, or just plain brass exercising its authoritative power to keep their powers from atrophying. The government wants to keep people away from that area of New Mexico, as this could very well start a stampede of curiosity seekers, as well as a panic among certain types of people who are easily frightened. I've talked to religious leaders, and they ridicule any idea that this would upset theological concepts. So I can't imagine what the Air Force had in mind. All I know is that they ruined our chances of working on 'live' models, and have left themselves groping and guessing ever since. I think we have some of the answers by now, but by no means all of them. My guess is that the visitors are at least 500 years ahead of us in their knowledge of propulsion at any rate."

That the UFOnauts showed improvement in each ship they sent out, the doctor didn't doubt. He pointed out a three-point landing gear on a sketch he had made of the smallest UFO. It held steel-like balls in vacuum cups which permitted the balls to revolve. While the balls were moving in one direction, nothing could tilt or tip the ship, but when they were motionless a child could tilt it. To solve that secret alone, Dr. Gee contended, would take years of research.

They asked the doctor what he thought were the chances of the Air Force's eventually admitting that the flying saucers had come from another planet. He replied that as nearly as he could judge from all the work he and his associates had done, the Air Force was not interested in admitting the discovery of a new method of flight. They were zeroed in on jet propulsion, and that was likely to be their preoccupation for the foreseeable future.

Dr. Gee explained his theory of how the UFOs fly. He said that there are 1,257 magnetic lines of force to the square centimeter. These are counted in the tenescope as one would count strands of wire at the cut end of a cable. He said that the crossing of two or more lines of force made it possible in effect to permit movement in a manner previously unknown in aerodynamics.

METHOD OF PROPULSION

"The saucer-like construction," said the doctor, "is the most ideal type of vehicle to move in the air. The whirling motion observed would be in order to maintain balance, because there is no forward thrust from the wing surface.

"What actually happens," he explained, "is that even though the wing part is whirling, the saucer actually crawls forward from one crossed magnetic line of force to another. Now, when you consider that there are 1,257 lines to the square centimeter and no two cross, we have the problem of combustion or propulsion, or power created when they are crossed under control. The successive crossing of these lines of force under control makes possible the speeding up of the whirling action of the wing part of the saucer, because the saucer is attempting to get to the next succeeding line of force; or perhaps we could say, seeking to get back in balance.

"In other words, the ship is trying to get away from itself, or trying to get away from the position it finds itself in, when combustion power is created by the crossing of magnetic lines of force."

He added that when the craft moves out of our atmosphere, there is no weight and of course no resistance. At that stage, there is nothing left but magnetic lines of force in an undisturbed state, out to where they approach similar lines of force from another planet. Since these forces are identical, they repel each other, just as the two north poles of a magnet would repel. In such a manner, the planet Venus and the planet Earth are each held in their respective positions by reason of magnetic repulsion. All the planets in our solar system are in universal balance, and all move in their orbits in the same fashion.

Dr. Gee's reason for appraising the interplanetary visitors as being 500 years ahead of us is based on the fact (writes Scully) that they appear to come and go at will. Somehow they can cross from their magnetic lines of force on to ours, despite the fact that the two planets involved are "positive," and would therefore repel any object's effort to move from one to the other. Scully notes that it is easy to conceive of them traveling up and down "as on a scenic railway," once given sufficient push. But hopping from one "scenic railway" to another going in the opposite direction represents "a triumph of magic over experience."

He writes that this is precisely what the saucerians seem to have achieved. "They fly singly and in groups and, as reported in Farmington, New Mexico during the month of March, 1950, they even appear in groups of hundreds. It is as if they were demonstrating that where one, two and even three of their number had failed, they later corrected the faults that caused the failures and came over in strength, flying over the very area where their pioneers had died trying.

And nimble-witted Scully ends this section of his story with a sting-like jab at the skeptics:

"Those whose doubts exceed those of the Pentagonians have harped on the size of the little men piloting the flying saucers. It has seemed to them like a rewrite of Gulliver's Travels. These scoffers should not be allowed to forget that Jonathan Swift's little friends measured six inches high, whereas the Saucerians measured three to three-and-a-half feet tall, and are therefore at least as believable as Mickey Rooney!"

Scully adds his comment that all the scientists involved in the examinations of the landed saucers deeply regretted the way the ships were dismantled, since the way the various pieces related to each other contained the secret of their magnetic propulsion. Dr. Gee told him that some of the Air Force men helped themselves to "souvenirs"—small parts of the craft, and Dr. Gee then proceeded to take what he could, "not to put in his trophy cabinet, but to use for research".

MOTION PICTURE FOOTAGE

There was some motion picture film which the Air Force men took, but it was a special film made to fade out in two hours. A special chemical obtainable only on license restored the image for another two hours. "Naturally, this film was not available to Dr. Gee," writes Scully. However, the doctor shot some film of his own, but it was not very clear, unfortunately.

By early 1950, there began what the author calls the "reign of error." The Air Force closed down its investigative Project Saucer and went underground. All were told to forget what they knew. "Hallucinations" became a routine answer. "Psycho" became a veiled threat.

"Everybody shut up but the people." said Scully. "The official dams were closed, but the public spilled its observations into the lake of a free press. The conflict between free inquiry and official censorship grew. Men who talked freely in the summer of 1940 wouldn't tell their story for $20,000,000 by the summer of 1950. But I remembered. Better than elephants, I remembered. In fact, elephants come to me when they forget."

In the years that followed the appearance of Scully's landmark book there were many detractors who tried to disprove its authenticity. None were totally successful and, although they did stir up an on-going controversy, the book still stands today as a pioneer in UFO annals.

Foremost among the attackers was one J. P. Kahn, a writer in *True* magazine (September, 1952). He denigrated the two main sources quoted in Scully's work, and smeared Scully himself by innuendo. He called Silas Newton "a shady oil speculator," despite all the credentials given in the book which he did not deny. He claimed to have identified the pseudonymous Dr. Gee as Herman Gebauer, proprietor of a radio-TV parts supply house. To those who studied all the elements of the controversy judiciously, it was apparent that if Kahn's theories were correct a colossal hoax was perpetrated by Newton and Gebauer, which totally fooled

Scully and the conservative publishing house of Henry Holt & Co.

But where was the motive for such a flim-flam? There was nothing to be gained, and everything to be lost in the reputations of the hoaxers, if indeed they were hoaxers. Newton had spent years building his name in the business and social worlds; why would he risk being torn down for a "publicity stunt" of this type?

On the contrary, those flying saucer researchers who have been around since the Scully book first appeared, and have carefully weighed all the elements of the story as they relate to developments in subsequent years, conclude almost unanimously that Scully was indeed telling the truth. They believe that Newton was harassed by the government after his name became known as a UFO proponent, and he was brought up on false charges of alleged oil manipulation (which of course reflected on his testimony in Scully's book).

These researchers believe that the real "Dr. Gee" was not Gebauer, but a bonafide magnetic scientist who could not come forward because of his Top Secret commitments to the government. Gebauer was nothing more than the proverbial "red herring!"

If today, the government decided to persecute executives of the major oil companies for alleged misconduct and shady business practices, our prisons would probably be crowded to the bursting point with rich oil profiteers.

Harold Salkin (left) with Albert Einstein, his sister and Sigfried Schweitzer.

Based upon the description of various eyewitnesses, this is a good approximation of the humanoid-type beings found near the site of crashed UFOs.

3

UNCLE SAM'S "TOP SECRET" DOCUMENTS

It takes a certain kind of dedication to be a serious UFO investigator. It's much easier to accept a statement at face value rather than go out and find out the truth for yourself. Lack of financial support and the necessity to make a living all cut into the time any researcher can spend trying to track down the ever elusive flying saucers; occasionally an individual will come forward who is so determined to solve the UFO mystery that nothing else matters. Antonio Huneeus is one of these unique individuals.

A native South American, Antonio now makes New York his base of operations. A full-time freelance writer, he has published over 250 articles in numerous newspapers, magazines and bulletins both in this country as well as Spanish speaking nations. These publications include *El Tiempo* and *Revista Alternative* in Bogota, Columbia, and *Revista Que Pasa* in Santiago, Chile. For the last several years he has published stories regularly in *High Times* magazine and *Ideal's UFO Magazine*. He has also contributed work for *The Complete Flying Saucer Book.*

One of Antonio's main areas of interest has been in determining the legitimacy of the various crashed saucer stories. While going over some previously classified government documents released recently under the Freedom of Information Act, Antonio discovered that several CIA, FBI, and State Department memorandums actually referred to instances where UFOs had landed in various parts of the United States and in a few instances on foreign soil. In all these incidents it appears as if the government was overly anxious to confiscate the wreckage. J. Edgar Hoover and Henry Kissinger even play a part in this amazing drama, as the following special report by Antonio Huneeus clearly points out.

In a letter to President Carter's Science Advisor, Frank Press, NASA administrator Robert Frosch remarked that "there is an absence of tangible or physical (UFO) evidence available for thorough laboratory analysis." The letter, dated December 21, 1977 was the final document in a series of correspondence between the White House and NASA regarding the possibility that the latter could reopen an official government investigation of unidentified flying objects.

Interestingly enough, an internal NASA memorandum of November 8th of the same year, on 'UFO Study Considerations", had stated that "there is a general feeling among the UFO organizations at least, that the United States Government 'knows' far more than it has released, and may even have pieces of UFO hardware in hand." After assessing the different options available to NASA with regard to the White House UFO request, the memo noted that, "all in all, undertaking a formal study at this time appears fraught with perils."

The story of the alleged crashed saucer(s) in the hands of the U.S. military and intelligence establishments has haunted the UFO literature since the very beginnings of the emergence of the phenomenon in North America. The famous initial sighting by Kenneth Arnold on June 24, 1947 near Mount Rainier, Washington State, was apparently followed less than two weeks later by the crash of an unknown spacecraft near Roswell, New Mexico.

And so, even before the U.S. Air Force began their official pre-Project Bluebook UFO investigations, Projects Sign and Grudge, the Army Air Force had already acquired the "tangible and physical evidence" that we humans are not alone in the universe. From there on, it was all a question of public relations, secrecy and debunking campaigns to mislead the American citizenry a job that the Air Force, the CIA and other Federal agencies accomplished very successfully. But as government people well know, it is a tough job to hide a secret forever in a democratic system like the American one.

What was once simply considered rumors, legends, hearsay, hoaxes or sci-fi fantasies, is now being presented in popular books and TV programs like Charles Berlitz and William Moore's *"The Roswell Incident."* NBC's *"In Search of UFO Cover-Ups"* has been impressively corroborated by dedicated researchers like Len Stringfield, and is even being presented to the public in a fictionalized format as in the recent movie Hangar 18.

THE DOCUMENTS

What concerns us now, however, is to corroborate further the case of the crashed saucer(s) in the hands of the U.S. military by the government's own admissions. As the readers probably know, over 5,000 pages of government documents on UFOs were declassified under the Freedom of Information Act during the Carter administration. These included memoranda, letters and field reports from the Defense Department, Army, Navy and Air Force, the State Department, the CIA, the FBI, the Defense Intelligence Agency (DIA) and the National Security Agency (NSA), NASA, the White House, the Atomic Energy Commission, etc. Although the majority of these documents were carefully screened, censored and sanitized in order to avoid releasing any data that could blow the government's 'double think' on the matter, we have been able to find some loops in the apparently impenetrable wall of government secrecy. Consider, for instance, the following March 22, 1950 memorandum to the Director, FBI by the Washington Special Agent in Charge (SAC), Guy Hottel:

"An investigator for the Air Force stated that three so-called flying saucers had been recovered in New Mexico. They were described as being circular in shape with raised centers, approximately 50 feet in diameter. Each one was occupied by three bodies of human shape but only 3 feet tall, dressed in metallic cloth of a very fine texture. Each body was bandaged in a manner similar to the blackout suits used by speed flyers and test pilots.

According to Mr. (deleted) informant, the saucers were found in New Mexico due to the fact that the Government has a very high-powered radar set-up in that area and it is believed the radar set-up in that area interferes with the controlling mechanism of the saucers."

J. EDGAR HOOVER AND THE FBI

On July 15, 1947, all-powerful FBI Director J. Edgar Hoover was very angry with the fact that the military would not let the FBI examine a "disc recovered." Titled "Memorandum for Mr. Ladd," the document begins with a short remark about a certain Colonel Forney, who thought "that inasmuch as it has been established that the flying discs are not the result of any Army or Navy experiments, the matter is of interest to the FBI." Therefore, Colonel Forney was lobbying for a previous official Army Air Force request that the Bureau help them to weed through the current saucer hysteria. Next came an "Addendum" suggesting that the Bureau should not assist the Army since "a great bulk of those alleged discs reported found have been pranks." J. Edgar Hoover was of a different opinion. "I would do it," he annotated at the end of the page in his own handwriting but before agreeing to it we must insist upon full access to discs recovered. For instance, in the SW case, the Army grabbed it and would not let us have it for cursory examination."

A previous FBI teletype, dated July 8, 1947, referred directly to the Roswell Incident and to the "high altitude weather balloon with a radar reflector" cover story. However, it added that "telephonic conversation between their office and Wright Field had not borne out this belief."

Furthermore, the FBI teletype also added that "disc and balloon being transported to Wright Field by special plane for examination," which contradicts General Ramey's reassurance to the press that the flight to Wright Field had been cancelled, since the flying disc was nothing more than a mundane weather balloon.

According to pioneer researcher Leonard Stringfield's two classic studies, *"Retrievals of the Third Kind"* and *"The UFO Crash Retrieval Syndrome",* a number of crashes occurred in the American Southwest between the late 1940s and the early 1950s. By this time, the Air Force was well plugged into a public disinformation campaign through their much-touted Project Bluebook at Wright-Patterson Air Force Base and under apparent instructions of the Central Intelligence Agency. According to one of Stringfield's informants, "at certain military bases, highly trained mobilized units were in constant 'ready' state for dispatch to any area in the U.S.A. to recover downed or crashed UFOs. These special forces, at the time, were known as the 'Blue Berets' which can operate secretly and effectively by using diversionary tactics to prevent public interference. Such diversions include creating power blackouts. At the same time, the Air Force has been absolutely adamant against releasing even one inch of the Blue Berets' existence or operations.

When noted UFO researcher Colman Von Keviczky requested the Air Force to release data under the Freedom of Information Act relating to the so-called Fritz Werner affidavit (the pseudonym for an Atomic Energy Commission engineer who examined for the AF a crashed saucer in Kingman, Arizona in 1953), the USAF responded that "records for that time period would have been destroyed in accordance with pertinent Air Force directives in effect at that time." In a letter provided to me by Colman Von Keviczky, the Wright-Patterson Air Force Museum used a more humoristic approach in responding to a query about the real "Hangar 18" where tiny extraterrestrials are supposedly preserved in deep frozen chambers. "We have no knowledge of such creatures ever having been found," said the letter. "If any are ever discovered, we certainly would like to have one for exhibition here. The crowds of visitors such a display would attract would be beyond imagination!"

ADDITIONAL CASES

But while the Air Force is still sticking strongly to a position to the effect that the crashed saucers and the little men never happened, CIA, DIA and State Dept. documents give us a rare glimpse of obscure foreign cases in which UFOs were reported to crash. Some of these include:

* From the CIA Worldwide UFO Reporting System, a brief transcription of a French radio broadcast extracted from a German magazine, stating that "a flying saucer which recently fell at Spitsbergen has been studied by eminent Norwegian and German rocket experts." The saucer was reported to carry no crew, having a diameter of 47 meters, constructed of "an unknown steel alloy" and carrying a "transmitter with a nucleus of plutonium transmitting on all wavelengths with

934 hertz, a measure that has been unknown so far." The report also mentioned that what seemed to be Russian inscriptions had been found aboard. The CIA field agent noted that "no one puts any credence in the story" but that, nevertheless, the Military Attache had been asked to "find out about it."

* A series of 1960 "Top Secret" Air Intelligence Information Reports from Hong Kong document a wave of UFO sightings over Sinkiang Province in the People's Republic of China in late 1958 and/or early 1959. One of these reports mentions that a Kazakh peasant "had found an object in the hills, which they believed had emitted the light seen over Arsalan, and had handed it in to the local government office at Arsalan."

* Still another heavily censored CIA foreign Intelligence Information Report about an "International Congress of Space Medicine" held in Mexico in September 1975, comments on the influence of magnetic fields on astronauts in space. "There is a theory that such fields are closely associated with superconductivity at very low temperatures, such as in space," states the document. "This in turn is related to the possible propulsion system of UFOs. There is a rumor that fragments of a possible UFO found in Brazil bore a relationship to superconductors and magneto hydrodynamics."

These rumors may or may not refer to the famous incident of a UFO which exploded near Ubatubain, Brazil in 1957, and of which magnesium pieces were examined by Brazilian and American scientists. (See *"Alien Metals"* by Harry Lebelson, OMNI, 'UFO Update" column).

CRASHES IN CHINA

One of the most colorful incidents occurred in Thailand in 1958. As told in a document written by the American Consul in Chiangmai to his superiors in Washington D.C.., on February 9, 1958, "various people in Chiangmai sighted a low flying object moving at a high speed." The witnesses included several Americans, described the object "like a ball of fire with white vapor or smoke tailing behind... "The Consulate went into a rush when it was reported on the next morning "that the object had landed in the mountains east of the town (Sankam Paeng, 14 Km. west of Chiangmai) and that tremors as from an explosion had been felt." Vice consul Robert G. Brewster and Political Analyst (possible euphemism for a CIA agent) Banchop joined immediately local newspapermen, local officers and policemen and proceeded by Land Rover into the mountains and on foot when the oxcart track ended."

Interviews with several local woodsmen were conducted and they confirmed the crash and the earth tremors felt after the explosion. "Due to the lateness in the day and lack of camping equipment to stay in the mountains," continues the report, "the party then returned to Sankam Paeng and Chiangmai. Vice consul Brewster gave the woodsmen a sum of money to hunt for the object." Whether the object was ever found, Uncle Sam is not telling us.

HENRY KISSINGER

There are more reports of mysterious crashes of "space objects" over South African, Mexican and Bolivian territory. Although it seems likely that some of these objects were really parts of rocket boosters or other earth-made satellite debris, the atmosphere of vagueness and denial on the part of the U.S. authorities usually contributes to fan more energy to those who propose that flying saucers are either crashing at a quite surprising rate, or else are deliberately sending small probes to give earthlings something to chew. The South African case is interesting because of Henry Kissinger's passing involvement in it. A series of telexes during 1975 and 1976 between the American Embassy in Pretoria, South Africa and Henry Kissinger in Washington, refer to a metallic ball with an "unidentified faint lettering" that had fallen in Cape Province and had been recovered and analyzed by South African authorities. Embassy personnel were allowed to see the object and photos were sent to the U.S. to see if it was manufactured here. The key section of Kissinger's instructions on the matter, for "limited official use," was that "the best way to determine whether the object is of U.S. origin is to examine it in the U.S." But then again, we don't know if the South African Government finally sent the object or what it was.

There are still more reports of strange pieces of metal falling from space or exploding near the earth. The government's official line continues to be that UFOs do not exist and are no longer investigated by the Air Force or any other Federal agency. "We dropped the whole UFO stuff back in 1969," is the essence of the Air Force form letters to queries from the public. There is no evidence and there never was. During the 1977 PR ruse with the White House described in the beginning of this article, NASA itself admitted that they are open-minded and that "we stand ready to respond to any bona fide physical evidence from credible sources." But, we may respond to NASA, aren't the USA, the CIA and the State Dept. impeccable examples of "credible sources?" The UFO business, as every private researcher well knows, can be sometimes quite frustrating.

4

THE LOS ALAMOS SAUCER AND THE U.S. GOVERNMENT

"Most of those individuals who were in any way involved with the inspection of the crashed discs, or watched the removal of the alien bodies have done their best to keep out of the public spotlight," concedes Gray Barker, a veteran UFOlogist who has been trying to track down UFOs since the early fifties. "If they were in the military or otherwise employed by Uncle Sam, their hesitancy to talk might be based on orders they were given to take the 'secret' to the grave with them, or on the misguided assumption that the nation's national security would somehow be compromised if word were to leak out pertaining to crashed saucers and dead little men. Some civilians who were involved in this hush-hush policy tend to feel reprisals will be taken against them if they dare blab a word of what they have seen. In addition, they also have the fear of ridicule attached to this, in that no one wants to be among the first to come forward and not be able to offer tangible proof of their claims."

Barker has looked hard and long at the reported episodes involving crashed spaceships and was not convinced one way or the other until he read an advanced proof of the *"Roswell Incident"* by Charles Berlitz and William Moore, and saw the State Department and other government documents reproduced along with the book.

Having been convinced that this aspect of the UFO controversy needed further probing, Barker went to his files and dusted off a folder pertaining to a strange Baron von Poppon who was supposedly involved in one of these crashed craft cases.

"Hopefully this report may help to shed some light on a subject still cloaked in intrigue," Barker acknowledges. "As head of my own UFO publishing company, Saucerian Press, and editor of a widely circulated newspaper (Gray Barker's Newsletter), I feel I owe the UFOlogical community something and thus I'm releasing my updated findings on this case to be included in this book. The Baron may have been involved in something that he was afraid to talk about."

I first heard of Dr. George C. Tyler from a West Coast researcher who had assisted me materially a year before in my investigations of a particular UFO case.

"I just got hold of a most peculiar manuscript written by Dr. Tyler," he told me by telephone, "and I think you should have it."

As usual he wouldn't divulge the contents over the telephone; nor would he tell me where he had obtained it. "I'll write you about the source," he promised; but thereafter he avoided that particular question.

PROFESSOR "P"

The manuscript was headed, **"THE FLYING SAUCER STORY OF DR. GEORGE C. TYLER, U.S.A.,"** with a subhead, **"THE LOS ALAMOS SAUCER AND THE U.S. GOVERNMENT."**

I sat back and began to read what obviously was a retyped copy of an original not in my possession:

"The hero of this story (and I mean hero, because of what he suffered) is a noted scientist whose name for the purpose of anonymity I will call 'Professor P' (Author's note: later the man's true identity was revealed as being Baron Von Poppon). As to our personal relationship, I was, 25 years ago, president of the Shale and Metal Co. in Denver, where we made the first successful shale oil mill in the U.S. It worked successfully, but was not economical.

"One day the Baron (the noble title of Professor—G.B.) arrived in Los Angeles at the head of a delegation from France. He had trailed me all over the country after being informed that I was the only person who had engineered such a mill in this country.

"The Baron wanted me to visit his land of Estonia, in the Balkans, which together with Lawia and Lithuania, made up a population of 17 million, and build a shale oil mill-in fact many of them. His country had developed oil fields with fine shale beds, and oil was needed.

"I was afraid of the rising tide of Communism, which was beginning to wash against their borders on the east, but he assured me there was no real danger. I finally consented to go after he made his offer more financially substantial.

"He had their Reichstag elect me Premier of the little country with full power to rejuvenate the commerce. On the strength of this move, they borrowed 30 million dollars in New York, bought an old steamer of large capacity, and loaded it with old cars, discarded radios and so on, to be made over in their land by mechanics who at that time were starving.

"Shortly afterward, however, and before I could get my affairs in shape here, Secret Servicemen of a certain people came to me with the information that the entire end of Europe would soon be conquered by the Bolsheviks, and that persons such as myself would be hastily liquidated. The information was so definite that I backed out, much to the Baron's dismay.

"He departed for his country at once. They carried out the plans as we had made them, or tried to; but all was brought to an end by the disaster I feared would happen. The Baron saw his beautiful wife cut to pieces and his two children dashed against the wall of a stone cellar, as he hid under some driftwood, wounded and helpless."

STRANGE PHOTOGRAPHIC ASSIGNMENT

Now the foregoing certainly has nothing to do with saucers, but we include it because of the background it offers to the narrative which follows.

Our West Coast correspondent, mentioned previously, loyally went to work on the case and managed to interview Dr. Tyler, a man in his 70's. Although he gave her the very same account his manuscript contained, her report filled in some missing points.

"The Baron was wounded," the staccato-type form of report advised. "Hid in basement. They tortured his wife to tell where he was. Wouldn't. Took his children and bashed their heads against the wall, spilled their brains out. This part might easily be true, but it is pretty horrible. Dr. Tyler inferred that it happened right before the Baron's eyes. The Baron was finally smuggled out of the basement and he returned to this country. He had dabbled in photography and continued that interest here, making a profession of it. Finally became a top man in the field. Don't know how he and Dr. Tyler got together again..".".

Dr. Tyler's manuscript takes up the story at this point:

'After we met I learned to love the personality of this frail man. Already a scientist, he had to do constructive work, so he became a scientific photographer, and his work grew to be so well recognized e was repeatedly called on for difficult work along this line.

"I was a little surprised one day when his voice came over the telephone, asking me to meet him in the coffee room of a downtown hotel. "'I have a matter I must discuss with you. Get there at once; it will take an hour to tell you.'

"It took not an hour, but several, before I left the meeting, my head spinning. Here is his story as he told it to me, without small details, since these would require a book:

"The Baron's story which I paraphrase:

'Last week two Secret Service men came to my home. They told me that they had a photographic job to be done, to please go with them. We went by plane and landed inside the vast Los Alamos Field, where I was met by the superintendent of that part of the field. We walked to the fringe of a crowd of several hundred men who were milling around a large, flat object, lying on the ground.

'When a lane was opened, I was led through the crowd and found myself viewing what one might term a Flying Saucer. There it was, surrounded by an estimated 1000 men- technicians and experts of all kinds, the best the government can hire. To say I was astonished would be putting it mildly.

'They gave me the finest equipment I had ever handled and told me to photograph the thing. For two days I crawled all over it, on top, underside, photographing it both close-up and from a distance-literally within inches of special pieces of equipment. In particular they wished my photographs to show the texture of the metal of which it was composed. In actuality, there seemed to be different kinds. Most of it appeared to be steel, but different than any I'd ever seen. Some of it was actually translucent.

'Now I'll try to describe it to you. It was a fraction of a foot less than 100 ft. across. They, the builders, seem to have a different basic mathematical number, the difference between 6 and 9. It was about eight feet thick in the middle.

'The technicians managed to open a door on the side, with its base on the chine of the rim. The door was so finely machined that when closed it left no indication that it was there. I suppose this served to insure against any seepage of air when in space.

'Inside was a circular room about 30 ft. across, a curving ceiling in conformity to the outside of the machine. Between the sides and outside edge of the ship seemed to be cargo space and around the side, next to the chine, were very heavy cables, some of which looked like copper. The rest I couldn't determine, and nobody expressed an opinion in my presence. It was like that all the time, very much hushed up. All of them seemed to be afraid of each other, and almost of themselves.

'Approximately in the center of this room was a panel control board, covered with push-buttons and tiny levers, somewhat similar to those we have on Earth.

'Before this small board were four swivel, bucket-type seats. And in all four seats were men-strapped in, dead.

41

THE LITTLE MEN

'The largest, who seemed to be the captain, was four feet, nine inches tall, and weighed about 35 pounds. The smallest and obviously the youngest was 23 inches tall and weighed about 22 pounds. They were white men, with very pale skin, as if they had come from a cold world with little air. Their faces were intellectual and refined—I have never seen anything like them here on Earth.

'The captain's right arm hung down as he lay slumped over the controls, and his fingers touched what must have been the ship's log book, lying open on the floor, the exposed pages covered with glyphs, nothing like I had ever seen before. But the book was made of some sort of indestructible material which was not paper at all, but could be written on.

'On the floor were some 15 little machines, beautifully welded to the floor, with welds that left no indication of any difference in appearance with the rest of the floor-though I could see they were indeed welds. I am particular about this, for here is some secret which an expert should be able to discover. The machines appeared somewhat like typewriters, beautifully made, though not so intricate as you would imagine.

'It showed me that these people have long ago passed through the period of technological development we are now in, and have again tended toward the simplification of life, thus eliminating the intricacies which tend to obscure the natural laws of being.

'I concluded the machines were the different pieces of apparatus which controlled the cosmic space motor which was made up, it seemed, of the big cables coiled around the inside of the ship's chine, and of some mechanism which they did not let me photograph.

'Beyond the central control center of the ship was a kind of garret, which I'll try to describe.

'Against the sides were several Pullman-like bunks, but suitable only for these pygmies. Against the wall was clipped a water bottle, out of which we drew water. I drank some of it, and it tasted good. In fact that was all they would let me have. You could tell no difference between this bottle and any water cooler we have in our offices, except that it was not made of glass, but was nevertheless translucent. There was a toilet, with peculiar arrangements, all very modest.

'One thing in this compartment drew my attention above everything else. What appeared to be a regular radio tube (or at least it looked like one of our tubes) was clipped against the wall. Every now and then it delivered a BEEP! BEEP! sound, which I judged was a call from space, since I had the idea that other ships connected with this one were anxiously trying to communicate with it. That went on all day until I was ready to leave. When I had finished my work, I slipped the tube out of its clip, wrapped it in my handkerchief and another rag as firmly as I could in order to muffle its sound, and tucked it into my pocket. But as we went to the plane which was to carry me back to Los Angeles, it sounded off again, and the superintendent who had met me and who had been with me all the time, heard it and said, 'Ah, so that's it! You are trying to snitch on us. Give, young fellow!" And naturally I had to return it; so I don't have a single thing to back my story except my word to you.'"

Dr. Tyler continues:

"That was the conclusion of the report Professor Von Poppon gave me at the coffee shop. Although he had sworn me to confidence, I found it difficult to keep quiet about it. For one thing, it made me almost doubt my sanity, and I felt I must have the reaction of some other person to it to help me make up my mind about it.

'At my next Friday evening lecture, I decided to give this story to my class, disguised so that my students could accept it as fiction if they so desired. Everybody highly enjoyed my narrative, though it was not presented as fact and I did not expect them to believe it. One member of the class, however, appeared to be deeply disturbed by the story, and considering his connections which I later found out, it was not surprising that two days later I was visited by two men who accused me of telling a false story. I agreed that I had told the story but insisted it wasn't false. They threatened to put me in jail if I persisted. But being a down-east Yankee, my anger was aroused and I told them I would now lecture on the subject every chance I got. This cooled them off but after a hurried consultation they asked me not to reveal the information because of security reasons. With this I complied at the time.

"Considering the developments, I decided to get in touch with the Baron and apprise him of what had transpired. I telephoned him and arranged to meet him at the coffee shop again. When we got together I told him what had happened as a result of his saucer story.

"His face turned white, and he asked in a frightened voice, 'WHAT SAUCER STORY?'

"I reminded him of the strange narrative he had given me. 'Why, I never told you a story about any saucer. What on earth are you talking about?'

"I leaped from the table in anger at this terrible about-face from my trusted friend. Then I looked at his face. His lips trembled as a look of utmost horror came over it. I knew he was remembering his gruesome experience in Estonia, was reliving the slaughter of his wife and children.

43

"I knew at that moment I must forgive him, and await the proper time to retell this amazing story.

"I kept silent four long years. Finally on a visit to George Adamski at Mt. Palomar Gardens Inn, on Dec. 29, 1953, I mentioned some details of the story to a confidante who was also present. This confidante gave me a roguish smile and told me the story was already out. At a party given in Hollywood a few weeks previous for a group of important people, was the very same superintendent who had supervised the work of Professor Von Poppon. When he got some drinks under his belt, he told the group the same story you have just read, the only difference being that he was the man who had bossed the job. The hostess, greatly impressed, rushed home and told her writer husband, who wrote it down and circulated it among a few friends, among whom was my confidante.

"I saw the notes, and the details were essentially the same, except for one added payoff. The ship was dismantled carefully, piece by piece, and shipped east to Dayton, Ohio, where every piece was carefully studied and a duplicate built. But when completed, the duplicate would not fly-nor could they activate the damaged original. Doing what they could—fume, fret, fuss and call each other names-the ship just sat there placidly, refusing to budge. Thank God for that! I offer such thanks advisedly, for knowing the human race, such a discovery would be one of the most terrible things imaginable. If we could make one which would fly, the first thing we'd do would be to put machine guns on it, fill it with bombs and go off trying to find and destroy some good world in space. 'God forbid!' is my prayer."

I CHECK THE STORY

That was the end of Dr. Tyler's manuscript, insofar as it concerned the alleged experiences of his informant, whom we shall refer to as follows: Baron Von Poppon. (The writings detailed two other incidents, consisting of interesting sightings which Dr. Tyler had collected).

My first impression was that no Baron Von Poppon might exist, so I addressed a letter to that name, using the address given in the Tyler manuscript.

Surprisingly enough, an air mail letter, dated Sept. 29, 1954, was not long in reaching me. In the communication, Baron Von Poppon thoroughly denied the circumstances described in the manuscript; though he did admit that Dr. Tyler had been "a very casual acquaintance," though he "never was a close friend of mine." The letter concluded with one factor which has led me to retain this information in my files rather than publish it:

"I believe you were well inspired," he wrote, "by checking Tyler's story with me before publishing it in your magazine. This possibly saved you a lot of embarrassment and trouble."

I had also written direct to Dr. Tyler, asking him for confirmation by letter of the material in his manuscript. My letter was returned from the address given to me by an informant, marked "Unclaimed," but a few days later the same informant wired me that Dr. Tyler had been admitted to the Los Angeles County Hospital to undergo surgery and I returned the letter there.

Meanwhile, I managed to reach my regular West Coast investigator, and she agreed, somewhat nervously, to go to Baron Von Poppon's residence and interview him personally. I think it best to quote her report, again in her characteristic literary style:

"It was rather late when I received the message, so it was 9:00 P.M.. when I arrived at Baron Von Poppon's place. He lives in oldish California-type bungalow—two apartments downstairs, two upstairs-in so-so neighborhood with lots of court-type apartments.

"I rang the bell. Could hear somebody shuffling downstairs. Little man opened door—not much bigger than me with my high heels on. I talked fast and furiously and winningly (?) as is my wont. He seemed to listen with a blank stare without catching a word I said, until I mentioned FLYING SAUCERS. This he CAUGHT, and he interrupted with a horrified protest that he had absolutely no interest in 'dem' (He talks with quite noticeable accent). I gave him some business about story being widely circulated which concerned him; wanted to know if there was a grain of truth in it before repeating it, came to HIM naturally first thing etc., etc.

"I didn't mention what story, who told it or anything. He looked at me a couple of seconds, and said 'You must mean that story that man, Taylor, Taylor?-tro, Tyler, told'.

"He grew quite indignant and assured me over and over that Tyler was 'insane' -all the while tapping his temple to illustrate his point. The most fantastic thing he had ever heard—absolutely no word of truth in the ridiculous story at all. Hadn't seen Tyler in 6 years—didn't really know the man at all. He got letters about the tale. Received one from 'way in other part of U.S. Was real nice letter. It was smart of this man (guess who?) to write him before printing the story, etc.

"I didn't get inside Baron Von Poppon's apt.-he had a fancy silk-type robe on, scarf around neck-quite a distinguished looking little guy, or at least I imagine he would be, or could be, when he wasn't so upset over a strange leering female putting questions to him about flying saucers. He evidently lives alone, and I had no chaperone, so I hope you'll understand my not getting into the house.

"One thing I can tell you for sure, Gray—if anybody would ever give you any trouble, it would be Baron Von Poppon. That's not very clear, but definitely got the impression that he doesn't want anything published about this Tyler business, and woe be to the guy who went any farther with it. He was pleasant enough, but he seemed the kind who would NOT brush off casually anything which irritated or annoyed him. And he looked every inch a Baron."

A SAD POSTSCRIPT

It seemed the next step should be to contact Dr. Tyler himself, and I waited for a reply to the communication I had re-routed to the hospital. Finally it was returned, marked "discharged." Other letters failed to reach him, nor could any of my West Coast informants manage to locate him.

A rather strange follow-up arrived one year later, surprisingly from the Baron, after hearing a rumor that copies of the photographs he had made at Los Alamos were being circulated privately in California. This he vehemently denied; though he added a quite interesting paragraph:

"Before ever receiving your letter I made certain investigations. I thus learned from Tyler's former landlord that Tyler died about a year ago in the Los Angeles County General Hospital of cancer. Before the landlord was notified of Tyler's death, a 'friend' of Tyler had gone to Tyler's room, to which he had a key and removed all of his papers, particularly everything pertaining to Tyler's work relative to the flying saucer business. The landlord has not been able to get any of these papers back."

Which leaves us, I suppose, not far from where we started, not unlike we have often been left after investigating a fantastic chapter in the Flying Saucer Mystery.

Was Dr. Tyler's manuscript really true, or possibly a re-hash of the account printed in Frank Scully's book *"BEHIND THE FLYING SAUCERS"?* Did Dr. Tyler die of natural causes, or did he really die at all? (My letter was returned marked "discharged.") Or was it really a "friend" who entered Dr. Tyler's apartment and removed any proof he may have had to back up his fantastic manuscript?

Researcher Antonio Huneeus has made a detailed study of the various "crashed saucer" documents released under the Freedom of Information Act.

Memorandum for Mr. Ladd

Mr. [ ] also discussed this matter with Colonel L. R. Forney of MID. Colonel Forney indicated that it was his attitude that inasmuch as it has been established that the flying disks are not the result of any Army or Navy experiments, the matter is of interest to the FBI. He stated that he was of the opinion that the Bureau, if at all possible, should accede to General Schulgen's request.

SWR:AJB

7-15

(J.Edgar Hoover)

I would do it but before agreeing to it we must insist upon full access to discs recovered. For instance in the La. case the Army grabbed it & would not let us have it for cursory examination - 2 -

A search of FBI files shows that the late J. Edgar Hoover expressed interest in at least one reported case of a downed disc though there is no record of any followup investigation on the part of the Bureau.

5

HANGAR 18 AND WRIGHT-PATTERSON AIR FORCE BASE

During the wee hours of the night throughout the 1950's and 1960's, if you were to tune your radio dial in some 30 States to WOR in New York, you would probably hear the easily recognizable voice of talk show host Long John Nebel discussing a variety of off-beat topics. If the program happened to be about UFOs, chances are one of the panelists would be James W. Moseley, editor and publisher of Saucer News, among the first UFO publications issued in this country.

Jim first became interested in the subject after Frank Scully's book was published, and he spent several years traveling around the U.S. in an effort to put together a volume of his own. He talked to many of the early contactees and spoke to dozens of eyewitnesses. He even saw a UFO of his own which sped across the sky. In those early years of UFOlogy, Jim was convinced that the majority of flying saucers were actually secret devices manufactured by Uncle Sam. As it became obvious that this explanation would not fit the existing pattern, he speculated that they might come from another dimension. However, one of the stories he encountered which he realized might tend to prove the interplanetary theory, centered around a woman who said she was directly involved in the military's retrieval of a crashed UFO. Until his death, Moseley kept an open mind about this episode, and admitted that the woman's story continued to puzzle him.

Jim Moseley published a privately circulated newsletter for "insiders" in the field. He is the author of *"The Book of Saucer News"* and *"The Wright-Patterson Story"* (Saucerian Publications), as well as being chairman of the National UFO Conference. He was responsible for promoting the largest indoor UFO Conference which attracted 8,000 people at the Hotel Commodore in New York in 1967.

The scene had been perfectly set for a weird bit of business. An odd weather condition had added a note of unreality and spectral quality to the Ohio city. It was sunset, and the sky had taken on a frightening red color. Somehow it seemed appropriate, for I had gone to this city to visit an Air Force base where a flying saucer had reportedly crashed. I was locating the base so that I could find it easily the next day.

I planned to find a nearby motel and look for "Miss Y" tomorrow. If my lead had been reliable, she would have a fantastic story to tell.

In looking through the Air Force files I hadn't expected to find, nor found, any reports of captured saucers or little men. Despite official AF denials, however, such rumors still persisted.

The late Frank Scully, well known and highly respected Hollywood writer, had caused a sensation with his book, *"Behind the Flying Saucers,"* in which he related how a government scientist had been called in to examine a saucer which had allegedly crashed in New Mexico. Few people now believe Scully's story, which he had obtained from two acquaintances, Silas Newton and Leo Gebauer; for a *True* magazine article had pretty well exposed it as a hoax. It probably wasn't Scully's fault. The article and other reports suggested that the author had simply been taken in.

But at that time the basic rumor, with many variations, vividly haunted the saucer scene. Every month or so a new crashed saucer report, complete with little men, would appear. Most of these reports came from the southwestern U.S., but there was one from Scandinavia and another from Europe.

I had little faith in the accounts until I bumped into a bizarre investigation of a saucer said to be in the possession of the AF at Wright-Patterson Air Force Base!

Since my perusal of the AF files late in 1953 I had begun corresponding with people all over the U.S. and was becoming fairly well known as a civilian UFO researcher. In April, 1954, one of these correspondents floored me with a letter, from which I quote:

My opinion is that the Air Force in holding a saucer or parts thereof at Wright-Patterson Field. I base this opinion on a great number of collective items, and one solid item—the testimony of a woman who was a WAC at Wright in the fall of 1952 when there was a Red and White aircraft attack alert for two weeks. She learned that a saucer had been brought to Wright Field and she saw a picture of it!

According to the correspondent, the Air Force had found an operative radio transmitting device inside the machine which regularly gave off "beep's". They were afraid the saucer had signalled for help and might attract other craft and a possible attack. The correspondent believed the saucer had crashed near Columbus, Ohio, but wasn't certain. He also said that bodies of six little men had been found and hauled to the base, along with the machine. I put down the letter and pulled out my special file on crash rumors. I had dozens of them.

A professor of anthropology at Columbia had supposedly been called out to Wright-Patterson to examine these creatures; a scientist in Massachusetts had made X-rays of the bodies; a man in Los Angeles knew of a saucer that landed in Mexico; a man in Florida had talked to a man who knew of, in turn, a man who had driven a truck for the Army, in which a captured saucer had been carried from the place it had "crashed" to a nearby military base; a doctor in New York had examined bodies of little men in a funeral parlor there....

And so it went. The reports had a great deal in common besides crashed saucers; the people involved were not named, so most of them were uncheckable.

The ones I had been able to check turned out to be hoaxes, or else they had no discoverable factual evidence to back them up. I finally decided that all of the accounts had been appropriated right out of the pages of Scully's book.

So I stuck the letter into the "crash file" to lie with the many unsubstantiated claims. I would have forgotten it had I not found myself routed through the correspondent's home town about a month later. I decided to stay overnight, got myself a hotel room and rang him up. The man, whom I will call Bill, greeted me enthusiastically on the phone and invited me to his house. From his conversation I gathered he might be the first informant who could provide any real, concrete lead on a captured saucer, for he claimed to have a tape recording of a key informant. For the first time I became really enthusiastic about such a matter. I wished I had not waited so long to follow it up.

THE MYSTERIOUS "MISS Y"

When I arrived at Bill's house he already had his recorder set up, and after a preliminary cup of coffee, I began to hear a tape made by a woman who sounded very much as if she really knew what she was talking about

Immediately impressed by her apparent sincerity, I quickly decided that here at last was something concrete, a firsthand account of what a woman working for the government had seen and heard in the course of her duties. Although uncertain about many details (just as many people would be in relating an event which had transpired months before), she in general told her story in such a manner that I could not help feeling that she was probably telling the truth.

There was only one fly in the UFOlogical ointment. Although the woman's first name (I will refer to her as Miss Y) was on the tape, Bill would not give me her full name, nor tell me how to get in touch with her.

"The fellow who made the recording promised her she would receive absolutely no personal publicity, and made me pledge likewise when he entrusted the tape to my safekeeping. When I wrote you, I had no idea that you would take the trouble to come out here and follow it up."

"But Bill," I pressed, "you may be sitting on the hottest news story of all time. Don't you think the public should know about this if it's true?"

"I agree with you, Jim, but a pledge is a pledge. Miss Y is already sorry she made the tape for she fears repercussions should her story leak out."

Miss Y's apparent sincerity on the tape made me determined to smoke her out and talk to her personally for I was convinced that this was one "crash" report really worth following up.

How I finally located Miss Y, three months later, is certainly worth telling, for it is almost like a detective story. But to tell the story I would have to give out many details which most likely would violate the secrecy of the identities of not only her, but others involved; and this I will not do, even at the expense of reader disbelief that these people do really exist. I know this is not good reporting, but if the reader will go along with me in this respect, I will relate what is to me the most fascinating part of this book.

Miss Y turned out to be a rather fragile looking woman: probably in her late thirties, bespectacled, with her hair neatly done up in a bun. Her entire demeanor was that of meekness, and I think she finally decided to talk with me because she felt sorry for me after my expressions of disappointment.

Now I know that some fragile little old ladies, and middle-aged ones as well, embezzle banks and other employers by the dozens, but I must say that Miss Y seemed to me to be almost the last person in the world who would make up a real whopper-and if Miss Y were lying, she had manufactured a colossal one!

First she straightened me out on some points which Bill had either assumed or got confused. She did not work at Wright-Patterson, but at another large military base in that area which I will not name; she was not a WAC, but rather a civilian employee of the Signal Corps, working under the Army and the FBI (she has since retired and moved away). Her duties, those of a night girl on teletype, included decoding messages and handling classified material of many different sorts. If this were true, I thought, this alone would vouch for her trustworthiness, for such work would require a security clearance granted only after a very thorough check of her background.

Miss Y went on: "In August-or was it September-of 1952, I walked into the photographic lab to get an aspirin from _____, who was in charge of this section (The Army photographer in charge of the lab will be referred to as Mr. Z.). This lab was in the same section of the communication building on the base which I worked in. When I walked in, he was developing a number of prints, and I couldn't help noticing that about a dozen of them looked like the newspaper drawings I had seen of flying saucers.

"At first he expressed some concern that I had seen the photos; he thought he had the door locked, but had gone to the rest room and forgotten to relock it. Knowing that I had a clearance and being a good friend of mine, he apparently decided to relieve my curiosity."

Mr. Z had personally taken the photos during a recent special assignment at a location Miss Y described simply as "north of the Base." There, according to the technician, a flying saucer had crashed. That in essence was all the information he would give her, as he warned her that the pictures were classified and carried top security designation.

"At the time," Miss Y told me, "I thought this was more or less a routine photographic record of experimental military aircraft which frequently were tested at the base, and thought little more of it until I handled some startling messages.

"The first communications involved information that the aircraft, which was thought to be of interplanetary nature, was being brought first to our Base, under very heavy guard, where it would receive a preliminary examination and then be trucked to Wright Field.

Further messages ordered a Red and White Alert for the Base, since it was feared that the crashed saucer had communicated with other similar craft still flying. This made me very nervous, for it sounded to me as if the Base Commander believed that other machines might attack in an effort to recover the disabled craft.

"Security had been clamped down very tightly. Officers and one scientist were brought in from other bases to complement the staff, and no enlisted men except Mr. Z had anything to do with the matter. No less than a major," Miss Y told me," drove the truck that hauled the craft to the base. Enlisted men were told that the alert was for practice only and that the officers had been flown in to observe how well it was carried out."

"How large do you think the saucer was, from seeing the photographs?" I asked.

"I'm not good at this, but I would say thirty feet in diameter. In a couple or three of the pictures there was a jeep parked by it and this gave a good frame of reference. It would be forty feet at the most, I would say.

"It had no protrusions, other than a rim where the upper and lower halves of the machine met.

"It appeared to be made of pieces of metal riveted together, though I couldn't see any rivets, only the different sections. It didn't have any windows that I could see. Some of the messages, however, mentioned that it had windows or portholes of one-way glass which you couldn't see through from the outside."

Miss Y also said she had heard from Mr. Z that scientists employed by the government had trouble getting inside the saucer, and that it was composed of one or more alloys not found on Earth.

And here her description departed from the classic tale: this saucer contained no dead little men. It was a remotely controlled device, evidently equipped with devices to collect and transmit information. Also, the saucer hadn't really crashed, having floated gently to the ground due to a "lack of magnetic power on which they run."

Miss Y had heard vague information about other saucers which had previously been captured, these actually containing bodies of humanoid creatures. I discounted this part of her story however, feeling that she had perhaps overheard conversations about the Scully book (she had never read it).

I was still greatly convinced with her sincerity, but I felt I still didn't have quite enough to warrant the conclusion that the Government did actually have a captured saucer and possibly little men.

So I begged Miss Y for the name of Mr. Z, the photographer, which she finally gave me after much hesitation.

"He won't talk, though. I can tell you that right now. He's still on active duty with the Army. He's getting almost ready for retirement and fears anything that might get him discharged."

THE MYSTERY DEEPENS

Whether for the reason that Miss Y gave, or whether she had, for some almost unbelievable reason, concocted the story and was indeed lying, she was certainly correct about one thing. Although Mr. Z did talk, it wasn't in confirmation of her account.

He began with a summary denial of having any knowledge of Flying Saucers, to say nothing of photographing one. During the two-hour conversation, the latter part of which was in the presence of his superior, a Signal Corps officer, he completely refuted her claims.

Miss Y did work as a night girl on teletype during the period she claimed to have been there, but she had never read any highly secret messages. She most likely had handled coded messages, but she had no way of decoding them. If any highly classified messages had indeed come through she would not have known what they contained.

"Sure we know about flying saucers," Mr. Z told me, "but only what we read in the papers. If you run around and investigate these sightings, you know a lot more than we do." Certainly no saucer had ever passed through their base, and they certainly had no knowledge of saucers captured anywhere by the government—or so they said.

They described Miss Y as a very efficient worker and "an upstanding woman." They couldn't guess why she would be telling such a story.

SOMEONE WAS LYING!

Walking out of the officer's club, where I interviewed the two, the seemingly almost organized confusion of the saucer mystery began to trouble me. If the two men were telling the truth, Miss Y was lying. One thing was obvious: Somebody was lying!

As I drove by the rows of barracks to the base exit, I tried to analyze the situation.

First I assumed that Miss Y was telling the truth. She had said that the facts she gave me were "public knowledge" and that she was not breaking security to tell them to me—though at that point I tended to disagree. It was quite understandable that she didn't want her name connected, even though it may have been public knowledge. She also had said that the government was holding back the facts from the public because of fear of panic, and also because they didn't have all the answers yet themselves—these observations probably were only her own personal opinion.

If indeed Miss Y had been telling the truth, it certainly would fit in with Mr. Z's statements. He would be required to say she was lying, and deny having made the photographs or having knowledge of them.

If the government did indeed have captured saucers, it probably would be known to only a few people, which would include a few with the necessary skills, such as photography, for investigative purposes. Probably none such people would know the full story; only his or her tiny part in the drama. Only a handful of brass at the very top would have all the details, anyhow.

The whole thing would be guarded as well, if not better, than the atomic bomb. If all that Miss Y had told me were true, I doubted if even the people at the Pentagon, whom I had talked with and who had let me see the files, knew it. It was then that I got a fantastic idea. Suppose that Project Blue Book was merely a cover-up, which analyzed routine saucer sightings; while somewhere else, within a highly guarded section of Wright Field—or some other base—a super-secret group was prying open saucers and desperately trying, in an attempt to get ahead of the Russians, to find out what made them and their extraterrestrial operators tick!

In keeping these secrets, the government had many advantages, and the main one probably was that the saucers themselves carried a ridiculous connotation in the minds of most of the public. Quite possibly, of course, there were very effective ways of dealing with individuals, in or out of the service, who knew too much or/and talked too much.

In Scully's case (if his story had some truth to it) it was fairly simple: he was not dealt with in any dire cloak-and-dagger manner, but by the simple technique of ridicule. At first his book caused a sensation; now very few people believe it, for every possible effort has apparently been made to discredit it and make him look ridiculous. Two principal characters of the book had been arrested on fraud charges, and they, their cases then undisposed of, were claiming that they were being persecuted for their saucer revelations. Could they be right and could Miss Y be right? There probably was a fifty-fifty choice either way. I thought of the flying saucer the Canadian Government had first started building and later sold to the U.S. Department of Defense. Were we desperately trying to build such a machine, basing our design on what we had learned from the possible inspection of genuine interplanetary craft? True, the news releases said the AVRO Saucer would employ conventional jet power. Later the government put the AVRO saucer on public display and indicated its design was unsuccessful. But its design would be strangely changed from that of the much publicized jet craft and turn out to be a ducted-fan hover-craft much like the model the British experimented with about the same time. Was the AVRO saucer a red herring or a possible preparation of the public to accept some startling announcements and increased congressional appropriations?

If saucers were real, they certainly didn't run on jet power. Many technicians had suggested that they must employ control of gravity and likely involve an electromagnetic drive. If the government had indeed captured a saucer or saucers it certainly appeared likely that they could unravel the power secrets involved.

When would the public be informed about the entire matter? Probably only when the government was good and ready, and only after they had mastered the secrets of the captured discs and learned from their operators the purpose of the visits. We would probably be told only after years of being gradually prepared and indoctrinated. This could be done in many ways, with more red herrings, such as George Adamski; with carefully conceived reports such as the AVRO saucer.

I wondered if the public should know sooner. After all, I was part of the public, and I didn't think I would panic if I suddenly knew the saucers were real. And I was becoming convinced, more and more each day, that they certainly weren't temperature inversions and all the other things the government said they were.

Yes, somebody was lying. If Miss Y were lying, there wasn't anything to the captured saucer. Yet if Miss Y were not lying, somebody should be able to prove it, and somebody should tell the public. If Miss Y were not lying, Mr. Z would have to lie!

The following is reprinted from "Retrievals of the Third Kind" (Ohio UFO Yearbook) by Len Stringfield, and is copyrighted by UFO Info. Network.

From anonymous medical and military sources, the following composite or general data were obtained:

1. The approximate height of the alien humanoid is 3-1/2 to 4- 1/2 feet tall. One source approximated five feet.

2. The head, by human standards, is large, when compared with the size of the torso and limbs. (See drawing of head Exhibit A)

3. The facial features show a pair of eyes described variously as large, sunken or deep set, far apart or distended more than human; and slightly slanted, appearing "Oriental" or "Mongoloid."

4. No ear lobes or flesh extending beyond apertures on each side of the head.

5. Nose is vague. Apeilures or nares are indicated with slight protuberance. One, and two, nares have been mentioned.

6. Mouth indicated as small "slit" or fissure. In some instances, no mouth described. Mouth appears not to function as a means for communication or as orifice for food ingestion.

7. Neck, described as being thin; and in some instances, not being visible because of garment in that section of the body.

8. Hair. Some observers describe the humanoids as hairless. Some say that the pate shows a slight fuzz. Bodies are described as hairless.

9. Torso. Small and thin fits the general description. In many instances the body was observed wearing a garment. From medical authorities, no comment. No abdominal navel indicated.

10. Arms are described as long and thin and reaching down to the knee section.

11 . Hands. Four fingers, no thumb. Two fingers appear longer than others. Some observers had seen fingernails; others without. A webbing effect between fingers was noted by three authoritative observers. (See drawing of hand, Exhibit

B)

12. No description available on legs or feet.

13. Skin description is not green, thank you! It is grey according to most observers. Some claim beige, tan, brown, or tannish or pinkish gray, and one said it looked almost "bluish gray" under deep freeze lights. In one instance, the bodies were charred to a dark brown.

14. Teeth unknown. No data from dental authorities.

15. Reproductive organs. This biological region is "sensitive." That is, to qualify a point, secret. One observer claims no male or female organs were identified. No phallus, no womb. In my nonprofessional judgment, the absence of sexual organs suggests some and perhaps all of the aliens do not reproduce as do the homo sapiens, or, that some of the bodies studied are produced perhaps by a system of cloning or other unknown means.

16. In some incidents of retrievals, the humanoids appear to be "formed out of a mold" or sharing identical biological characteristics.

17. Brain capacity, unknown.

18. Blood. Liquid is prevalent, but not blood as we know it.

19. Sustenance for existence. No food or water intake is known. No food found on craft in one known retrieval. No alimentary canal or rectal area described.

20. Humanoid types. Unknown. Descriptive variations of anatomy may be no more diverse than those known among earth homo sapiens. Other alien types, reportedly varying in range from human to more grotesque configurations are unknown to me. Speculatively, if these types exist, they may have their origins in other solar systems or have roots on different planets within one solar system.

21. I know of the names of two major medical centers in the Eastern United States where continuing specialized intensive research is conducted on deceased alien bodies. Other hospitals where research reportedly has been conducted are in Indiana, Illinois, Texas, Southwestern and Western U.S.A.

The late UFOlogist Gray Barker looks over the previously classified documents at his office in Clarksburg, W. Va.

Artist rendering of the way the UFO might have appeared on the ground at Los Alamos surrounded by MPs. From movie poster courtesy of Scotia Films.

6

THE CONTROVERSIAL ALIEN BODY PHOTOS

In 1980 two highly unusual photographs supposedly showing the remains of a humanoid being found among the wreckage of a crashed UFO were released to the news media. The pictures and accompanying story were first carried by the Associated Press, and almost immediately headlined in the tabloids such as *GLOBE* and *THE WEEKLY WORLD NEWS.*

According to the information released at the time, the photos were said to have been leaked by a retired military man to a group of independent UFO researchers. The group, known as the "Coalition of Concerned UFOlogists," is made up of investigators Williard F. McIntyre, Charles J. Wilhelm and Dennis Pilichis, all of whom have been involved in the field for years.

Because of the nature of this material, I immediately placed long distance telephone calls to two of the individuals involved, with whom I had maintained contact in the past. Both Charles Wilhelm and Dennis Pilichis were more than anxious to cooperate in supplying me with prints made from the original negatives, and extended considerable time allowing me to interview them for an article I planned to run in a forthcoming issue of *UFO REVIEW.*

As it turned out, the completed article, along with the photos in question, were the main feature in issue Number Nine. The reaction from our readers was, as might be expected, given the circumstances, PHENOMENAL!

There were those who believed the pictures were legitimate—the real McCoy—while others among our audience questioned their validity. A controversy developed, with almost everyone taking sides. The saucer press (mainly several relatively limited circulation bulletins and newsletters) printed every bit of data they could get their hands on, both pro and con. Unfortunately, the majority of those airing their views only had the opportunity to view poor reproductions, usually printed on pulp paper from which a considerable amount of detail was missing. As in any serious scientific study, it is necessary to spend considerable time and effort to piece together the many parts to such a great puzzle. Quick decisions cannot be made. All the evidence must be weighed and every scrap of information taken into consideration.

One thing is for sure, no one was trying to withhold anything. When another group analyzed the photos and declared that they were probably monkeys, the Coalition didn't sweep that fact under the rug but set out to prove otherwise. Putting their collective heads together, they patiently organized all the facts at their disposal and attempted to straighten out some of the misinformation which had been circulating in the UFOlogical community.

It is my feeling that, should these photos prove to be legitimate, they can provide all the evidence necessary to prove that the government does have the wreckage of UFOs that have crash landed, as well as their alien occupants. Such proof could rock the scientific community and make international headlines.

On the following pages you will find a detailed report on these shocking photographs. In the long run, it is up to you to decide if they are for real—they could very well be!

THIS CHAPTER ON THE UFO CRASH OF JULY 7TH, 1948 and the reproduction of the alleged alien body photos is COPYRIGHT 1980

BY THE COALITION OF CONCERNED UFOLOGISTS OF AMERICA

Reprinted by permission

The following material is from a report prepared by The Coalition of Concerned Ufologists of America. The coalition founders are:

The Mutual Anomaly Research Center and Evaluation Network

(MARCEN)

123 Olney-Sandy Spring Road

Sandy Spring, MD 20860

The UFO Information Network (UFOIN)

P. O. Box 5012

Rome, OH 44085

The Ohio UFO Investigation League (OUFOIL)

1139 Senate Drive

Fairfield, OH 45014

Editors:

Williard F. McIntyre (MARCEN)

Dennis J. Pilichis (UFOIN)

Charles J. Wilhelm (OUFOIL)

The material reproduced in this book is part of a much larger report that may be obtained along with current updated research exploring other aspects of the UFO crash case(s) along with comments from scientific sources that the alien body photos do not represent monkeys, from: ($6.00 postpaid) The UFO Information Network, Box 5012, Rome, OH 44085

The Mutual Anomaly Research Center and Evaluation Network Inc.

(MARCEN)

123 Olney-Sandy Spring Road

Sandy Spring MD. 20860

MARCEN was a fledgling organization in November, 1978, having just mailed out its first journal, and was the recipient of much mail from interested and curious persons. Little did we know, when we answered an inquiry with a lot of questions about our motivation and goals that we would be handed the ufological story or hoax of all times.

After exchanging three letters with a gentleman in Tennessee, we received from him a letter in mid December 1978 that came with an 8 by 10 glossy print of a lot of debris and the charred remains of some type of body. The accompanying letter extolled our virtues that the writer approved of and complained of the shortcomings of other organizations. Most cryptically, the letter contained a challenge to identify the contents of the photo.

We promptly fired off a letter giving our guess that it showed the remains of a light aircraft crash and its burned pilot. The response came in early January, 1979 in the form of a three page, typed, single-spaced letter detailing a fantastic odyssey of a young Navy photographer flown to Mexico in 1948 as part of a team to document the crash of a 90 foot in diameter 'flying saucer' and its dead pilot. A fantastic adventure unfolded in those three pages, ending with the writer's concern for his own security since he was still in the service and fearful of prosecution for breaches of security.

We responded with our assurances of anonymity for the source and expressed our doubt he would ever be prosecuted.

In mid-March 1979 we received another three page letter reiterating his concerns over prosecution, detailing the episode in more detail, and giving us personal data upon which to check on his credentials.

For the next several months, we proceeded to check into the man's background; everything checked out exactly as he had said. We kept the print lying around MARCEN offices, periodically showed it to visitors, and asked their opinion of its contents without revealing what it purported to show. No one was very impressed with the photo, not even the few to whom we revealed what it was supposed to be. Most were disappointed that the debris looked earthly but no one could describe what unearthly debris should look like.

By October, 1979, we told the source what we had learned, and signed an agreement to keep his identity secret.

In the meantime, we had microscopic and microdensitometer tests made on the print, and found no evidence of double exposure or paste up photography.

By the end of November, 1979, the source responded by sending us the negative from which the print was made and an acceptance of our agreement. We had agreed that we would use a pseudonym in corresponding with the source to further protect his identity in case MARCEN's security was breached.

In early 1980 we made the other members of the organizing committee of the Coalition of Concerned Ufologists (Dennis Pilichis and Charles Wilhelm) aware of our possession, and sent them Xerox copies of the print while we had the negative analyzed by Kodak and other laboratories.

The conclusion of Eastman Kodak, which we initially felt was of dubious value because of the methodology used, pointed to a negative processed at least 30 years previously. Microdensitometer traces of the negative showed us that no deliberate hoaxing had been done, at least photographically, in the production of the negative.

In May, 1980, the source sent us the second negative showing the body lying in vegetation on a hillside. By now we had begun believing this fantastic story at least partially, and asked for more details and his permission to make the photos and part of the story public as a joint release of the coalition (MARCEN, UFOIN, OUFOIL).

In August, 1980, the source gave his permission and warned of the possible consequences of such a release. Little did he know or visualize the explosion that would really come, or who would detonate it.

The coalition organizers recognized the significance of the story and decided that the best course would be to release the pictures to the public. It was hoped that this action would give everyone a chance to see the photos, so that if they were a hoax or misidentification, someone would be able to set us straight. It was also hoped that the publication of the photos would encourage others with evidence they may have been hoarding to come forward.

Prints were made from the negatives, and the actual negatives were submitted to Ground Saucer Watch (GSW) for extensive computer analysis. Just prior to the coalition organizational meeting on August 22nd at Kent State University, the photos were released to the Associated Press in two areas and to numerous newspaper and broadcast stations. The next several weeks were bedlam, as the media clamored for more information and the coalition officers were kept busy with the radio and television interviews.

All of the public attention over the photos was expected to generate jealousy from other segments of the ufological community who were pushed out of the limelight. It did rear its head in the form of condemnation, snubbing and outright lies and character assassination of the coalition members involved and the entire Coalition of Concerned Ufologists.

Ninety days later the hullabaloo had not abated, as the wrath of the ufological hierarchy intensified when various tabloids publicized the photos and story.

Was it all worth the hassle we were subjected to? And what do we think of the photos and story at this point in time?

Universally condemned as hoaxes by skeptics and establishment ufologists alike, the photos remain unidentified. No legitimate explanation has emerged, and not even a plausible theory that can hold up. There has been no lack of attempts at explaining away the veracity of the photos but none even held up more than a week.

It has been suggested that the photographer was duped when he took the photos, and was told it was a UFO to cover up some sinister testing failure of the U.S. Government. I cannot buy that theory any more than I can accept that anyone would perpetrate a hoax in 1948 and wait three decades to spring it on the public. It has also been suggested that some members of the coalition were responsible for the photos but the problem here is that since the age of the photos was so old (also confirmed by GSW) the ages of these coalition members would have ranged from not born to nine years old. We don't think so...

I personally believe that these photos and the story surrounding them are either completely authentic as told by our source, or it is a complete hoax perpetrated in a sophisticated manner that has thus far defied detection, and done for reasons thus far unknown.

There are problems with the case that we have just learned as this report was being printed. In an attempt to convince the source to release more of the negatives he says he has, we sent a representative to the current address where we have been communicating with him in San Antonio, Texas, only to learn he did not live there, but was known at that address.

We have since learned that this was a mail drop used by the source to protect his actual identity even from us, and that the name we knew him by and checked out was actually the name of another member of the photographic team that supposedly documented the UFO crash and has since died.

We received another call from the source, and he stated that he will be in Washington, D.C. on Thanksgiving; he will meet with us and will reveal and prove his true identity, and will bring more of his negatives.

We know we are dealing with presumably a career military man, very fearful of some sort of prosecution for his transgressions in this affair who is doing his best to remain anonymous. He has presented us with a story and supporting evidence that has not yet been disproved, no matter how hard anyone has tried. When the final verdict is in, we will make it known to the entire ufological field. Until then, we can only say that we strongly believe, but honestly do not know.

The following facts and photos will allow the reader to form his or her own judgment on the case and available evidence.

Sincerely,

For the rest of the coalition membership,

WILLIARD F. MCINTYRE

Director of MARCEN

THE DETAILED STORY OF THE UFO CRASH OF JULY 7, 1948

AND EVENTS THAT LED UP TO PHOTOGRAPHING THE ALIEN BODY

The following material has been taken from actual letters from our source sent to Williard McIntyre of the Mutual Anomaly Research And Evaluation Network. The letters date from December 11th 1978 to August 2nd 1980.

Nothing has been done to distort what the actual letters have to say, although some material has been edited in order to protect the identification of certain people mentioned and to present a coherent flow of the correct sequence of events that took place.

At the time this UFO incident took place our source was photographer assigned at White Sands, New Mexico. Most of his time was spent photographing and documenting fatigue and stress results on various metallic alloys after a variety of shock distresses. Before July 7th, 1948, the most exciting part of his duty was sporadic visits to the atomic test sites to document various aftereffects of the blasts.

Our source had heard that at approximately 1322 hours, the DEW line early warning radar was tracking an object moving at speeds in excess of 2,000 mph when it crossed into Washington State flying south by southeast.

Attempts by our interceptors to identify it resulted only in seeing a metallic streak go by. Apparently the airwaves were filled with talk of the object because two fighter pilots operating out of Dias Air Base in Texas heard the flight path of the bogey and got themselves into position over Albuquerque, New Mexico to attempt to either intercept it or to identify it.

As the UFO approached the two F-94s it was about 2,000 feet above their altitude of 9,000 feet and it made a 90 degree turn without slowing down and headed east over Texas. This maneuver took place at approximately 1401 hours. Other pilots in the new flight path reported that the object seemed to be slowing down and was wobbling in flight. Several radar units tracking the object reported that it had slowed to a speed of approximately 90 mph by 1413 hours and by 1429 hours it had disappeared from all of the radar screens.

Using triangulation from all of the radar stations, it was determined that the object either landed or crashed in Mexico in the state of Nuevo Leon at a point midway between Nuevo Laredo and the Sabinas River, approximately 30 miles south of Laredo, Texas.

RECOVERY TEAMS ARE SENT TO THE LOCATION

The Mexican military authorities were notified of this incident and the U.S. Army and Air Force units were rushed to the site and arrived there at about 1830 hours. Commander Smith (real name on file), a Naval Intelligence officer, was in Mexico City when he heard of the crash and went to the scene with Mexican authorities, arriving about 2010 hours. After surveying the site, he apparently called his superiors in Washington or wherever because at 2050 hours our source's team received a call to prepare a photographic team to be airlifted to the site. They were told they were going to the site of a top secret airplane crash.

At 2130 hours they were picked up by a U.S. Army L-19 Bird Dog and it was rather uncomfortable cramming five of them and their bulky equipment into that plane. They landed in Del Rio, Texas around midnight to refuel and then arrived at the site about 0215 hours.

As they circled the site before landing, they saw the remains of the frame and structure of an apparently disc shaped craft still smoldering and smoking some 12 hours after it had crashed. The crash site was a deserted valley surrounded by heavily vegetated hills rising a few hundred feet on three sides.

They landed at a makeshift runway about half a mile from the crash site and were immediately taken to the site by U.S. Army trucks. Commander Smith had apparently been given command or at least as far as their mission, and told them to photograph everything in as much detail as possible.

THE CONTROVERSIAL ALIEN BODY PHOTOS

WHAT THEY OBSERVED AND PHOTOGRAPHED

Details of the object:

What they observed and photographed was an unearthly shaped craft made up of earthly looking debris. The basic structure looked as if it could have been built by earthly hands. Things were badly burned by the time they got to the site, but they noticed a complete absence of any type of wiring, rubber, glass, plastic, wood, or paper products.

Our source noticed what was some supportive structures, which were held together by what appeared to be conventional bolts, but when the mechanics attempted to unscrew them with wrenches, they would not turn at all. They had to be eventually chiseled off and the metal was very hard. The Army was using carbide and diamond drills and diamond saws for the final disassembly.

There appeared to be two kinds of metal involved. The first and most abundant could not be cut by the oxy-acetylene cutting torches brought in. The second immediately began burning when the cutting torches were used on it.

The structural skin of the craft was apparently blown away in the explosion when the device crashed, as the whole valley was scattered with fragments of what appeared to be foil, very much like our cigarette packages, only much harder. You could not bend the material. Before anyone could leave the site, the MPs searched them and confiscated all fragments that had been collected..

As best the source could ascertain, the craft was nearly perfectly circular and was about 90 feet in diameter and about 28 feet in thickness at the center and tapering off to about 5 feet thick at the perimeter.

There appeared to be five or six levels in the center of the craft, and they were told some sort of instrumentation and machinery were removed before they had arrived. No propulsion system or mechanism was apparent to the source.

Details of the body:

There was only one body, and it was badly burned at that, still in the structure. Our source photographed it in place in the structure as best he could with the intense heat from the still smoldering structure and the burning hot sand. After they had taken photos of the entire scene and attempted to use multiple flashguns and a tripod to record the overall scene from a nearby hillside, the Air Force crash and rescue firemen on the scene dragged the body from the craft and put it on a nearby bank so they could photograph it away from the intense heat.

During their briefing, before photographic work began, one of the team members asked what this was and where it came from. Commander Smith told him not too ask. An Army captain who assisted them said the little fellow we were photographing did not come from this Earth.

They only saw and photographed one body but rumors were floating around the site that two or more creatures had been blown out of the vehicle and were captured and taken away—injured severely but still alive. Our source said he had no confirmation of this aspect of the case.

The body they photographed was 4 feet 6 inches long. Its head was extremely large for the body size by human proportions. The eyes were gone from the fire but the eye sockets were much larger than in humans and were almost wraparound as if to give it 180 degree vision. There were no visible ears or nose but there were openings where ears and nostrils would have been in humans. There were no lips and the mouth was just a sort of slit with no teeth or tongue. There were two legs of normal proportions with short feet having no discernible toes. The two arms were longer than in humans and the hands had four claw-like fingers each with no apparent thumbs. The arms and legs appeared to have joints in approximately the same place as in humans.

There were two Army doctors that arrived on the morning of July 8th, and they made a superficial examination of the body. Our source listened to them while taking photos of their work.

There were no teeth or tongue in the mouth, and no apparent duct connecting the mouth to any kind of digestive system. There were no reproductive organs visible by human standards. The most remarkable thing he overheard was that no stratified muscle fiber was discovered in any of the extremities. The tissue, which was grey in color, was extremely smooth, and the doctors compared its consistency to the tissue of a human female breast. They said that the bone structure in the extremities was more complicated than in humans, and speculated that motion may have been accomplished through the supporting bones instead of muscles. The entire abdomen was encased by a rib-like structure all the way to the hips. The doctors were amazed that the right arm extremity had a metallic joint at the elbow. No internal examinations were made at the site.

The hands each had four digits, longer than human fingers, and they tapered to an almost claw-like appearance at the tip. There were no opposing digits like thumbs. There was no visible evidence of toes, and the feet came to a blunt point. The body appeared to have been clothed in a metallic-like material, most of which had been burned away.

The doctors said there was no evidence of hair growing on the head or other areas of the body, as they found no immediate evidence of hair roots. The only fluid found in the apparent veins in the extremities was colorless, with a slight green cast and a strong sulfurous odor.

THE CONTROVERSIAL ALIEN BODY PHOTOS

Our source noticed a strong sulfurous odor and an ozone smell when working around the burned structure.

MISCELLANEOUS DETAILS OF THE CASE

They worked until about 0430 hours, and then were allowed to get some coffee and breakfast at a rudimentary camp that had been setup, after being cautioned not to discuss what they had seen with each other or the Army troops. They went to a tent and caught some sleep until 0800, when they were awakened to begin documenting the scene in daylight. They worked steadily until 1300 hours when a C-47 arrived. The body was taken away, and the Army units began cutting up the wreckage and putting the dismantled parts on U.S. and Mexican trucks. The Mexican trucks departed toward Monterey, and the U.S. trucks left in the direction of Laredo, Texas. The source does not know the final destination of any of them.

The source also overheard a conversation by a metallurgist who was brought to the site on July 8th, saying that the metal seemed to have a honeycomb crystalline structure unlike anything known on earth, and he believed that the metal was an alloy containing silicon, which could also account for some of the phenomenal hardness.

At 1830 hours on July 8th, 1948, they packed up all of their equipment and their more than 500 exposed negatives. They were picked up by a C-47, along with Commander Smith, and flown to Alamogordo, New Mexico. When they got back to White Sands, they were taken off all other duties for three weeks, and spent all of their time developing negatives and making prints. No one else was allowed near their darkroom while they were working there. In fact, Marine guards were posted around the darkroom area to insure security.

As soon as a complete set of 8 x 10s of all negatives was made, Commander Smith left for Washington and the source never saw him again. In fact, some of the guys began talking about Commander Smith, and decided that he probably was not even a Naval Officer, since they never saw him in uniform and his speech was decidedly non-Naval. Various other intelligence officers visited them sporadically and they were cautioned about disclosing what they had seen or photographed.

A few years later, when our Source's transfer was obviously imminent, he removed 40 negatives from the file and made duplicate negatives which he put back into the files. He took the original negatives, figuring the whole episode would be forever buried in bureaucratic bungling and secrecy unless one of those involved was able to reveal the secret someday in a credible way.

In answer to a question about radiation, the source did not know if measurements were made or not. They were asked to bring a scintillometer, which they did bring on the trip, but apparently it was damaged because it did not operate in a proper way. The source did not notice anyone else with radiation measuring equipment but he told us that a sizeable number of his negatives were badly fogged when he processed them. The source feels it could have been radiation, or it could have been the heat from the crash, but they did notice that all of the film that was loaded on the site inside of changing bags was fogged to some degree or other.

RESEARCH WORK DONE ON THE NEGATIVES

About August 10th, 1980 Williard McIntyre submitted by certified mail the two original negatives to the Ground Saucer Watch [13238 N. 7th Drive, Phoenix, Arizona 85029] for their evaluation by computer enhancement photographic research. Their findings are reproduced here:

LAREDO TEXAS INCIDENT JULY 7th, 1948

COMPUTER ENHANCEMENT PHOTOGRAPHIC EVALUATION (Critique)

COPYRIGHT 1980 GSW

Two original b & w negatives were submitted to GSW for computer photographic analysis. The negatives, although extremely age-dated, contained photographic images of a severely burned humanoid-like creature/animal lying on the ground and what appears to be wreckage, consisting of twisted metal.

Although GSW's computerized enhancement technique works well on photographs of purported UFOs, only some sparse data can be gleaned from photographic images, relatively close to the camera, of the conventional variety. When analyzing photo of UFOs, such items as verification of the time of day based on image shadows is obtainable, details of lumen dispersion, information on surface reflectivity and the approximation of distance-to-camera based on the effects of the atmosphere to groupings of pixels [picture cells].

All major modes of computerized enhancement were utilized, with the exception of color contouring, including high resolution averaging to gain further information. The following was obtained after a careful review of the negatives:

THE CONTROVERSIAL ALIEN BODY PHOTOS

1. The negatives have been non-destructively age-dated using a powerful microscope and empirically comparing these negatives and photographic medium existing close to 30 years ago.

2. The larger of the two negatives has an extremely shallow depth of field and portions of the top of the photo are out of focus.

3. There is evidence of the "creature" being severely burned and mutilated as a result of an obvious accident.

4. The disfiguration of the body and signs of rigor mortis are indicative of the time after death that the photographs were taken. The time is calculated at twelve hours.

5. Measurement of the head and jaw bone area on the face, the arm/leg lengths and a careful study of the extremities, i.e. hands and feet, and then comparison with forensic pathology records, revealed a commonality between these measurements and that of a laboratory monkey.

6. A close computer scrutiny of the wreckage materials in the smaller negative revealed common "terrestrial" geometric shapes and signs of manufacture.

7. The size of the "creature" is 863mm. measured from head to buttocks.

8. There is evidence of a horny sheath covering the toe portion of the primate. The nail, which is covered by hair, is very similar to that of a monkey.

9. In the smaller negative there is photographic evidence of burning of the skull of the primate. The blistering is indicative of a short duration, high temperature flash burn. There is also evidence of the torso being disintegrated due to crushing/ripping during the fall.

10. There is no evidence of a hoax or deliberate manipulation of the film.

CONCLUSIONS AND SPECULATION BY GSW ON THEIR ANALYSIS:

It is the consensus of the GSW photographic review staff that the photographs in question represent a misinterpretation of a normal laboratory monkey [either a rhesus or orangutan] that has been badly burned and partially dismembered. If the narrative portion of this purported UFO incident is accurate, there are grave implications to the origin of this crash /accident. If the incident actually did occur as reported, which is a reasonable assumption, then it indicates that the U.S. Government was illegally testing rockets in cross-state firings, i.e. rocket launching in New Mexico [White Sands] and cross-launching into Texas over populous areas.

It is known that the U.S. Government was firing rockets and monkeys (pre-space development) into space for experimentation purposes. We know that the government/military has had numerous failures ,especially in the early days of rocket development [after WWII].

The questions now arise about all purported crashed saucer incidents. Why, after all these years, are "crashed saucer" photographs surfacing?

Why would any trained anthropologist even remotely consider pictures of this caliber to be connected with an alien creature? Are these photographs, and similar ones, being disseminated for misinformation purposes?

If the answers to the above questions are based on a plot to filter misinformation to the body politic and UFO researchers to cover the obvious sinister motives of government wrongdoings, then all of the valid crashed saucer cases make logical sense. The reasons for the security was the location of the crashes, i.e., off of military bases or testing areas, as opposed to the actuality of the incident.

It is of little concern that some monkeys were killed as hundreds of test animals are killed every day for reasons ranging from warfare development to medical research. What is important is the fact the U.S. Government was firing rockets over populous areas, and luckily they never killed or injured a high quantity of that same populous.

GSW has copied the negatives onto our computer discs, and will contact additional zoologists and quantify our measurements for absolute identification of the creature. However, at this time there is not one data point to even suggest that an alien creature was attributable to the imagery on the analyzed negatives.

End of Report

FRED ARDLAN

GSW PHOTOGRAPHIC CONSULTANT

WILLIAM H. SPAULDING

DIRECTOR/ WESTERN DIVISION

COALITION RESPONSE TO THE

GROUND SAUCER WATCH ANALYSIS

While the first reading of the Ground Saucer Watch [GSW] analysis of the alleged alien body negatives appears to cast doubt on their authenticity as actual photos of an alien, in reality the analysis strengthens the veracity of the testimony of their contents.

We know from the GSW analysis and from those done by other laboratories that the negatives were processed about 30 years ago and definitely within the time span of 1947 to 1953. This alone casts doubt on someone waiting 30 years to spring a hoax perpetrated three decades ago.

GSW's unique finding of rigor mortis calculated at 12 hours after death confirms exactly the source's testimony of the time lapse between the crash and when the photos were taken. GSW was not given this information prior to the analysis.

The GSW analysis confirms there is no evidence of a hoax with the negatives, ruling out miniaturization, double exposure, pasteups, or any of the normally employed hoaxing techniques.

The main problem we have with the analysis is when GSW begins speculation that the body is of a Rhesus Monkey or an Orangutan.

Mr. Spaulding indicated to Charles Wilhelm that GSW is involved in investigating five or six other incidents involving crashes containing monkeys and dating back to 1945 or 1946, and that is why he additionally believes these photos are of a monkey or an Orangutan.

We don't honestly know why Mr. Spaulding is attempting to manipulate this case toward an explanation of a monkey. We would also only be speculating to advance the hypothesis that:

[1] Mr. Spaulding may be part of the MUFON-Stringfield plot to discredit these photos because they take the wind out of the sails of Stringfield's photos of "The creature from under the Empire State Building and the creature from the Chicago Sewer" which MUFON planned to hype at the 1981 convention, already having set the stage at the 1980 MUFON Convention.

[2] Mr. Spaulding may be trying to mold the evidence to fit his own personal theory advanced on national television that UFOs are not extraterrestrial an originate from mundane sources on Earth.

[3] Mr. Spaulding may honestly believe the pictures are of a monkey. We are inclined to believe that #2 is the case since Mr. Spaulding has never shown any inclination to engage in the kind of lying, character assassination and outright deceit that has accompanied the response to the public release of these photos.

If we are to believe that the photos were taken in 1948, as stated by the source and confirmed by GSW, and that they are actually the corpse of a monkey in rocket debris, then the only rocket the United States possessed was the captured German V2 which was brought in numbers to White Sands, New Mexico.

To find out more about the V2, we went to the National Air and Space Museum of the Smithsonian Institute in Washington, D.C. and talked to Dr. Gregory Kennedy, who is described by his colleagues as the most knowledgeable person on the subject of V2s in America today. A talk with Dr. Kennedy convinced us of the accuracy of this, and he documented his statement with the report of U.S. Army Project Hermes, which was started in 1944 to study the V2 and continued with the testing of the captured V2s brought to the United States.

According to Dr. Kennedy and the Project Hermes report, only four V2 launches were ever made containing monkeys in experiments to study the effects of launching primates. The first was V2 #37 launched on June 11, 1948 in which the Rhesus monkey died before launch. The next primate launch on June 14, 1949 and the next two following it resulted in the V2 exploding in flight, so that no monkey was ever recovered alive.

All of the V2 primate experiments only utilized Rhesus monkeys which attain a maximum length of about two feet—far smaller than the 34.6 inch [863mm] head to buttock dimensions of the pictured creature as measured by Ground Saucer Watch.

The fact that a maximum of four V2 primate launches were made would also appear to shoot holes in Mr. Spaulding's investigation of five or six crashes of V2s carrying monkeys, some of which would have occurred two to three years before the first actual V2 primate launch.

We find we have a problem accepting point #5 of the GSW analysis stating a commonality of measurement between the pictured creature and a laboratory monkey [or Rhesus monkey] when point #7 states a head to buttocks measurement of 863mm [34.6 inches]—considerably longer than the maximum total length attained by a Rhesus monkey. There is also no evidence of a tail in the photo.

While the measurements of the pictured creature could match those of an Orangutan, which reached a length of about four and a half feet, no Orangutans were ever launched in V2s according to Dr. Kennedy. After examining the instrument capsule which replaced the warhead on the front of the V2, we can understand why Orangutans were not launched. The capsule, which is cone shaped, is 30 inches in diameter at the base and tapers to a point 78 inches above. It would be quite a feat to cram a live Orangutan, four and a half feet long with a seven and a half foot arm span into this tiny space, along with breathing apparatus and any sort of seat or protective enclosure. There would certainly not be any room for any sort of instrumentation or recovery devices if the cone were filled with wall to wall monkey.

There are other factors that contradict the theory that a V2 rocket crash is pictured in the photos. The V2 had a theoretical maximum range of 200 to 225 miles. Dr. Wernher Von Braun, writing in the History of Rocketry and Space Travel [Thomas Y. Crowell Company, 1969] stated that a maximum range of any V2 fired in the United States was 111.1 miles. Dr. Kennedy indicated the maximum range attained in the United States was actually only 68 miles. In any event, any and all of the above figures fall far short of the almost 1,000 miles from the White Sands launch site to the crash site in Mexico where the debris and the body were photographed.

Arguments have been advanced that the U.S. did have V2s go astray and land in Mexico. "That is true," said Dr. Kennedy, "and in fact in 1948, a wayward V2 hit Juarez, Mexico, a mere 68 miles due south of White Sands."

Could a rocket have been launched from somewhere else and landed at the crashsite? "No," said Dr. Kennedy. "All of the V2s were launched at White Sands, New Mexico except for two tested at Cape Canaveral, Florida and two fired from the deck of the aircraft carrier U.S.S. Midway, and all far out of range.

Also very bothersome in the GSW analysis and report is the accompanying page of photos that GSW xeroxed from some unidentified source to try and bolster the monkey theory. These three photos may have been from three different sources and some may have had nothing to do with V2s, since there is no documentation to check.

On the whole, the GSW analysis and report tend to enhance the veracity of these photos being of an alien creature. It confirms the age of the negatives and the fact that no hanky panky took place in the photography or in manipulating the negatives. We are not bothered that earthly geometric shapes appear in the photos. Do not the same laws of geometry apply throughout the universe? Are science and manufacturing abilities unique only to an intelligence on Earth?

The similarity between the creature photographed and a Chimpanzee or Orangutan bears out the eyewitness accounts of many encounters with reported aliens under five feet tall with large heads and long arms.

If in fact a UFO with an unearthly alien did crash in Mexico on July 7, 1948, we would expect the body of the pilot to resemble the reports of other aliens encountered, and not look like an elephant or something totally bizarre.

In summary, we believe the issue of a V2 rocket with a monkey has been put to rest and is not the subject of the aforementioned photographs.

POSTSCRIPT TO THE COALITION RESPONSE TO THE GSW ANALYSIS

In reading the complete GSW report, reproduced in this Alien Body Photo Report, it clearly indicates that GSW felt "rocket" experiments had taken place and that this sort of technology was responsible for these "crashed saucer reports." There was never at any time any sort of mention whatsoever of "flying discs" or "circular aircraft" involvement.

A news clipping has come to our attention relating to a special investigation GSW is now involved in. The clipping is dated September 21, 1980 from the Mesa, Arizona Tribune. It says in part:

"Spaulding and other members of GSW currently are investigating reports of three crashes near Roswell, N.M., and Laredo and El Paso, Texas, of circular surfaced aircraft—"flying discs" that reportedly are super secret U.S. military projects."

The reason they have been hushed is because it's political. We intend to reveal the whole story in December with names and everything because the public has a right to know. Manipulation and suppression of known UFO data by government agencies has created misinformation that is misleading the public.

So, apparently now we are dealing with "flying discs"! Are we led to believe that monkeys are driving around complicated hover-craft objects?

We are rather puzzled by the shift in word terminology from rocket firings, monkeys, V2s, pre-space development, cross-state firings, etc., etc., to flying discs, circular aircraft and super secret U.S. military experiments.

We apparently had some pretty "cool" orangutans manoeuvering the friendly skies of the United States in the late 1940s and early 1950s!

COALITION MEMBERS CONFRONT GOSSIP

AND DISTORTION BY UFOLOGISTS

After the release of the "alien" body photo to the public, coalition members Dennis Pilichis and Charles Wilhelm began hearing confirmed stories from other researchers in the UFO field that members of the ufological hierarchy were saying our photos were a hoax. They were informed that something regarding our photos was going to take place at a local gathering of the Cleveland UfOlogy Project meeting in Cleveland, Ohio the night of September 20th, 1980.

Pilichis and Wilhelm felt these stories were rather strange, in that none of these "researchers" had once bothered to correspond with them to find out more details on the authenticity of the case in question.

After learning that Mr. Len Stringfield was involved in this sort of game playing and distortion of the facts, Mr. Pilichis and Mr. Wilhelm decided to attend the UFO meeting in Cleveland, Ohio to confront Mr. Stringfield with the "allegations" they had been hearing.

Mr. Stringfield was attending the local UFO meeting to speak on his alien body photos [for a complete report on this, please see the second part of this study].

When asked if he was indeed claiming our photos were a hoax and not authentic, Mr. Stringfield said he was not doing so, and would not do so, as he knew very little about our alien body photo case and could not make any sort of judgment as to their authenticity.

Later that evening after the meeting, the subject of Williard McIntyre came up. Mr. Pilichis and Mr. Wilhelm told Mr. Stringfield they were very aware of the fact that certain "unreliable" people were saying things about Mr. McIntyre and that they had very questionable motives for doing so.

Mr. Stringfield said he really knew nothing about Mr. McIntyre, and alluded to "East Coast contacts" telling him things. Mr. Stringfield did say he was interested in checking into Mr. McIntyre in a kind way, so as not to hurt his standing or reputation. We might add that Mr. Pilichis and Mr. Wilhelm attended the local UFO meeting also in order to see Stringfield's photos and to be able to clearly identify them. They had their suspicions that his photos were the ridiculous "alien creature photos taken under the Empire State Building" which appeared in the past issue of the totally unreliable Ancient Astronauts Magazine. When Len's slides came on the screen, they were shocked to learn their worst fears were confirmed. These were indeed the same pictures! A complete report follows in these pages on Mr. Stringfield's pictures.

We now ask you to read the following material taken from a broadcast over the MUFON AMATEUR RADIO NETWORK on Saturday, September 13th, 1980, a week before the above mentioned Cleveland UFOlogy Project meeting, which took place on Sept. 20, 1980.

The broadcast was made by David Dobbs, a Cincinnati resident and science writer, also a very close friend of Len Stringfield's. Mr. Pilichis wrote Mr. Dobbs a letter on Nov. 4, 1980 concerning this broadcast he made, and to the date of publication of this report, he has not received any sort of reply.

We might add here that at no time did any MUFON representative contact either Mr. Pilichis, Mr. McIntyre, or Mr. Wilhelm in regard to the alien body photos, the actual background of the case, or other factors involved, before issuing this information out over the radio airwaves. This is not the way so-called respectable researchers should be acting.

Note the following transcript of that MUFON radio broadcast on Sept 1, 1980. [The actual tape recording of this broadcast is on file]:

"Len has information about the photographs which were published locally here and were seen on television in Cincinnati and Dayton and were publicized by Charles Wilhelm, our local MUFON representative.

"Len's information is that these pictures are not authentic, but they originated with a doctor, so-called 'doctor' McIntyre in the Washington, D.C. area, who apparently does not have too good a reputation for veracity.

"I did have an opportunity to study the photographs, the one photograph in detail, as it was published n an Ohio newspaper. What is purported to be the head was absolutely round and had no structure whatever. It looked like a ball that had been thrown into a fire and the paint had charred and sort of bubbled. As I say, it was completely round and when you looked at the picture for some time, not for a second on television, it didn't have too good an appearance. I certainly was not impressed with it myself.

"There has been no follow-up or any further publicity on these pictures and...." [at this point in the taped broadcast there is strong interference and the remaining part of the sentence is not understandable].

"In brief, to summarize the news we had here this morning, other than the photographs which Len Stringfield has which he showed at the MUFON Symposium, they now appear to be perhaps infrared photographs designed to show some of the bone structure. The rotary joints and the nature of the bone structure has been verified by his medical authorities. They are not familiar with the photographs, but they did say the bone structure is authentic, so he feels that he is accumulating evidence that this is an authentic photoset, and feels that other sets may be being released and planted in order to discount them. It's a possibility, anyway. . ."

END OF BROADCAST.

So, it all began to make a lot of sense to coalition members what was really taking place here! To add more to the confusion and to create a more sinister flavor to the situation, it appears Mr. Stringfield feels our photos were released in order to discredit his. We take great offense to this statement, as we have had our photos since late 1978, and our release has nothing whatsoever to do with his photos. In the first place, his photos don't need any outside help in discrediting themselves, as our complete report clearly details!

To add insult to injury Mr. Stringfield is now denying he made the above statements to David Dobbs, and when brought up refers to them as "alleged" comments! We have a direct copy of the broadcast and have no problem in authenticating the actual tape recording.

We are very concerned over Stringfield's "East Coast contacts" as he called them, as we know for a fact he has been in touch with one totally unreliable individual who has long-ago established a reputation in the UFO field as an antagonist and troublemaker, and is directly responsible for spreading false material to other ufologists in order to cause conflict.

PUBLISHER'S UPDATE: At press time, one of those involved in the preparation of this report—Charles Wilhelm—has changed his opinion on the seeming authenticity of the alien photos and now believes they may represent the remains of a dead primate used in early top secret rocket tests by the Military. Mr. McIntyre has since vanished and Dennis Pilichis has moved to Pennsylvania, so requests for more information are likely to be ignored.

The object in question either landed or crashed in Mexico in the State of Nuevo Leon at a point midway between Nuevo Laredo and Sabinas River, approximately 30 miles south of Laredo, Texas on July 7, 1948.

7

DID A UFO EVER CRASH IN CENTRAL PARK?

One of the questions often posed to UFO researchers is: Why do most sightings occur in rural areas with only a handful of witnesses present? For instance, why has not one of these objects landed on the White House lawn or somewhere in New York City, where millions of people could see it?

Surprising as it may seem, such happenings have taken place; and not entirely unobserved. Readers are probably familiar with the series of UFO events which transpired in the sky over our nation's capital during the months of July and August of 1952—this is recorded history.

During this period more than fifty unidentified objects appeared almost nightly over Washington, D.C. On several occasions they were actually tracked on radar, and jet interceptors were scrambled in an attempt to identify these unknown occurrences. Each time the UFOs would pull away at fantastic speed, leaving the radar screens in a matter of seconds, to say nothing of the bewildered military pilots who had been sent up to identify them.

However, only a few persons within a small area of New York City's Harlem realized that during the same period, a UFO was not only sighted, but that part of it was actually shot off and fell in New York's famous Central Park-at least that is what one seemingly reliable person has revealed to us.

If this case really took place, undoubtedly hundreds, perhaps thousands, of New Yorkers must know of this incident, but because of a tight wall of security and seventeen years of absolute press silence, this important and dramatic UFO event has never been publicized.

Some time ago I spoke to the one witness who is willing to talk about this unusual episode. Barbara Hudson, an attractive middle-aged black woman who has lived most of her life in New York City, says that the event in question happened in late July of 1952—she is not certain of the exact date after all these years.

The time was 8:30 and dusk was just beginning to creep upon the city. Barbara, her mother and brother were on their way home to 115th Street from a sightseeing tour of Broadway and 42nd Street, the mecca of the city whose population numbers seven million persons of every creed and nationality.

"As we drove past the 110th Street entrance of Morningside Park, we were puzzled to see a group of people gathering and pointing at something in the sky.

"Getting out of our auto and looking up for ourselves, we saw a strange craft gliding from a clear evening-blue sky. Although still some distance up in the air, the object seemed to be hovering directly over the entrance to Morningside Park.

"It was larger than a full moon, and barrel-shaped with dark ridges going down the front, which formed a large bay window. The UFO glowed a yellowish orange, with flashes of pink. The craft apparently was surrounded by a blue, pulsating force-field. You could actually make out the dark sky between the object itself and this halo. A blue flame was shooting out from the rear of the UFO. Surprisingly enough, no sound was coming from the object. It just seemed to hang there as if supported by some invisible hand.

"By this time hundreds of cars had stopped, as their occupants watched this strange happening.

"The object was really quite colorful and beautiful. It looked so peaceful and serene as it glided down and hovered over the park," recalled Miss Hudson.

The UFO, according to Barbara Hudson, then continued on its way and passed at a low altitude over Eighth Avenue—passing over Wadleigh High School. The people in this vicinity said the object lit up the street as brightly as if it were day, and that it looked enormous when it was flying very low.

About five minutes passed, when suddenly several loud explosions shattered store front windows and knocked a heavy glass ornament off the dashboard of Miss Hudson's auto.

Leaving her car in front of her apartment building, Barbara joined the crowd of people hurrying down to the 110th Street entrance of Central Park, where all the excitement seemed to be centered.

Apparently the alerted military had setup anti-aircraft weapons near the entrance to the park, and a section of the UFO had actually been shot off and was lying on the grass in full view over the low stone wall that surrounds Central Park.

"The huge chunk of metal rose at least two feet above the wall," said Hudson. "One side was a dull metallic-like color, similar to aluminum, and the other side was a pale lavender color. The outside rim of the jagged chunk of metal seemed to be glowing a blue shade, exactly as it had done in the sky. We couldn't get any closer because of the police barriers that had been set up. Military Police stationed at the entrance of the park were attempting to push back the crowd. People were shouting. Some women screamed. Everyone was getting excited."

Unable to get any closer, Barbara began walking home. "All along the street we heard the neighbors talking about how low the thing had been flying over the area and how another part of it had fallen in flames on Seventh Avenue and 115th Street.

"When I got into the house, I went directly to the fire escape and looked toward Seventh Avenue. From this vantage point I could see another large piece of metal lying in the middle of the avenue. It remained there for several hours before the Military Police towed it away in an unmarked truck. After it had been carted off they immediately covered the hole, which had been made by the UFO, with tar. Floodlights such as they use for making movies illuminated Seventh Avenue as far as Lenox Avenue, and everyone was now being ordered off the street and into their homes."

"Dozens of searchlights had been set up, and they continued to search the star-filled sky for the elusive object. Moments later at least a dozen MPs marched up the street, three abreast, and entered various apartment buildings on both sides of the street.

"Within a few minutes after entering our building there was a heavy knock on our neighbor's door, which we could hear clearly from our dining room. It sounded as if the MPs were asking her some questions, but most of their conversation was inaudible.

"A few minutes later, two steel-helmeted MPs knocked on our door and inquired if everything was all right. They suggested that we should lock the windows leading to the fire escape and other exits, and only open the door to people we know. We couldn't be too careful, one of them said.

"My mother asked the MPs what this was all about. One of them said that if he knew what they were looking for, he would be glad to tell us. After leaving us they went up the stairway to the roof where the third member of their party was stationed."

Miss Hudson went to the back window in her apartment and noticed several other MPs in the backyard. They seemed to be looking for something. As she watched, four of them walked around the tiny place—two of them carried powerful flashlights, the other two had carbines at the ready.

"I watched for several minutes, and then decided there was really nothing to see. Half an hour later I looked again, and they were still there. Another man had joined them. He was carrying some kind of instrument that looked like a metal disk on the end of a pole.

"About 3:00 A.M. my father arrived home from his hotel job. He told me that while he was cleaning up on the penthouse terrace, he had seen a mysterious brightly lit object in the sky heading toward the park."

Mr. Hudson confirmed this to the writer. He described the UFO as being a fire-ball with a long tail. He also said that from his position on the hotel rooftop he could see a number of heavy duty military tanks heading in a downtown direction.

On returning home, he noticed that Seventh Avenue was blocked to all traffic. Searchlights were focused on various apartment houses. Others continued to scan the sky, apparently trying to locate the UFO from which the various pieces had been shot off.

The next morning everything seemed to be back to normal. Fire trucks, military vehicles and the blockade had all disappeared-and traffic was flowing normally into all avenues and streets.

"Nothing ever appeared in the newspapers or was broadcast on radio or TV to explain what happened; something I find hard to explain to many people," continued Miss Hudson. "This sighting, and the torn-off hunks of the object, were certainly seen by hundreds of eye-witnesses. Thousands must have heard the anti-aircraft guns firing."

Although many of those persons involved have since moved away, witnesses are still around, and many are willing to talk about the events of that summer.

Other saucer sightings were made in the New York City area around the same time as the Central Park incident. On July 28, 1952, August C. Roberts was keeping watch on the New York City skyline from his position on the roof of the Sixth Precinct police station in Jersey City, directly across the Hudson River. With him were two other Civil Defense personnel.

At exactly 12:11 a.m. a bright object hovered in the vicinity of the Empire State Building. Through binoculars it looked like a large ball of light, orange in color, with a dark brownish rim, very bright and flickering. It also had what seemed to be a reddish dot in the center.

As it began to move toward the southeast, the rim of the object turned a bright red. "As it moved up and away I got a good glimpse at its bulk. Whatever the object was, I am sure it was not like any type of aircraft I have ever seen," commented Roberts.

Roberts managed to get a photo of the UFO as it hung in the sky over New York City. Then he immediately called the local air filter center and a nearby Air Force base. Before he knew it, he was being grilled by a knowledgeable group of officials.

I talked to Augie, as his friends call him, in his Wayne, New Jersey, home. Still as puzzled today as he had been on the evening of the sighting, he remarked that he could still remember the seventy-two-hour grilling he received from the police and newspapers. One of the men who interrogated him stated that he was an FBI man.

"For a combined total of three days, my life was a virtual hell. They just wouldn't let me alone. What did you see? How is it possible? What do you think it was? They just never stopped questioning me. I was so worn out that I had to spend the rest of the week resting up at my sister's home. I was questioned, badgered, threatened, laughed at and insulted. In the end they accepted my story. I hope I never go through that again!"

Perhaps the weirdest of all New York saucer incidents was related some years back by the celebrated astronomer, the late Dr. Morris K. Jessup. During the summer months of 1952, men were busy working on a high scaffolding on the Cathedral of St. John the Divine. One Monday morning when workmen returned to the job and mounted the scaffolding they found the body of a little man with one eye in the middle of his forehead.

According to Jessup, a New York Times reporter came and wrote up the incident, but it was killed by the paper for fear of being charged with sensationalism. The Army was told about the incident, and they cam and removed the body of the dead little man.

Said Dr. Jessup with a smile, "Perhaps little men occasionally fall from the sky-as well as frogs, snakes, periwinkles and fish.'

Whether this account has any merit to it or not is impossible to say. Had it come from any other source, we would discount it entirely. The late Dr. Jessup was respected for his factual, scientific, matter-of-fact attitude toward the UFO enigma. However, the story of the Central Park UFO is backed up by signed statements.

As we turned into the street, we heard sounds of large guns being fired, and a loud explosion was heard. Rest of the UFO was laying in the entrance of Central Park at 110th Sts and 8th Ave. It was a dull polished metal on oneside and a lavender color on the other side, it was still hot looking because it was still glowing . The object glowed IT DID NOT BURN OR SMOKE.

Barbara Hudson gave this book's author the above sketch showing path taken by UFO before it crashed in Central Park.

8

ALIEN ARTIFACT UNCOVERED

While the rest of the nation was experiencing a cold snap that sent temperatures plunging well below freezing, Orlando was registering temperatures of 80 degrees, making it the warmest city anywhere in the entire country. I had already been in Florida for more than a week, making appearances on various TV and radio talk shows, promoting UFO REVIEW. While back in New York before venturing South after Christmas, I had received an urgent call from Karen Alt, a UFO REVIEW correspondent who has covered fast-breaking UFO stories in the past. This time her conversation had centered around an unusual "artifact" supposedly found at the site of a UFO crash. She had heard a remarkable story from a student attending Seminole Community College in nearby Sanford, where she works as a secretary. Realizing that UFO skeptics such as Philip Klass and NASA's James Oberg are always clamoring for "physical evidence," Karen was understandably excited over what she thought might be an important breakthrough in the field. She wanted to know if I'd be willing to talk with the person who owned the artifact and get the inside scoop.

Naturally, I was fascinated. However, I was determined to make certain this wasn't some type of crude hoax. After all, if this was the 'real McCoy' and not a fraud, UFOlogists would at long last have something concrete to rub in the noses of the nonbelievers.

A three decades-long search for physical evidence that would conclusively prove that flying saucers are "somebody else's spacecraft," may have recently reached the exciting climax with the discovery of actual "hardware" from a crashed UFO.

The important discovery was made in late 1977 by an Orlando, Florida, health food store owner when jogging across the United States. While he was unable to carry all of what he found back across the country with him, John Peele now has in his possession what he maintains is a glove once worn by an alien astronaut that crashed to Earth. Moreover, the owner of this glove—a glove that is far too small for any earthly pilot to wear—is confident that the entire craft which brought the alien to our planet is still under the sifting sands, just waiting to be retrieved at some future date.

A firm believer in physical fitness, John Peele and his wife Nancy, exercise daily and have adopted a strict vegetarian diet. In order to promote their particular lifestyle, the couple—along with their young son and a close friend—ran some 3,100 miles to call attention to the fact that jogging is healthy for the body and a perfect way to get (and remain) in shape.

They began their adventure over the 1977 Labor Day weekend, leaving Daytona, Florida and heading West. Their 91-day run took them through both large and small towns as well as along shores, through steaming deserts and over mountainous terrain.

For the most part, the weather was nearly perfect, making it possible for John to cover an appropriate distance during the daylight hours. Later, just before sunset, John and his jogging partner would join up with Nancy Peele and their son, who were driving ahead in a camper-van.

"We were preparing to leave El Centro, California, when a bad wind storm came up, toppling cars and semi's along I-10. John Peele began his extensive narrative as we sat in the livingroom of his nicely furnished, Spanish-style townhouse. "The wind was blowing upwards to 125 miles per hour and so we knew it would be foolish to think we could get any further that day.

"By the next morning, however, the sky had cleared and the day promised to be near excellent for jogging. We had headed out over the desert through the town of Ocotillo, a stone's throw from the Mexican border. The road we were running on quickly came to an end, and we soon started to cross what appeared to be an old, dried up river bed. Around the next bend was a railroad trestle that was almost totally demolished."

John admits that he isn't sure just how old the trestle was, or what a railroad was doing in this particular location. "The rails didn't look as if they were particularly old—they weren't rusty or anything—but the desert does tend to be deceiving, and the lack of rain in the area could have kept them looking relatively new, when, in reality, they might have dated back many years."

Keeping a slower than normal pace, John and his companion tried to run along the tracks. But the rails would buckle up and down in the desert making it difficult to jog without spraining an ankle in the twisted metal.

Leaving the track, they headed toward a mountain peak that loomed in the distance. At this point, John admits to feeling something "very odd" in the air. Suddenly, they were confronted by what appeared to be an aerial wreck of some sort.

"There, jutting up out of the desert, were several large pieces of what resembled plexiglass." Having been an army helicopter pilot stationed in Viet Nam for over a year, John was positive they could not have been pieces from the windshield of a crashed Army or Air Force vehicle.

"First off, the material was a deep royal blue, not the color used in military windshields." John explained that to his knowledge, Phantom and Cobra helicopters use plexiglass that is tinted light blue toward the top of the windshield to block out the harsh rays of the sun. "But this was much too dark to see through," he continued. "The largest piece of this strange royal blue glass measured some two square feet. There were many other smaller pieces of two or three inches in diameter lying all over the place."

A little further on, something else on the ground caught his eye. "There was all this lightweight metal that felt similar to aluminum, except that it was smooth on one side, honeycombed on the other, and when I tried to bend it the metal wouldn't give."

Realizing that he had probably come across something highly unusual, John picked up several of the smaller pieces and put them into his pocket for safekeeping.

Author took these photos while making Poole. Note size of glove when held in the average size hand of a human.

Yet this was not all he was to find. For there on the ground not far away was a glove not totally unlike the pressurized gloves worn by our high altitude test pilots and astronauts. What made John do a double-take was the fact that this pressurized glove was in miniature form as if it had been made for a child. Of course, children do not pilot high altitude planes, nor does the government allow individuals under a certain size to join the service, ruling out that the glove might have been manufactured for a midget.

Only a few feet away was a second glove, this one having apparently been burned in a crash. It was not in prefect condition like the other glove, having obviously been badly scorched by extreme heat.

While John held an intense curiosity about what he had found, his jogging partner did not share the same sense of discovery. "You'd better drop that thing," he warned. "If it's radioactive, your hand will fall off!"

Disturbed over what he considered to be a distinct possibility at the time, and realizing that they had already far too much to carry John took the good glove, along with some pieces of the strange blue glass as well as the aluminum-like metal, and buried them.

"I found a natural cave under some rocks and placed everything carefully inside, expecting to return shortly and reclaim my findings. Luckily, at the last minute, I decided to take the partly burned glove along with me, as I thought it might be relatively safe compared to the glove that was in perfect condition."

John placed markers around the area where he hid the items, so that the exact spot would be known to him when he returned in the future.

However, when he tried to reclaim his discovery, a peculiar storm came up, sending him scurrying out of the desert for safety"

"We were driving back after the last leg of our run. With my wife Nancy at the wheel, my jogging companion and my son in the back of the van, I joked about how when we got back to the cave there would probably be an alien guarding the spot.

"All of a sudden a tremendous storm came up out of nowhere. The sky turned pitch black as if it were in the middle of the night. Later, we talked to local residents who told us they couldn't remember the last time it stormed in this part of the desert."

A firm believer in physical fitness, John finds himself mysterious alien glove as he jogged across the desert. To this day, he's uncertain what his discovery indicates, but he is positive the artifact is genuine.

As hard as it might be for him to accept, John can't help feel that "cosmic forces were at work," preventing him from returning to reclaim the good glove, and the other artifacts. "I'm positive that it's still where I put it, and I can't help but believe that the remains of an entire ship that crashed is buried in the desert nearby." If this is the case, then this would definitely prove the validity of UFOs and would be the clincher in proving that alien beings are coming to Earth on a regular basis. In addition, being that the gloves have five fingers, this would indicate that their wearer was a humanoid similar to our own race of homo sapiens; except that they are probably smaller in stature, a factor often reported in the sighting of UFO occupants.

The return trip to Florida was uneventful, although John couldn't get over the nagging feeling that his discovery was earth shaking in its implications. In Healing Waters, Arizona, the party got additional confirmation that we are not the only individuals capable of flight.

"Overhead, late one night," Nancy Peele told **UFO REVIEW**, "we saw an object as bright as a street lamp zipping back and forth across the darkened sky. I watched it for over 35 minutes through the windshield of our van, and I was amazed at the way it would move from one part of the star-filled heavens to another, and then drop down before eventually shooting straight up into space."

Arriving back in the Orlando area, John remained excited over the one glove he still had with him. And while he never advertised that he owned such a strange artifact, he sealed the partially burned glove in a transparent pack and kept it under the counter of his newly opened 21st Century Health Food Store located in Winter Park. From time to time he would show it to customers, who would usually walk off after examining it, nodding their heads in total wonderment.

One of the things that was immediately noticed was the manner in which the glove was stitched. "It was double stitched, unlike anything of the type our military makes. Also, the stitching had not shrunk, despite the fact that it had quite obviously been exposed to a high temperature." Also, it was ascertained that the zipper of the glove seemed to zip from the inside, a most peculiar feature. The glove appears to be made out of a leather-like material, and is composed of three layers that have been peeled back partially, no doubt due to the nature of the crash the wearer of the glove had to go through. The alien glove is maybe half the size of a glove worn by a normal-sized human, and when compared to the size of paper money it is easy to see just how small the glove really is.

Without a doubt, the strangest feature is the stamping of the word 'LARGE' in English on the innermost layer of material. Almost immediately one would assume that this would rule out the glove being of extraterrestrial origin. But, the fact remains that no pressurized glove of this size would ever be marked 'LARGE' if it were manufactured by our military.

John has gone over all the possibilities in his mind and still comes up with a blank. "Someone suggested that the glove might have been worn by a monkey, since NASA did send several monkeys into space in the early days of our space program. However, this doesn't hold water either, since the thumb of a monkey is further down on its hand than the thumb on a man. Interestingly, the thumb of this glove is higher up, indicating advanced species."

More questions pop up, but few answers have been forthcoming to date regarding John Peele's discovery. Understandably because of its potential value, the glove's owner has been very reluctant to let the glove out of his sight. "One time I allowed someone from the Martin-Marietta Company, a firm with government connections that is responsible for the manufacture of parts in our guided missile systems, to take it out of the shop back to his firm to have it examined by scientists. He was convinced that I had come across something highly unusual. But once he had the glove in his hands, his attitude changed. He had promised to return it right away, and now I wasn't even able to get him to come to the phone. Finally, he sent it back without any type of analysis or even a letter.

Representatives of Rockwell International as well as NASA have privately looked at the glove and have told me that to their knowledge the glove was not manufactured by private contractor. Each time they come back to the peculiar stitching and the location of the thumb placement on the glove."

Of course, John is well aware of the value of what he accidentally came across in the California desert, but to date he hasn't had any luck profiting from his unique discovery.

"When the movie 'Close Encounters of the Third Kind' opened in Orlando, I introduced myself to the manager of the theater, telling him what I had and offering to put the glove on display in the theater for his patrons to examine in the lobby. He agreed that the artifact would be a good draw, but when I brought in the glove and showed it to him, the manager really 'freaked out' and refused to put it on exhibit. An assistant informed me later that he thought the glove would really frighten people who came in expecting to see a science fiction film."

John acknowledges that he is in no way opposed to having the glove examined by those who are competent to do so. But, on the other hand, he is quite familiar with the various ill-fated attempts to analyze what was thought to be physical evidence of a UFO that supposedly crashed in Brazil—the material under inspection having been "accidentally" washed down the drain by a scientist involved in the inquiry.

John Peele is the first to admit he isn't completely certain what the extent of his discovery may be, but he is convinced that the glove is some sort of outer space artifact, and that furthermore, below the desert outside of a small California town, are the remains of a vehicle that carried a humanoid being to this planet. Perhaps the alien itself is still among the wreckage. Maybe he escaped. But, John Peele plans to eventually go back to the "crash site" and look for himself. What he uncovers could well be the most important discovery of all time and remember- where you read about it first.

KEN LANDGRAF

Supposed cases of crashed UFOs are not just the product of "daydreamers" in the States. Artist Ken Landgraf shows what the ship that went down in frozen-over lake inside Russian might have looked like.

9

THE DAY A UFO CRASHED INSIDE RUSSIA

For several years shocking reports involving the observation of UFOs have been filtering out of the USSR. Many of the reports that have reached the West from inside Russia would indicate that the Soviet Union is experiencing a continuing wave of UFO sightings. These sightings are similar in intensity and nature to those the United States originally went through when disc-shaped craft buzzed many of our large cities for the first time in the late 1940s and early '50s. Despite the official party line that UFOs are an invention of a Capitalistic society, observations apparently persist in almost all Communist satellite nations around the world.

Victor Demidov is a trained Soviet investigator who is not about to rule out the possibility—despite any governmental pressure—that space ships have arrived from other planets. He investigated firsthand what he strongly believes may have been the crash of a UFO inside Russia. This report is being presented for the first time in America, and adds weight to the growing belief that accidental mishaps have transpired more than once in our atmosphere. It could be true that the U.S. military has pieces of crashed UFOs, and now perhaps our counterparts in the Soviet Union also have fragments of an extraterrestrial vehicle.

At 8:00 A.M. on April 28, 1961, Vassili Brodsky, a forester who was inspecting the shore of one of the many lakes near the Southern boundary of Karelia, discovered a huge funnel-shaped crater which had not been there the day before.

Brodsky thought the matter so important that he made a long trek to the nearest forestry station and radioed Leningrad: "Mysterious crater found at lakeside. Experts and divers needed."

At 6:00 A.M. the next morning I was already on the way to the scene, aboard a train with a group which included divers.

We reached the small, rather long lake and saw that a huge section of earth had been gouged out of a bluff. The crater was about 88 feet long, 50 feet wide and 20 feet deep. Near the shore there was a large hole in the ice; floating in the open water were a few jagged blocks of ice. Everywhere else the ice on the lake was smooth. Close to the water the bottom of the crater narrowed.

Such a crater could have been the result of an explosion. But where were the telltale signs? I searched thoroughly for any, but couldn't find even a scorch mark on the previous year's grass. And the ice on the lake showed no cracks; there was only the single hole.

In the grayish foam near the hole I noticed some little black balls which looked like scorched grains of millet. I scooped up a handful and rubbed them between my fingers—they were brittle, and not like millet grains at all. I dropped some in my pocket.

We decided that the clue to the secret probably lay on the lake bottom, and a diver was sent down.

Near the crater, the bottom of the lake was covered with loose earth and frozen sod, he reported. That explained why so few ice blocks were floating in the hole-they were pressed to the bottom. The whole mass of loose soil on the lake bottom formed a long, narrow tongue. On both sides of it, the floor of the lake was clean and firm.

It looked as though a mysterious something had hit the shore and ricocheted into the water. We hoped to find other traces in addition to the crater and air hole, but the readings of a metal detector disappointed us, for they were weak and inconclusive. With a long probe, a diver covered the lake bottom beneath the hole. Now and again the steel rod found a boulder or a block of ice, but that was all.

Brodsky, who was acting as our guide, had been sitting silently smoking shag. Now he rose to his feet, relit his strong-smelling pipe and said: "I'm going to walk around the end of the lake and take a look at the other side."

The thought of a ricochet had occurred to us, too. If an unknown body, travelling at a colossal speed, had hit the edge of the shore and ricocheted like a flat stone skipping across water, it could conceivably have reached the far shore.

We asked Brodsky to take a close look at the soil, the trees and the ice. While he was gone, we found something we couldn't explain. A diver, climbing out of the hole, happened to overturn a block of ice; its immersed part was emerald green to a depth of a couple of inches. We examined several blocks and the story was the same; but when we whacked off a chunk from the solid ice it showed no green. Apparently the hole was the center of some strange physio-chemical process which had colored the ice fragments.

97

So we took samples of the ice, fished out more scorched "millet grains" and sat around a bonfire to warm up and have a meal and rest.

Then our guide came back. He had found absolutely nothing on the other shore that could help shed light on our mystery.

"Well, let's compare ideas," said the head of our expedition.

A rocket?

But there have been no launchings recently; we checked before leaving Leningrad. Anyway, a rocket would scatter some fragments around.

A bomb?

There were no signs of an explosion.

Ball-lightning?

It would leave no fragments, but the probability of ball-lightning is very low.

A meteorite?

Toward the end of our "conference" this theory found the most backers. But where was the celestial visitor now? Lost in the earth at the bottom of the lake? In that case, surely the probe would have located it.

The divers gave us their detailed reports.

"I was treading along the furrow when I suddenly felt a knob," said one.

"What do you mean?" I broke in. "What furrow? What knob?"

"Down there, on the bottom. A very narrow furrow..."

This had to be checked! In a few minutes the diver was again under water. He reappeared at the outer edge of the hole and asked for the probe. I stepped into a rubber dinghy, rowed out and handed him the instrument.

Minutes later his head again broke the surface of the water. He was excited. "From the shore to where you gave me the probe there is a silt-covered trail," he reported. "It looks like a bed hollowed out by a huge pipe. Behind it is a small bank of earth some five feet high. It seems as though some force had been pushing the earth in front of it and then stopped. Further on there is nothing unusual— I walked about 300 feet and the lake bottom is perfectly smooth."

Where did that Something disappear? After all, it couldn't have flown back. But then who knows? Why couldn't it have done just that?

Giving free play to our imaginations, we did some rough calculating; our mysterious Something must have landed at a tremendous speed, torn some 35,000 cubic feet of earth out of the bluff at the lakeside, plunged into the lake and advanced about 65 feet, then made a sharp turn, pierced a 16-foot layer of water and zoomed skywards. The attending stress would have reached incredible proportions, and no human pilots could have survived.... Some bits of information came from woodcutters in the area when we questioned them. They said that during the night, they believed between 2:00 A.M. and 4:00 A.M., they heard a sort of rolling thunder, like the roar of aero engines, from the direction of the lake.

Our speculations continued during our return journey to Leningrad, where we hoped scientists would help us unravel the enigma. Leningrad has about 20,000 scientists in its university, its 40 colleges and 200 research institutions. Which of them should we approach? When we made several telephone calls to various centers, the answers followed one pattern: "Sorry that is outside the competence of our Institute (faculty, laboratory, etc.)." Everyone was working on some specific problem and we came disturbing them with a fantastic Something.

Finally the Laboratory of Fine Chemical Analysis of Leningrad Technological College agreed to examine our samples. Meanwhile I was checking our meteorite theory.

"I don't think it could be a meteorite," said Professor Vsevolod Sharonov of Leningrad University. "A meteorite normally leaves a pit at least five times its own size. Your hypothetical meteorite must have been large, and astronomers never miss them; they get white-hot when they burst into the atmosphere and their dazzle betrays them hundreds of mile away."

That killed one of our most credible theories. Our ball-lightening hypothesis "burnt out" too—at the High Energy Faculty of the Polytechnical College.

One institute found nothing out of the ordinary in our earth sample. In another we were told categorically that there was nothing unusual about them from the point of view of radioactivity.

At Leningrad University we heard that our crater had nothing in common with a natural cave-in, while an expert in soil mechanics swamped our idea of a landslide.

We were left with our most fantastic explanation: that a spaceship had landed and taken off again. But on examining photos of the pit and the sketches of the underwater imprints of our Something, experienced engineers said they very much doubted that any device could stand such a powerful impact with frozen ground without being smashed to pieces.

Discouraged, I kept vigil in the Chemical Laboratory of Leningrad Technological College, waiting for the results of the analysis. Finally a woman member of the lab staff came up to me and said:

"I'm sorry to disappoint you, but we cannot explain or even confirm the emerald green color of your ice. The elements we have found in your samples refused to be green in any of the combinations we know...."

All right. Suppose I had turned color blind that day. But the ice blocks had been examined by seven people!

The laboratory verdict said: "The elements identified in the melted ice offer no explanation of the green color pointed out by members of the expedition."

So that was that. We were left with only the scorched "millet grains." The chemists shrugged their shoulders, but politely agreed to examine them under the microscope.

Unexpectedly the grains revealed a metallic lustre! No seed or other organic substances shine like that!

In an hour I was holding in my hands a conclusion which read: "In the infrared spectrum of the powder obtained by rubbing the grains, the absorption band characteristic of all organic compounds is absent."

The grain particles would not dissolve either in concentrated sulfuric acid or in a mixture of it and hydrofluoric acid, which even corrodes glass. Rubbed to powder, these particles refused to dissolve in hydrochloric acid.

I found out later that grains of such a shape may appear in high-temperature processes, such as welding. The scientists wrote: "These grains have an inorganic origin and are apparently non-natural formations." Sometimes I open my desk drawer and again examine our photographs and finger the black, ball-shaped grains. WHAT WAS IT? The question gives me no peace.

ART BY CAROL RODRIGUEZ

10

ALIEN DIES ON AIR FORCE BASE

Evidence keeps mounting and virtual proof is at hand that UFOs have crashed, and alien bodies have been retrieved by the U.S. Government in a cover-up that makes Watergate look like child's play," or so says Diane Tessman, former Mutual UFO Network State Section Director for Florida, who during her many years as a UFO investigator has researched extensively the crashed saucer syndrome. Tessman—herself an abductee—has corresponded with the likes of Leonard Stringfield and others in order to get to the bottom of this puzzle. Her special report follows:

In his latest scientific report entitled *UFO CRASH RETRIEVALS:*

AMASSING THE EVIDENCE (Status Report III), UFOlogist Leonard H. Stringfield presents truly incredible, but fully documented accounts of flying saucer crashes. Also, he has published, for the first time, an X-ray of the remains of an "unknown creature," allegedly found in shale, which further proves the existence of fetus-type humanoids. The hand, arm and clavicle in the X-ray are exactly like those of the aliens in *CLOSE ENCOUNTERS OF THE THIRD KIND.* It is generally thought that producer Steven Spielberg had access to "classified" information, and had consulted with J. Allen Hynek and other UFO researchers before designing the aliens in that awe-inspiring film. The small, "fetus" humanoid is indeed a reality! If one could capture a variety of UFOs and open the portals of each, it is a certainty that in at least a few of them, ET or one of his cousins, would be staring back at you.

In researching and documenting reports of crashed saucers and alien bodies, Leonard Stringfield has literally risked his life. He has been threatened on several occasions by sinister unknown agents and his topic is so explosive—so hot— that he has carefully dispersed his new-found information to a few chosen friends so that if his life is taken, his files will not be lost.

Near Camp Polk, Louisiana, summer 1953, an informant whom Stringfield identified only as HJ was on U.S. Army maneuvers. At dusk, his entire patrol watched an egg-shaped UFO crash into the soft, sandy soil. HJ reports that both A and B companies were ordered to guard the crashed disc until a special detachment could arrive. Once the detachment showed up (an ambulance and other special equipment), the companies were immediately ordered to pull back about 100 yards. "Peons like me had to get out of the way," says HJ.

HJ told Stringfield that the oval UFO was without windows or lights and was surrounded by a fin-like protrusion at its equator which was still rotating. The ground around it was burnt into a powdery substance like crushed rock and was still hot.

The top brass and medics arrived soon and approached the hatch on the side, which was open. After hesitating, two medics went in and emerged carrying a stretcher which contained a body. They took it off to the ambulance. And then, HJ reports, three UFO crewmembers emerged, aided by the medics as though injured. "One of them," says HJ, "kept looking at the one on the stretcher and making strange noises. I couldn't believe what I was seeing!"

Softening his voice, HJ reports that the occupants of the saucer were only three and a half feet tall, of very slight build and walked as if they had no knees...very stiff, only bending at the hips. HJ could not distinguish any features of the hands, commenting, "It looked like they were wearing mittens." (Publisher's Note: Could this be reference to "alien glove" described in a previous chapter?) He believed the large heads, also without features, were covered by helmets. Their uniforms were dull metallic green (which is the closest that we've ever come to a "little green man").

HJ later heard that the survivors had been sent to a hospital and "put in isolation," but all had soon died. He also heard the bodies were sent to a medical center near Washington.

The crash site was roped off for a 50 mile radius, and MPs were put on guard everywhere. HJ and the other men of his company were grilled by an intelligence officer, who told them to forget what they had seen, that it was a secret Army experiment and that they were never to talk about it. The men of HJ's company were put through "every conceivable test" for three days at the base hospital. And researcher Stringfield has a collaborating witness, a Mr. J., who independently substantiated everything HJ reported. Mr. J. was also in the Army undergoing basic training at Camp Polk; his account lines up perfectly with HJ's! Like so many of Stringfield's brave informants, HJ's phone was suddenly disconnected when Stringfield attempted a routine call to him, and HJ has apparently dropped from sight. A signed statement HJ made regarding his involvement in a crash/retrieval experience was mailed by HJ's wife at the local post office, but it never arrived in

Leonard's mailbox.

And so, the cover-up which would make Watergate look like child's play goes on...and on.

The next personal account which Stringfield managed to unearth is one from a Mr. KA, a member of the U.S. Air Force from 1954-1955. KA was part of a military mission, a UFO crash retrieval operation which took place near Walker Air Force Base, Roswell, New Mexico in 1954. Of course, the significance of Roswell in the crashed saucer cover-ups is well-known and documented in the book *THE ROSWELL INCIDENT.*

On April 12, 1954, KA and his fellow crew members were playing ping pong when they were ordered by an officer to pack their gear. He told them they had 15 minutes to report to the flight line, that there had been a "crash in the desert." KA was an excellent aerial photographer (this was his specialty in the Air Force), and his assignment was to take photos of the crash. Before he left the base the announcement was made, "Men, this is not a drill. This is a red alert scramble." KA reports that a total stranger, rather than the usual crew member, was waiting in the cockpit of the helicopter, and that he took complete command and gave all the orders.

As KA's helicopter cleared a small cliff about 10 miles away from the base, the crew spotted brightly flashing red, blue and yellow/white lights, and at their altitude of 40 feet, they could plainly see the outline of a round, silvery object. After descending to 30 feet, the stranger in command of the helicopter gave the order to turn on the spotlight. KA then plainly saw a round, metallic, saucer-like object approximately 40 to 50 feet in diameter. The craft appeared to have crashed head-long into the sand!

The UFO had a stationary center dome, but the outer rim was still spinning in a counterclockwise direction and the lights on the outer edge were rotating in the same direction. However, KA reports that what the crew saw next was even more incredible: outside the craft were four bodies...small bodies, scattered helter-skelter. They were not moving and seemed to be dead. The bodies looked to be four feet in height, and their heads were disproportionately large for the rest of the bodies. They wore no helmets, had the same tight-fitting dark blue uniforms. With the spotlight shining on their faces, a green luminous tint could be observed. KA reports that he and his fellow crew members looked at each other in total disbelief.

Suddenly, the stranger in command ordered KA to take photos from many different angles, and then he gave the order to land the helicopter about 100 feet away from the crashed UFO.

As soon as KA leaped from the helicopter, he became aware of an overpowering stench like auto battery acid that permeated the area. Also, there were headlights of approaching ground vehicles. At this point, KA tried to get a glimpse of the stranger who was commanding his helicopter (the man had not let the crew see his face.) KA could only see the outline of the head and shoulders of the man.

Now the ground vehicles had arrived and soldiers wearing side arms jumped out. They warned KA not to go closer than 40 feet, but to take pictures from where he stood. At this point, members of the ground crew began to vomit from the stench arising from the crashed UFO; nonetheless, the ground crew put tags on the four small bodies.

KA engaged one member of the ground crew in conversation long enough to learn that through a small hatch door in the side of the saucer two more alien bodies could be seen, and it looked as though they had been trying to crawl out of the craft on their hands and knees.

Soon after, KA and his crew were ordered to return to Roswell, but could not leave the helicopter upon landing until several staff cars approached and the helicopter crew was divided into groups of two. Each pair was driven to an old barracks building known as Building No. 5, and there the "living hell" began.

In Building No.5, KA was grilled by "intelligence officers" wearing civilian clothes and black ties. These strangers worked on KA in staggered intervals, first one asking him to repeat what he saw, then leaving the room while two others came in and told him he "did not see the crashed saucer," then a fourth coming in to read him a treatise about being court martialed, fined, imprisonment, hard labor, if he ever breathed a word of what he had witnessed. Then the first man returned, and so it went for three days. The other crew members were experiencing the same tactics in other rooms of the same building.

Scuttlebutt had it that the saucer was brought to the base and hidden in a Hangar 46. But, as it turned out, the hangar was too small, so the object was moved to Hangar 18!

The day after KA was released from undergoing brutal interrogation, he was flown over the crash site which had been cleaned with a fine tooth comb. He was told, "See, you guys didn't see anything." However, the pilot of KA's helicopter had an ULTRA F-5 camera which was not supposed to be in his possession, and as soon as he was returned from the jaunt, he went to the latrine, stood on the commode, and took photos of Hangar 18 and the activity around it. KA flopped down on his bunk exhausted. When he awoke, the pilot, his gear, and his camera were all gone. KA never saw him again.

In the months that followed, KA was harassed unmercifully by the military, and his mind finally snapped and he suffered a nervous breakdown. During his three months hospital stay, he remembers the doctor injecting him with a large needle, and then being led to a room where four or five people sat. On the table was a microphone. He was quizzed about the UFO crash, but due to the injection, is unsure how he answered their questions. On the day of his release from the hospital, he was called before a colonel who handed him his general discharge papers. KA protested, but was told that he had revealed details of the desert incident, luckily only to members of the Air Force. But he was considered "dangerous," so was being released.

KA's torment did not end there! He suffered hideous nightmares, not so much from the original experience of viewing a crashed saucer, but from the inhuman treatment the military heaped upon him for no logical reason. He and his fellow crew members had responded to a red alert and in return for executing the order, they have been punished for it ever since.

The stories go on and on—there seems to be no end of them, and always the military appears to go out of its way to keep the entire affair hushed up.

On September 16, 1980, Sergeant JM of the Air Force, who is a military policeman, sent a letter to Stringfield in which he revealed a bizarre UFO crash incident which he witnessed at McGuire Air Force Base, New Jersey.

The incident supposedly transpired in January of 1978. He told Len of assisting an MP who informed him that planes from Ft. Dix were pursuing a low flying object. Suddenly, the object appeared over his patrol car! His radio transmission was cut off. Then, in front of his police car, appeared a "thing" with a fat head, long, slender arms, grayish in color, and about four feet tall. The MP fired five rounds into the alien and another round into the object hanging in the air over his car.

The UFO then flew straight up to join eleven others which were high in the nighttime sky. The MP reported that the alien had run into the woods still moving after having five rounds from a .45 caliber gun fired into him.

However, JM reported that he and several other military police found the body of the alien. It had climbed a high fence and died while running. The entire area was roped off and hush-hush security ensued. A battery acid, ammonia-like stench continued to permeate the area. The next day, a special team from Wright-Patterson AFB arrived and loaded a metal container onto their plane. All personnel were warned that they would be punished if they ever breathed a word of the incident.

Unfortunately, no more information can be gained from JM because, as Stringfield reports, he has virtually vanished into thin air shortly before he was to be discharged. All attempts to contact him have failed.

In 1967, Mr. RT, another of Stringfield's informants, reports that he was flown from Camp Pendleton, California, to a crash site "somewhere in the desert." RT was given 45 minutes notice for his strange assignment. (He was a Marine at the time, PFC rank, with the Canine Corps. He spent six years in Viet Nam.)

For four days, RT was ordered to guard a makeshift hangar out in the middle of the desert. He was told to ask no questions and only follow assigned paths. Curiosity got the better of him, and on the fourth day he took a different route, sneaking a peek into the hangar itself. Inside he saw a metallic saucer about 30 feet in diameter. On top was a dome, but there were no windows. Men were at work examining instruments on tables, and there were several empty body bags. These men had no insignia on their uniforms, and the same kind of no-insignia personnel were reported by KA and HJ.

RT was grabbed by a security guard and subjected to days, months, and years of torment for his "one small peek" inside the hangar. He was harassed by "men in black" which his dog hated, sensing their strangeness. During one of the intimidating meetings with him, he was shown photos of alien cadavers with army doctors dissecting them. The men asked RT, "Do you see any blood?" Apparently the "message" was that either the aliens had no blood, or that it wasn't red.

RT and his wife moved from their apartment a day or two after talking with Stringfield, and RT insisted he wasn't going to talk about UFOs anymore.

Not only was the witness threatened, but a UFO investigator who attempted to get RT to talk again was "punished" by what may well have been the sinister Men in Black. Investigator RC's fiance was soon killed in a car crash in Florida; her car was forced off the road, leaving only black paint marks on the side of the auto, left there by the vehicle which was the instrument of her murder.

Was this "punishment" for RC, the investigator, caused by poking his nose into the above-mentioned UFO case? The last word Stringfield heard from the researcher was that he was going to meet with three men at the airport concerning crashed flying saucers. Since then, silence...total silence!

Not all of Leonard's informants tell him about four foot tall humanoids, with large heads. A professor from France who has worked with several Nobel Prize winners told Stringfield of an invitation he received from an American scientific group to lecture and also to perform an experiment about historic weight of particular cells. He was taken by USAF shuttle plane to Wright-Patterson AFB, and was somewhat surprised that he had not been told he would be going deep inside a military complex.

The French professor performed the tests on the cells he was given (he was considered top notch in this field), and was so amazed at his findings, that he felt he should do his experiments again (the historic weight was ridiculously low, much below what human cells could possibly be). After his second attempt came up with the same results as the first, he begged to see the corpse from which these cells came. He was taken into a special room where lay the bodies of two humanoids. These beings were 7 feet, 3 inches tall and bore hideous mutilations on their bodies as if they had been in a dreadful auto accident. Luckily, the heads were in good shape, and the professor could see that their foreheads were very high and broad. Their hair was long and blonde, eyes stretching toward their temples, which gave them an oriental look. The nose and lips were small, as was the chins. There were no beards or facial hair visible. The two humanoids looked like twins to the professor, but, of course, the cloning process is also a possibility.

The giant humanoids seemed to have no keratin granules under their skin, but had remained perfectly white, even in formalin. Their eyes were a light, almost "china" shade of blue, and their hands and feet were very humanlike, though delicate.

The professor was told that these were indeed extraterrestrials, but that he was to keep total secrecy about what he had seen for ten years. This he did. And the most macabre of all "secret rooms at Wright-Patterson" accounts was told to Stringfield by a Mrs. C.K. Her husband was an Air Force serviceman and her 18 month old son was therefore admitted to wright-Patterson Children's Ward in July, 1964 for a pediatric examination. While waiting in the lounge of the base hospital, her restless child "escaped" from her, ran down a corridor, and managed to squeeze through a swinging door into a room marked "Isolation. Keep out." Mrs. C.K., of course, ran after her child and in snatching him back from the isolated room saw a sight she will never forget: On a bed without sheets or pillow was a hunk of flesh which looked vaguely like a torso. Mrs. C.K. says it reminded her of an uncooked pot roast. It had no arms, no legs but had a crease down the middle and there were tubes at each end, pumping a clear liquid or fluid into the "hunk."

The light was dim and on windows were open. Her child had stood only about six feet away from the alien "blob", and just as Mrs. C.K. was about to yank the child away, a nurse appeared and harshly told her to leave.

When Mrs. C.K. returned the next day, she first started to apologize again for her child's behavior. The nurse was extremely friendly just the opposite of the previous day) and ushered her into the same room, which was now vacant, well-lighted, windows open...totally bright and cheery.

Dating back to 1944 is the strange encounter of E.L. of Los Angeles, who served with a construction battalion in World War II. At this time, the informant was a Seabee strolling along Kenohe Beach on Oahu, Hawaii, looking for shells. As he walked, his eyes caught the glint of something metal reflecting suniight near a wooded ridge which was close to a radar installation. As he neared the object, E.L. was faced with a strange globular craft about 50 feet in diameter. E.L. said, "It looked like an igloo, and on top of the clear dome was a gold device much like a weather vane."

Dressed in tight-fitting green uniforms, were a group of humanoids milling around the outside of the craft. They were short (about 4 feet tall), slight of build with no visible buttocks. Their faces and heads were humanlike, but they had short, lush black hair with large dark eyes and heavy eyebrows. One of them had large, fanged teeth and this one, E.L. was told, was a female. Each alien wore a heavy boxlike belt, and all of them seemed very intrigued and intent upon E.L., the human who had come across them by accident. One little man spoke to him in a heavy accent, but his voice was much to deep for his size.

What happened next is unusual in the many UFO encounters which have taken place throughout the years. After pressing a button on his belt which made E.L. dizzy and nauseous, one of the aliens lunged at E.L. with a swordlike weapon. E.L. drew his knife and a "life and death" battle ensued. E.L. was just winning (he had battled the small man down to the ground), when the others jumped into the fight. E.L. assumed that this was surely the end of him. But instead, the others killed their crewmate. E.L. sneaked the dead alien's box-like contraption from his belt and kept it.

The next day, E.L. was told to return to a special rock and he would hear about where they came from, how long they had been here, etc. They were indeed at the appointed place, telling him they had come from a world 21 light years away. However, E.L.'s meeting with them had been reported to Navy intelligence. E.L. was forced to surrender the black box to the Navy and he also was told by intelligence officers that they had captured the female alien. She was sent to the U.S. mainland under heavy guard.

E.L. also learned later that the Navy had shot down the alien ship as it tried to take off after its meeting with him. The Navy towed the UFO to San Diego, being unable to open the craft's metal skin with conventional tools, the Navy apparently left the six aliens inside to rot. E.L. told Stringfield that Navy Intelligence was greatly interested in the black box they took from him. He says that when the black box was aimed at a cat and one of the three buttons was pressed, the cat fell dead instantly, its bones liquefying to jelly. The varnish on the table where the cat had sat was burned and a foul odor permeated the air.

Though this report cannot possibly be documented, it is interesting to note that I had previously heard the story about a crashed UFO being held inside a once active military base in the San Diego area, and now it remains by itself in a secured building with only guards nearby to keep outsiders away. I often drive by this facility and wonder what secrets lurk behind the chained fence. Is there a crashed UFO inside or is it just another undocumented rumor?

Time will tell.

In recent times, researcher Leonard Stringfield has come under repeated attack from the rank and file members of various ultraconservative UFO groups in which he was once very active. Certainly, it is true that these reports are highly sensational and controversial. Yet, these accounts need to be looked into, as they may well offer the hard-core proof the scientific establishment has long been screaming its brains out for. If UFOs are space ships, chances are that they are highly developed, yet a few of them might have met with technical failure. Chances are the government knows what's going on, and yet they continue to try and keep the public in the dark about the most important topic of all times.

AUTOPSY REPORT FROM LEONARD STRINGFIELD'S FILES.

Researcher Leonard Stringfield first published this rendering of an alien hand (see box marked 1) which is based upon the report of a former CIA employee who claimed to have seen deceased aliens during a 1962 recovery in New Mexico. In panel 2, artist Al Reed shows hand structure and in panel 3 the all-important hypothetical bone structure.

11

THE MYSTERIOUS PROFESSOR

Gray Barker spent a great many years tracking down crashed saucer stories. During the course of his investigations he had the opportunity to meet with the rather mysterious Dr. Robert Spencer Carr, who at that time chaired the Department of Communications at the University of South Florida. His story is titillating:

Since the bulk of my contact with him was my attendance at a symposium he sponsored, I had little opportunity to talk with him about a subject I knew he was well versed on: the official cover-up of UFO crashes in the Southwestern U.S., involving the recovery of both machines and occupants by the military.

I could understand his reticence to discuss this subject at that time, for I knew he was in his last year before retirement and assumed he didn't want to send any shock waves through the relatively conservative institution.

I had first become aware of Carr while reading Maj. Donald E. Keyhoe's *Aliens From Space*, in which the professor was quoted as proposing what Keyhoe called "Operation Lure," a unique communication scheme to be installed on a remote New Mexico mountain top which might facilitate establishing friendly relationships with UFOs.

Although the plan reminded me of cargo cults among primitive natives in the South Pacific, I thought better of it when I learned more about Carr. The academician was a recognized expert in nonverbal communications. During World War II he had been retained by the Walt Disney studios to help develop their animated training films which depended upon action, rather than verbalization in order to speed comprehension and cross language barriers. After the war he had worked with scientific foundations and one huge corporation in their public relations programs.

Upon learning of his retirement, I again contacted Carr, this time by telephone. Although I found it difficult to draw him into an on-the-record interview, that and subsequent conversations gradually drew us into a friendly relationship.

Recently my efforts finally paid off. Carr not only permitted me to record the conversation, but also authorized me to print certain parts of it in UFO Review.

Although our 90-minute interview included many other things I would like to report—such as more recent UFO events and Carr's present Government connections—the conversation which follows is probably the most fascinating part of the recording, for it gives us new insights into the beginning of our modern UFO era, and astounding new confirmation that the U.S. Government has recovered hardware and little men from outer space! That part of our interview follows:

BARKER: Does the Government have captured hardware and....

CARR: (Interrupting) Yes!

BARKER: ....captured saucers, and the bodies of the occupants....

CARR: (Interrupting) Yes! And at least a couple of hundred top figures in the academic world, a few in the medical world, a few from the Naval Hospital, a few from the Pentagon, and of course Air Intelligence and CIA were then in it, up to their necks. And now their wings are clipped and they're sort of out of it. But they have that locked away in vaults. Some of it is in that big vault-like building behind the CIA headquarters in Langley, VA. You have to have an aerial view to see it. The two crashed UFOs are pretty badly damaged. They're charred, and some sort of corrosive liquid came out and messed them up. We found them; we didn't shoot them down. They don't tell very much. But the one perfect UFO that has no damage except a hole about the size of your fist in its canopy, is still at Wright-Patterson field.

You may recall when I was raising such a cry about Hangar 18. Well, about a hundred newspaper men and television men stormed the gates. And they had just cleaned out Hangar 18. It was absolutely empty—nothing, except a few pipes in the floor.

BARKER: Bob, let's backtrack and start at the beginning. First, I want to establish this: You were living in New Mexico, were you not, at the time Scully told of the saucer crash?

CARR: I was living in southern New Mexico and owned a small ranch at the time that the Aztec, New Mexico, dead-stick landing happened—it was a "dead-man" landing; it came down automatically. When the first helicopters from what was then Muroc Dry Lake Air Force Base (it wasn't renamed Edwards until several years later) came in, it was already standing there on its tripod landing gear.

BARKER: (Hearing squealing sound on line) I'm getting some interference, but

I can still hear you. Is this the incident reported in Scully's book, *Behind the Flying Saucers?*

CARR: Yes, it was reported by Scully, because one of the electronics experts, Dr. Leo DeBaur, who was Dutch, was such a top man that he also served as a consultant to the Air Force, and he is the one who told the oil man, who made the talk described in the book, all about it. The oil millionaire was the person who made the speech before faculty and students at the University of Colorado....

BARKER: (Interrupts) Of course we have both read that in the book, but do you have any independent confirmation?

CARR: The first confirmation I got was from a biologist who (this was already 1952 and the autopsy had already been performed) had a biological section of a larger report which had been torn out forcibly from the binding with jagged edges. It was a carbon copy—they didn't make Xeroxes in those days. At that time I was the public relations director for a scientific research foundation at Fort Meyers Beach, and we would have visiting scientists from all over the nation. This was the James Foundation, headed by the distinguished scientist, Dr. Robert L. James.

BARKER; I assume that you heard these reports direct from people who were actual witnesses.

CARR: He had the official report, although he had not been present at the autopsy. But he had been allowed to see the report, and he simply tore the biological section out. He wasn't interested in anything else, for example aeronautical engineering. To my great sorrow, he didn't take the whole report! That would have been priceless. It no doubt still exists.

BARKER: And you actually saw that part of the report he tore out?

CARR: He wouldn't let it out of his hands, but he read it to me verbatim.

BARKER: Where was this crashed UFO taken?

CARR: It was taken from a point twelve miles northwest of Aztec, New Mexico, near a locality known as Hart Canyon. Some people call it Hard Canyon, but the people who homesteaded it were named Hart....

BARKER: And this was taken to Wright-Patterson, am I correct?

CARR: No! No! It was taken to Muroc Dry Lake. It didn't get up to Wright-Patterson until after the autopsy and the CIA took command of the whole situation. You remember between 1947 and 1952 there was a period of chaos. The newspapers were front-paging UFO news, and everybody was free to speak. And then the Robertson Committee was appointed by the CIA, and they met in the autumn of 1952. That was after the Washington, D.C. flap, when UFO's flew in triangular formation over the White House. Now, we don't know what a triangular formation means. In an alien culture it might be some sort of honorific sign of peace. We don't know what it means—we never gave them a chance! We scrambled swarms of jet fighters after them and hit them on every side with radar, which they despise, because radar penetrated their electro-gravitic shields, and threw their instrumentation off. In fact, this may be what caused the Aztec, New Mexico, craft to go out of control, although it was also hit by something. The little men were dead of decompression.

The other wreck was found that summer in the desert in Arizona by visual observation. This one was burned and it had been out there in the desert for too long. There were organic materials left, but the predators and the heat of the desert had pretty well taken care of the occupants. But they scooped it up and took it along. Then about two years later, after the CIA was in complete control...You see, after the Washington flap, somebody had to take charge, and the CIA at that time was the most powerful, the most efficient, and the most coherent organization in the United States. And they took charge for the good of the people with the blessings of the President. About 1953 an object crashed into a mountainside on the East Coast of Mexico, not far from the U.S. border. The ties between the CIA and the Mexican military were so close that CIA personnel made the ascent to the crash site with the Mexican military. And it is believed, although I've never been able to get an eyewitness to admit it, that the mangled, crashed disc, with organic material in it, was taken by the CIA and added to its collection.

BARKER: Can you name your sources for this information?

CARR: No, I cannot. Keep in mind that I have, in some cases, multiple informants, all telling me the same things. One of the most convincing—the final clincher for me, was when I made my one and only lecture tour in the winter of 1974-1975. At every college campus where I lectured, ending up finally at a packed auditorium at Georgia Tech, there would always be one or two grey-haired, important-looking quiet men who kept their eyes on me and followed me around. I thought they were just tailing me, and so I would just smile at them. However I went into a washroom between a luncheon and a press conference, and one of them came in and stood beside me. He said, "Look, I'm a retired military person of high rank. I was in North Africa. I wanted to tell you, 'Keep it up!' I saw them in North Africa on the ground, up to 90 feet in diameter. You haven't even scratched the surface, Carr. Oh God, how I wish I could get up there on that platform with you! Now forget you ever saw me! Goodbye!"

BARKER: Do you think these men were officially giving you confirmation of your facts, or what?

CARR; No, no. They were on the level. They had to get it off their chests. They were like a retired, 71-year-old nurse out in Ohio, who had been sworn to secrecy because she assisted at an autopsy as the head surgical nurse.

BARKER: Where was that—at Wright-Patterson, or Muroc?

CARR: At Muroc. By the time the remains went up to Wright-Patterson, they went into deep-freeze. They didn't have the preservation facilities at Muroc, and the temperatures were too high; and besides, the security wasn't good.

In fact, this chap James Moseley, in his book, *The Wright Field Story,* got it all mixed up when he said there was a red and white alert at Wright-Patterson. The red and white alert was ordered at Muroc Dry Lake because the UFO had in it a little radio which at about eleven minutes after each earth hour gave out a sing-song beeping which lasted for about 15 seconds. The commanding general at Muroc made the only logical military decision: the thing was automatically signalling to the other members in its fleet, and that the base might be attacked. But in about twelve days the power pack died out, and the little radio no longer emitted the signals. Some Air Force technician took it for a souvenir. It's hard to believe that security was that lax, and it's just terrible how the thing was dismantled.

BARKER: Do you think he may still have the little radio?

CARR: Yes, it we could just find out who he is. But, you see, the CIA swung into action after it appeared that Washington was in danger of being overflown by alien craft. It was the CIA which, with great skill and diplomatic finesse, was able to convince the editors of the three great wire services to play down the crashed disc rumors. Not that they discouraged any local papers from running such stories. They wouldn't have cared if, for example, your Clarksburg Telegram ran a front page story—they just didn't want it to get on the wires. The CIA had high ranking military officers contact the top men at these wire services and tell them, "It is not in the national interest to propagate these cockamamie reports, because they clog intelligence channels at crucial moments, which might provide the Soviet Union opportunities to attack us. Second, don't you realize, sir, that when your editors put one of the local incidents on the wire that it costs the Government fantastic sums of money to follow up a rash of hoaxes, imitative and hysterical sightings. And if you don't propagate UFO reports, the whole thing will blow over."

They hired the Brookings Institute—it's in the Congressional Record—to conduct a socio-psychological study. This Institute put into plain English the pernicious doctrine which still prevails—that our behavior on the night of the Orson Wells radio broadcast of The War of the Worlds proves we are not ready for interplanetary contact. I think it's a damnable libel on the maturity and the intelligence of the American public! 1979 is not the late 1930s. We've put men on the moon. We've put a robot on Mars. We have a probe photographing Jupiter. A whole generation has grown up on Star Trek. We have polled every senior class of my students, up to the very month of my retirement, on what they would do if a flying saucer landed right there on the campus. They reply, "We would go toward it tossing flowers! We would hold up our arms and say, "'Welcome, brothers!'"

BARKER: Back to the autopsy of the little man—did he seem to be, let's say, roughly humanoid?

CARR: He was not only roughly humanoid, he was entirely human.

BARKER: I have another report indicating that these occupants in crash retrievals did not have human blood. They had some sort of fluid.

CARR: They have Type "O" blood. They could give you or me a transfusion tonight! The organs were all in the right places. The occupant was in excellent health. The only physical characteristic which produced shock and amazement was when the brain surgeon cut open the skull and looked at the brain. Now the head was a little bit large for the body. He was just a little bit megacephalic. But after all, we see megacephalic little people ourselves. Many little people have heads a little too big. If these occupants were given children's clothing, they could pass undetected on the streets of any large city like New York. Maybe they would be noticed in a small town where everybody knows everybody else, but in New York they wouldn't even draw a passing glance. Well, when they opened the skull, of course, you know the story.

BARKER: No, I don't.

CARR: They found a brain whose convolutions and the intricacy and depth of the brain furrows indicated they were looking at the brain of a man several hundred years old! Yet he appeared to be a vigorous young man which we, in human terms, would estimate to be between 20 and 30. An Olympic athlete, only small.

BARKER: But the brain...go on please.

CARR: But the brain... You see, the brain of Charles Darwin is preserved in the British Medical Museum in London. It is the most deeply convoluted brain known (you know, the brains of idiots are smooth). The brain of the alien was more deeply convoluted than any brain they had ever seen, and the entire staff bent down to see it and drew back with a shock of amazement. Their life spans must be longer than ours. That's how they can achieve interstellar travel.

BARKER: You're suggesting then, that this person was from outside our solar system?

CARR: That was the general consensus of the Air Intelligence in the original *Estimate of the Situation.* This was the report the chief of staff asked for. It was

Major General Twining who was chief of Air Staff. This Estimate said in effect: "The UFO's are real. They are metallic. They are propelled by a highly superior propulsion system, and they undoubtedly originate outside our solar system. They are piloted by intelligent, humanlike beings."

BARKER: What was Twining's reaction to the Estimate?

CARR: Twining hit the ceiling. He tore the report to shreds, and he ordered every copy burned! Only two copies are said to have survived, and if anybody in civilian UFO investigation knows where they are, it's Major Donald E. Keyhoe. I have never been able to get my hands on it.

Years before it was considered "fashionable,", Professor Robert Carr delivered a lecture at a Florida University on the subject of crashed saucers. His speech made headlines in several newspapers the next day and he was to be pestered by the press for months to come resulting in a lack of privacy for a very long while, until the furor he created died down.

12

CRASHED SAUCERS AND ALIEN BEINGS GALORE

As executive director of the Ohio UFO Investigators League and a mid-western correspondent for *UFO REVIEW*, Charles Wilhelm has a great interest in seeking out reports of crashed UFOs and the aliens said to have been found on board these disabled objects. Well known for his in-depth field investigations, Wilhelm has been approached on several occasions by individuals who profess to have "inside" information on this controversial topic. Opening his extensive files, researcher Wilhelm released the following cases exclusively for use in this publication.

Case 1: "This story was told to me by a Mrs. G. in 1959. She was very sick when I met her, and said she didn't want anyone to know of her experience while she was still alive. Since she was near death, Mrs. G. felt she had to relate what happened to someone she thought could be trusted, and who would keep the secret until the 'right moment.'

"According to what she told me, Mrs. G. had worked at Wright-Patterson Air Force Base in Dayton, Ohio during the 1940s and '50s until her retirement (due to health) in 1959. She was working in the Foreign Material Division with top security rating. Her job was one of cataloging any material, known or unknown. In 1955, she was assigned to a special job, cataloging the entire interior contents of a crashed UFO. Every little item inside the saucer was photographed and tagged. She couldn't remember how many items were listed, but she did say it ran over a thousand.

"During one of her breaks, she saw something which shocked her to no end. Wheeled past her from another room was what seemed to be two small individuals secured in ice or chemicals. The beings appeared to be about 4 1/2 to 5 feet tall with normal (earthly) features except for slanted eyes and a larger than normal sized head. Mrs. G. couldn't describe the clothing due to the short period of time the beings were in view. Mrs. G. appeared to me to be very sincere. She was well respected in the community and an active churchgoer. I questioned her as to why she was telling me this story and why wasn't she afraid of government pressure towards her. That's when she told me she was dying and said, 'Uncle Sam can't do anything to me once I'm in my grave!' This woman died six or seven months after telling me her story. I promised I would never reveal her true identify because she was well respected and I don't want to ruin her name."

Case 2: "I became friends with an individual whose father had also worked at Wright-Patterson during the 1940s and '50s. In 1966, Mr. D. told his son on his deathbed about two disc-shaped crafts, one intact and one damaged, crafts not of this planet. Also he mentioned seeing four alien bodies from the partial craft, and all four aliens were packed in dry ice.

"The bodies were around 5 feet tall, had larger heads than ours, slanted eyes, yet looked pretty humanoid. He thought the fingers were a little longer than a human's but couldn't be sure. Mr. D. had a high security clearance and was in charge of security at this particular time in 1956. His son told me the story after his father died, and had me promise that I would never make known his real name."

Case 3: "A Mr. Tomley related to me that back in April, 1953 he was flown to Ft. Monmouth, N.J. to observe a special film. He was an electronics expert for the Army and his job was to analyze from the film anything that he could define from his knowledge of radar technology.

"The day after arriving at the military base, he was escorted to a guarded building where the film was going to be shown. When he arrived, there were already nine other individuals plus a Major who was setting up the projector. Soon three or four other individuals arrived, and the Major said it was time to begin.

"Before the film was shown, all those present were told to take notes and when the film was over, no one was to discuss what they had seen to each other or anybody else. They even signed papers to that effect.

"The film started out by showing a strange disc-shaped craft with two guards (possibly MPs), one on each side of the craft. The object was sitting on two large blocks. He estimated the craft to be 15 to 18 feet in diameter.

Its surface, he said, was smooth, except for some tooled marks around the door. Where the door was located. A ramp extended to the ground. My informant estimated the door to be 2 feet wide and maybe 5 feet high. The craft was either silver or light gray in color.

"Then the interior of the craft was shown. There were no meters, radar screens, buttons or windows of any kind. The only thing he was able to see was a panel on which there were some types of levers that looked like sticks.

119

The interior of the craft was decorated in light pastel colors.

"Next the film came outside the craft, and off to the right a table was shown on which three small bodies had been placed. The film showed the bodies up close for a full five minutes.

"According to Mr. Tomley the small bodies were approximately 5 feet tall. He said their heads were quite large, and that their fingers were longer than a human's, their noses were sharper, ears longer, eyes closed but looked Oriental. Their bodies were a light green or ash. They were all dressed alike in yellow uniforms that were trimmed in black or a dark color. The skin on these beings looked wrinkled, as if they were quite old.

"Apparently a lot of questions were asked after the screening had come to an end. However, the Major refused to give any additional details, although he did say that the craft was found in New Mexico.

"Mr. Tomley told me that several of those who had seen the film were able to get together for a few moments and talk over what they had been privileged to see. All agreed that the technology was a thousand years ahead of ours."

Case 4: "I had been informed by a Mr. Daly that in 1953 he was flown to an undisclosed destination to examine the metal on an unknown ship. During this period of time, Mr. Daly was a metallurgist in the Air Force.

"Upon arriving at his destination at night, he was blindfolded, placed in a car and driven around for 30 minutes. When he got out of the military car, he expected to find hard ground, but almost fell due to the soft footing underneath him.

"When they took off his blindfold, he was inside a very large tent resting on sandy soil. Before him was an oddly shaped craft the likes of which he had never seen before. He was told to analyze the metal if he could. They brought him all the latest equipment and he began his work.

"The results were nonconclusive; he apparently didn't know what he was dealing with. Eventually the government men blindfolded him again and took it off when they reached the plane which took him back to the base he was stationed at.

"Mr. Daly never saw the inside of the craft. But he described the exterior as being 25 feet in diameter, silver in color, and with no apparent damage. An entrance way to the craft was 4 to 5 feet high and 2 to 3 feet wide. Mr. Daly couldn't give me any more details about his little trip. However, he did say that wherever they took him, it was very hot for the month of April."

Edward Lunguy first noticed strange object in the sky over the Magic City Shopping Plaza (top photo). Later he found peculiar substance which analysis shows may not be Earthly in origin. In bottom picture Lunguy holds piece of material in his hand.

13

THE NIGHT A UFO CAME CRASHING DOWN OVER OHIO

Here's one that maybe didn't get away!

A mysterious space fragment has NASA stumped, and a Kent University scientist admits weird object could be piece from an exploding spaceship. That's the story told by an Ohio man.

It was the steady, pulsating globe of strange orange light that caused Edward A. Lunguy to crane his neck through the window of his automobile that unforgettable Wednesday evening in July of 1972.

The driveway was dark, and the circular orb, glowing like a full moon, only larger, squatted weirdly in the sky about a mile away, directly over the Magic City shopping plaza where he was to meet his grandmother. Silent and wondrous, like something wholly unreal, it seemed frozen, put there by God-knows-who, for no other reason than to bedazzle the senses of man.

Awed, Edward Lunguy squinted, straining his eyes for another look. No, he wasn't dreaming. The object seemed to radiate an inner glow, like an amber-colored light bulb, hovering about 100 feet in the Ohio sky.

It was sticky and very humid, and fast approaching 10 P.M. when Lunguy's auto came to a halt outside of Moose Lodge, where his grandmother, 71-year old Mrs. Hazel M. Obney, was attending her usual once-a-week club meeting.

Now directly overhead, the thing loomed noiselessly, about the size and shape of a Klick market sign, Lunguy related.

"When I picked up my grandmother, I told her about the strange round object that was over the Plaza, and asked if she would like to see it. She agreed, and we stopped the car while coming down our street, at 962 Howe Road, Cuyahoga Falls. We both climbed from the car. It was about 9:50 P.M., and it was still overhead, hovering ghost like above the shopping center complex.

"Then the object began to move as though some invisible hand turned a switch to start a motor. It moved slowly, sluggishly, towards the other side of Barberton. It was as though whatever force controlled that movement didn't seem to care who saw it, and it didn't seem to be in any hurry at all.

"It was traveling, I'd say, 100-125 miles an hour, like a small airplane, a Piper Cub, toward the Sun Rubber company. And then, just as it passed over a water tower about two blocks from where we were standing in our back yard, the object exploded in a silent shower of sparks and disappeared. It looked like the Fourth of July!

"We didn't see anything fall to the ground, but we did see lots of sparks fly all over the sky, and we were somewhat disappointed to see it explode like that. And strange it is to say that it still made no noise—nothing at all—even while it was exploding. Then we went into the house and I told my mother and the children what we saw that night..."

Although unconfirmed by any authoritative sources at the time, police switchboards buzzed incessantly with reports of a UFO sighting, and a noiseless explosion of a huge orange ball in the sky that couldn't have been a meteor. Speculation that it might have been a balloon were dismissed because of its speed and the shower of sparks when it quietly exploded.

However, that spectacular sighting over Barberton, and what followed, are causing many in the scientific and UFOlogical communities to speculate that not only did a UFO visit Ohio that night during the summer of 1972, but that it left behind physical evidence that could once and for all prove the reality of space craft visiting from distant worlds.

It was the beginning of August, three weeks after the sighting, and conversation concerning the incident had all but ebbed into nearly forgotten kitchen-table small-talk. Lunguy was busily working around the yard early one morning smoothing the hedges and mowing the grass on his farm-size piece of property. It was while he was maneuvering the lawn mower around a pine tree that he found the substance that looked like a rock. It was under the tree, buried beneath an inch of soil. He was immediately drawn to its beauty. It was like nothing else he'd ever seen before. The nine-inch, 13-pound mass was smooth and black, and amber tones gleamed from it. It was such a beautiful specimen that Lunguy couldn't let it lie in the yard, and so he picked it up gently and took it into the house. The rock-like material was admired by the family and finally put aside, to be used as a decoration on the mantelpiece.

"My children were very small at the time, and quite often utilized it (the rock) as a footstool with which to watch television, and many times used it to reach a light switch in our home.

"After the passing of my grandmother in 1974, my wife suddenly asked me what kind of rock it was. I shrugged, telling her I didn't know. But she spurred my curiosity, and so I began looking through many books. I also went to the library, but I just wasn't able to find out what kind of rock it was. After a time, she asked me to take it to someone to see just exactly what it was. I told her I would."

In August of 1974, just before he took the mystery find to Kent State University, Kent, Ohio, the sudden flash of coincidence struck home, hitting like a door slamming him in the face.

The amber, beer-bottle color tones of the rock and the hue of the UFO sighted above Barberton two years before, were the same... With that "coincidence" fresh in his mind, the rock was taken to David Burns, assistant professor of geology at Kent State University.

Burns performed a series of spectrograph tests and came to the conclusion that the rock was too fresh to have been outside long. What's more, tests concluded that it was not a rock at all, but glass.

When Lunguy told Burns of the celestial explosion witnessed in 1972, and that the material was discovered some weeks afterward, it was suggested that Lunguy immediately notify NASA.

Before the still puzzling substance was submitted for testing to Robert Oldrieve, a NASA scientist at Cleveland's Lewis Research Center, Lunguy was visited by Earl Neff, director of the Cleveland UFO Club, and Mr. Canduso, of the Akron UFO Club. The interview was conducted on Thursday, September 11th, 1974, and their findings were that "Lunguy is a credible witness who sough no publicity either at the time of the sighting or now."

In the meantime, Edward Lunguy's 13" x 9" x 4" 'rock' was given over to Oldrieve, himself a 21-year veteran at NASA/Cleveland. A new diffractometer trace as well as a spectrochemical analysis was made.

Although a radioactivity test produced negative results, one of the most interesting coincidences NASA/Cleveland discovered is that the glass itself was not any of the volcanic or common natural glasses known.

Dr. Richard Grekila of the Westinghouse Research Laboratory was called in. He suggested Feldspar, Anorthite, or Orthiclose with limestone in solution. This proved out negative, as such a glass would not be clear, but crystalline.

Another major coincidence drawn by Oldrieve was how vastly different the unknown glass is from any natural glass, and how close in composition it is to glasses which were found to be desirable for rocket nozzle applications in NASA programs.

In part, Oldrieve's report states, "That such a composition should be associated with a UFO is curious, to say the least. Mr. Lunguy could not have known the color of the glass until his investigator cleaved it. When he saw it, he immediately exclaimed that this was the color (as he had described to us previously) of the UFO he had seen."

The report continued, "The unknown glass has the desirabilities for the protection of such hot items as jet engine combustor liners, or ram-jet or rocket parts."

In short, the mass was determined to be a natural glass similar to rocket glass-the substance used in space research, to guard space capsules entering the earth's atmosphere.

Scientists are continuing to test the as yet elusive material. Speculation runs high that it was not man-made; that it may possibly have been constructed by extraterrestrial life far beyond the earth's surface.

Tested, it has shown to be a fantastic refractory material, has great bonding strength, and that it has good thermal expansion. It could prove invaluable in the space race. Many experts have exclaimed that it could revolutionize the glass industry.

Expounded Oldrieve: "The only conclusion that can be made is that the unknown remains unknown. Apart from the fascinating possibility that the glass was part of a UFO, the glass is harder, less fusible, and in these respects more like a gemstone than is common glass. The properties which would make the 'UFO-glass' suitable for re-entry are: will bond to metals; expansion coefficient of tungsten; will not spall or flow off; and should prevent oxidation."

Glasses are so different in composition, he brought out, and are so abundant, that no conclusion can be made about uniqueness. The fact that it is like a rocket glass in composition is the only tie-in to a UFO sighting.

A "gossamer, thin-walled ornament with internal lighting device? An extraterrestrial 'experiment' to see if humans are perceptive of objects in the sky? Or just a rock?

Only time, and further testing will tell. In any event the UFO-glass, which is the name that has been applied to it, is, at last report, being kept safely under wraps-in a vault, deep in the basement of a bank in Barberton, Ohio.

14

OCCUPANTS REPAIR DISABLED CRAFT

In a most amazing report from the U.K., a disabled craft landed on a military base as startled servicemen watched alien beings repair the ship which remained for over four hours. Photos were taken of the encounter and high ranking personnel actually conversed with the stranded UFOnauts.

Names of witnesses in the following have been withheld for their protection. In Great Britain even civilians are subject to the Official Secrets Act, and the leaking of information revealed below by the late Gray Barker could subject these informants to severe criminal penalties. (Editor's note)

Have the military establishments of not only the U.S. but other nations already made contact with alien occupants of UFOs and withheld this information from the public? If this has indeed taken place, why has the greatest news story in the history of modern journalism been suppressed? Because the revelation would threaten Big Energy and break its stranglehold upon the common man? Because it might render banking systems obsolete by providing cheap and simple transmutation of "base metals" into gold, or by revealing how people on other planets manage without money and the interest charged thereon?

Or because the coming of the UFOnauts might herald massive planetary physical changes, the evacuation of humanity from Planet Earth and the resulting ruptures in established religions which cement society?

Or is it the Government itself which has the "saucers"? Our government along with other governments? Does the military-industrial complex, warned about by the late President Eisenhower, fear that revelation of such a secret could eliminate its bloated, fattening place at the public trough and its economic/political hold on the masses?

A well-documented "saucer crash" in Great Britain during 1980 and contact with its occupants by the U.S. Air Force can feed the "paranoia" suffered by the writer and no doubt some readers. Or perhaps some thoughtful reader can come up with a rational explanation that can set these fears to rest, at least for the time being. The "crash" itself has been investigated by the top civilian UFO researchers of the United Kingdom, along with our own lesser efforts.

THE MYSTERIOUS FOREST

Rendlesham Forest, an immense wooded area nestled among the hills in the sleepy farm country of East Anglia about eight miles northeast of Ipswich and close to the coast of England, has long been a subject for superstition and legend. Ancient tales of fairies and trolls harbored within its dark interior abound in the folklore of the area. J. R. Tolkien's foreboding forests of his Ring series may have been inspired by these woods.

Clusters of "ley lines" abound in the region, suggesting chains of ancient landmarks hat may have guided aerial navigation in the distant past.

But antiquity does not hold exclusive claim on unusual events transpiring in the Rendlesham Forest. In December, 1980, a flying saucer may have landed and its occupants contacted by the U.S. Air Force!

This fascinating account begins on a sunny June day when Jenny Randles could find no escape from her role as Britain's best known and most popular investigator-writer on the controversial subject of UFOs, especially since the publication of her popular book, *UFO Study*.

Entering a little pub and scouting a table to place her packages, her eyes suddenly met another familiar pair. The look of mild shock on both faces melted into sheepish grins as she recognized Paul Begg, a UFO skeptic with whom she had experienced many pyrotechnical verbal run-ins on television interviews and at "saucer" symposia.

"Please sit with me, and we will promise not to argue," Begg, author of the popular *Thin Air* book (in which mysterious disappearances are examined skeptically) persuaded.

As they sipped coffee and made small talk, Begg broke the ice.

"I've been thinking about you this week. In fact, I almost telephoned you. For I have a choice rumor for your UFO mill!"

The writer then told how he and his wife encountered a young man while dining out in their village. The informant had just come from work at a civil radar base, a part of the large East Anglican complex that monitors the strategic area. During the past week a friend going off duty took him aside and told him of a dramatic UFO tracking that had taken place the previous night.

The base had tracked the unusual target as it headed toward Suffolk and east of Ipswich at an incredible speed. Other bases tracked the same object.

"At first this sounded much like many unfounded rumors of UFO radar cases," Begg continued, "but the young man then turned up some additional details which intrigued me.

"Two or three days later U.S. Air Force officers-remember I said United States Air Force, not the RAF-came to the base and confiscated the taped recordings of the tracking. He thought they were from the USAF Base at Bentwaters."

Begg said he didn't have the time to follow up on the information provided him, but he suggested Randles tackle the case if she were interested.

THE LANDING AT WOODBRIDGE

Enlisting the aid of civilian radar experts, Randles contacted the witness, who confirmed his initial report to Begg and then added some attractive tidbits:

"We were led to believe that the object tracked on radar landed near the Woodbridge Air Force Base. Later scuttlebutt from our own officers indicated it landed inside the base! Obviously it was a metallic aircraft of alien nature. Its occupants were contacted by base personnel!"

After the interview (Randles told me during a transatlantic phone call) she and the experts sat down to analyze the case.

"The man seemed to be honest and truthful, and I concluded that behind the smoking rumor there surely must be some fire. But we really had nothing concrete to go on until good fortune struck in a contact with Norman Oliver."

Oliver, editor of BUFORA Journal, a British UFO magazine, forged another link in the Rendlesham Forest mystery.

One of the U.S. investigators had managed to obtain similar information from an American serviceman, who had returned to the States and felt more free to talk. According to this new information, "something big" had occurred at Woodbridge Air Force Base the first part of the year, probably December.

This reminded him of another report he had scanned briefly, then laid aside during the hectic preparation of the latest Journal issue: Two of his own British Associates had submitted the report in March, 1981, sometime before either his or Randles' involvement.

The interest of Brenda Butler and Dot Street, local Suffolk residents, had been piqued when a personal friend, an officer at the USAF base who had previously confided UFO information, gave them essentially the same account. He had informed her a month before any of the other rumors surfaced. After they promised secrecy, at least until the story might surface elsewhere and he thus could be taken off the hook, he told essentially the same story, but with dramatic additions:

This was not the first UFO incident which had taken place at the base. But this one was the most dramatic, because it had involved contact with the occupants of an alien craft!

A farmer on the edge of the forest called the base on December 30, 1980 to report a brilliant light and a possible crash in the area. Military police investigated and radioed back, "There's a bloody flying saucer out here in the woods!"

Rather oddly, a reporter from the base newspaper was the next person involved, possibly because of the inertia in the base commander's getting together "a high-level team" to investigate. The reporter obtained both still and motion pictures of the object on the ground, and possibly of its occupants!

The commander stripped the team of all weapons and briefed the men to "avoid showing any hostility to any unfamiliar personnel you encounter. Do not react hastily, no matter what unfamiliar circumstances you may face!"

At the site the team was amazed to confront a large, shiny metallic craft on the ground. It apparently had been damaged in landing, and three tiny beings, wearing silver-colored uniforms, seemed to be supported by rays or light beams emanating from the ground, as they were suspended in the air, while apparently repairing the machine's exterior.

The informant told quite freely how the commander had taken the cameras and film from the base reporter, still on the scene, and ordered a total information blackout. Then he conversed with the occupants while they worked. After about four hours the occupants halted their work and climbed back into the craft which rose slowly to treetop level before shooting off rapidly.

Although written reports by the two women made little importance of one facet, it could be an important clue to unraveling the mystery. Their informant talked freely of other aspects but he refused to discuss two important points: A more detailed description of the craft's appearance, and the conversation between the commander and the occupants.

CONFRONTING THE COMMANDER

Dot and Brenda personally confronted the Base Commander who had allegedly led the party to the crash scene and communicated with the occupants:

"On February 18th, Brenda and I went to the air base and made an appointment to see the Commander. While we were talking to his secretary and arranging the interview, we sensed reluctance on her part, until we mentioned the January sighting, to which she replied (without prompting), 'The beginning of January?'

"When we confirmed this to be so, this seemed to break the ice and she appeared to be more willing for us to see the Commander, which she was able to arrange later in the day.

'As we told him of the sighting we knew about, he began to smile. When we had finished, he said he didn't know anything about it. He then asked if we planned to continue our investigation. I replied in the affirmative."

"What do you plan to do with your information?" he asked.

"I told him we probably would make a written report for submission to UFO investigation groups.

"Although the Commander was entirely noncommittal, we got the distinct impression that he knew all the details we sought. He also seemed concerned that we planned to report it, but of course did not say so in actual words-he knew we were civilians and that he would have difficulty suppressing our findings.

"We then went to the forest location where the landing was said to have taken place, but by that time it was late in the day and we left. That might have ended our investigation had not Brenda heard from a man who insisted the landing report was true and gave her directions to the site.

"So on February 24th, we decided to pay another visit to Rendlesham Forest. However, we soon found that the directions were rather vague and were not leading us to the site.

"Finally we visited the Forestry Commission's office, where we had an interesting conversation with a person on duty. He told us that he had been working in the office on January 1st, when a man walked in and said he had just been talking to a farmer, who, on December 29,1980, had heard a very loud noise which frightened his animals. The farmer also said that his farm had been illuminated by a very bright, white light. He then called the RAF Base at Woodbridge, which promised to investigate.

"Unfortunately the Forestry worker had not thought it important to ask the farmer his name. We heard another rumor that people who had sighted anything unusual that night had been asked to keep quiet about it.

"While we were at the office, another Forestry worker came in and told us that his wife's friend's husband had also seen a UFO that same night.

"Neither worker mentioned a rumor we heard later to the effect that workers had discovered a section of forest with the tops of trees scorched. Our source said they had reported this to the Air Base, but had been told to keep quiet about it.

"After leaving the office we talked to people living in the immediate area. At one farm house we were told that the residents had been visited by two men on January 1st, who had asked the same questions as we. These people also told us of a rumor that 'something happened' that night on the Air Base bomb disposal site."

Though this concluded Gray Barker's early report on the incident, the entire affair has attracted some attention in the media. The Cable Network News was so impressed by their findings that they devoted several segments to the episode. In the book, *Clear Intent*, author Larry Fawcett interviews a young Serviceman, Larry Warren, who claims to have been at the base when the near landing took place.

Apparently he was one of those who witnessed the repair job being done on the disabled craft, saw the aliens, and was present when communication between the military and the saucer crew members was established. In our concluding chapter we discover that similar affiliations may be pretty common between them and us.

Are the mysterious MJ-12 UFO DOCUMENTS, which have received their share of attention, a proof of alien visitations?

At a recent UFO Conference in Burbank, California, those in attendance were treated to a display of documents supposedly of a Top-Secret "For the Eyes of the President Only" nature. The documents concerned the crash of a UFO in New Mexico in 1947, near Roswell Air Force Base and tell of a small group known as "Majestic 12" established by President Truman to take charge of the technical, sociological and other aspects of the landing which involved the demise of several small beings who were inside the craft when it exploded. The "MJ-12" group was made up of a number of outstanding scientists and military personnel. The following is a report issued at the Burbank Conference by William Moore, Stanton Friedman and Jaime Shandera, giving the surrounding circumstances as to how the document came to be received and subsequently released.

Nuclear physicist Stanton Friedman supports the authenticity of the MJ-12 documents based on the fact that he knows the government has managed to keep its share of secrets. Here he's shown holding "sanitized" documents released under the Freedom of Information Act with many key portions blacked out.

15

MAJESTIC-12

TOP SECRET UFO DOCUMENTS RELEASED!

For IMMEDIATE RELEASE: June 11th, 1987

The accompanying document is part of the research properties of William L. Moore, Jaime H. Shandera and Stanton T. Friedman. Moore (a professional writer) and Friedman (a well-known nuclear physicist) are recognized and respected UFO researchers of long standing with solid backgrounds for factual reporting. Both have written and lectured widely on the subject. Shandera is a Los Angeles television producer with a background that includes directing a variety of news and documentary shows. In 1982, after Moore had worked more than a year-and-a-half on his own, the three teamed up on a research project that would take them further into the strange world of government involvement with Unidentified Flying Objects than anyone in the civilian field is known to have ever gone before. This project involved anonymous government agents sharing research pointers and dialogue alleging that UFOs are indeed extraterrestrial spacecraft and that certain elements of the U.S. intelligence community continue to maintain a high-level but covert interest in this phenomenon at a time when official position statements assert that there is no government interest whatsoever.

Over the past seven years, the Moore-Shandera-Friedman team, working closely with a number of other associates both in the news media and within the civilian UFO community, has aggressively pursued contacts, developed sources, and carefully researched leads. Numerous interviews were conducted, and many days were spent combing through records at the National Archives in Washington, D.C. as well as both the Truman and Eisenhower Presidential Libraries and numerous similar facilities both federal and private. They can now report that considerable progress has been made.

The accompanying document arrived in the mail in a plain brown wrapper at the residence of Jaime Shandera in December, 1981. A detailed and exhaustive study of every aspect of this document has been under way since then. Although we are not in a position to endorse its authenticity at this time, it is our considered opinion, based upon research and interviews conducted thus far, that the document and its contents appear to be genuine.

At the very least, it is possible to state with certainty that absolutely nothing has surfaced during the course of our research which would seem to suggest otherwise. Indeed, one document was uncovered at the National Archives which unquestionably verifies the existence of an "M J 12 group in 1954 and definitely links both the National Security Council and the President of the United States to it. A copy of this document, with its authenticating stamp from the National Archives, is also attached for your examination.

These materials are being submitted for your examination and consideration, either as a member of the news media, or as one whose own interests and research lie along similar lines.

Please be advised that no use of this material may be made without crediting its source as the Moore-Shandera-Friedman Research Project into U.S. Government UFO Policy.

QUESTIONS AND ANSWERS ABOUT THE TOP SECRET EYES ONLY
UFO BRIEFING DOCUMENTS

1. Is there any other evidence that the U.S. government retrieved a crashed alien craft outside Roswell, New Mexico in July, 1947? Moore and Friedman have since 1978 conducted a very very extensive research project concerning the so-called Roswell Incident. To date, 92 different people have been located and interviewed about the event, 31 of whom had first-hand involvement. Included are several generals, the base security officer, counterintelligence corps personnel, the neighbors and family of the rancher who discovered the wrecked device, the public relations officer of the air base, local news media personnel, etc., etc. To date, one book and five research papers have been published presenting the data.

2. Is there any proof that the event was first publicized and then covered-up by the government? Yes. A press release was first distributed by the Army Air Force at Roswell stating that a crashed disc had been recovered. Then shortly afterwards the head of the 8th Air Force announced that a mistake had been made and that it was only a radar reflector from a weather balloon. The officer who took the call from Washington, D.C. with the instructions to cover-up the story has so testi-

fied to Friedman and Moore. Many people who handled the very strange materials have testified that the material could not have been from a radar reflector. Ten first-hand witnesses are on record as having stated that the object was, in fact, some sort of spacecraft.

3. Was there any evidence of strange writing on the retrieved material? Yes. Five persons who actually handled pieces of the wreckage have described very unusual symbols on pieces of the wreckage.

4. Is there any evidence that President-elect Eisenhower received a military briefing on 18 November, 1952? Yes. Information at the Eisenhower Library and in the Truman files indicates White House and Pentagon briefings on that date. A Washington Post article also confirms a briefing on that date.

5. Is there any evidence that Bush and Forrestal met with Truman on September 24th, 1947? Yes. Forrestal's diary, Bush's files and the Truman Library listing of Presidential Activities all establish that Bush and Forrestal first met with each other, and then with Truman on that date. Bush and Forrestal often met with each other during the 1947-49 time frame.

6. Is there any evidence that the Cutler to Twining "Top Secret-Eyes Only" memo is genuine? Yes. There are several factors to be considered here:

A. It was found in a file box at the National Archives by Moore and Shandera who were the first persons to go through the newly declassified materials.

B. The archivist Joanna Williamson who was in charge of the RG 341 file is quoted in the London Observer as saying "It was found in the files of the U.S. Air Force's Director of Intelligence and is certainly genuine."

C. A very similar in format and content "Top Secret-Eyes Only" memo was sent by Cutler to Twining in 1953 about a similar NSC meeting on another, unrelated, project.

7. Why is there no signature on the memo? The file copy was a carbon. Carbons are normally not signed.

8. Is there any reason at all to think that Harvard Astronomer Dr. Donald H. Menzel, who wrote three anti-UFO books and many articles, could really have been part of a Top Secret-Eyes Only group that knew some UFOs were "Identified Alien Craft"? As a result of extended research by Friedman at Harvard and elsewhere, these facts have been established about Menzel:

A. Menzel once mentioned in a letter written to President-elect Jack Kennedy that he possessed a Top Secret-Ultra security clearance.

B. Menzel claimed to JFK in 1960 that he had a longer continuous association with the highly classified National Security Agency (NSA) and its predecessor U.S. Navy agency than anyone else in the government at that time.

C. Menzel's association with Dr. Vannevar Bush, wartime head of the Office of Scientific Research and Development, dates back to 1934.

D. Bush was the staunchest Menzel defender at the USAF loyalty hearing in 1950. Indeed, Bush had instructed Menzel's attorney to notify him (Bush) immediately upon resolution of the loyalty problem.

E. Menzel worked on classified programs for more than 30 different companies.

F. Menzel is on record as having made numerous trips during 1947 to both Washington, DC and New Mexico on government research activities.

G. Menzel had learned Japanese for his cryptography work for the Navy, was familiar with disinformation, and would have been the perfect person to show the Roswell writing to.

H. Menzel had written science fiction and popular newspaper articles for major papers. He was the best qualified of the 12 to put out disinformation, and his first book was translated into Russian.

9. The documents indicate that a second object crashed in Texas on the night of December 6th-7th, 1950. Is there any indication that such an event ever occurred? Yes. A copy of an official communique was located in files released by the F.B.I. indicating a "high alert" status about UFOs had been called by the Air Force on December 8th, 1950. There are also several newspaper articles indicating that military leaves at various air bases were abruptly cancelled that same day.

10. What about other official documentary evidence? A formerly Top Secret Canadian memo dated November, 1950, states that "the matter (of UFOs) is the most highly classified subject in the United States government" and identified Dr. Vannevar Bush as head of a project which was trying to discover how UFOs work"

Note: The following is an accurate reproduction of the "Majestic 12' documents. Though the first few pages have been reset in type for purposes of easy reading, we have tried to stay as close to the original format as possible. The last two documents are easy to read and thus we have reproduced the originals.

COPY ONE OF ONE

BRIEFING DOCUMENT: OPERATION MAJESTIC 12

PREPARED FOR PRESIDENT-ELECT DWIGHT D. EISENHOWER:

18 NOVEMBER, 1952

WARNING! This is a document containing compartmentalized information essential to the national security of the United States. The material herein is strictly limited to those possessing Majestic-12 clearance level. Reproduction in any form or the taking of written or mechanically transcribed notes is strictly forbidden.

T52-EXEMPT (E)

"MAJESTIC 12

COPY ONE OF ONE

SUBJECT: OPERATION MAJESTIC-12 PRELIMINARY BRIEFING FOR

PRESIDENT-ELECT EISENHOWER.

DOCUMENT PREPARED 18 NOVEMBER, 1952.

BRIEFING OFFICER: ADM. ROSCOE H. HILLENKOETTER (MJ-1)

NOTE: This document has been prepared as a preliminary briefing only. It should be regarded as introductory to a full operations briefing intended to follow.

OPERATION MAJESTIC-12 is a TOP SECRET Research and Development Intelligence operation responsible directly and only to the President of the United States. Operations of the project are carried out under control of the Majestic-12 (Majic-12) Group which was established by special classified executive order of President Truman on 24 September, 1947, upon recommendation by Dr. Vannevar Bush and Secretary James Forrestal. (See Attachment "4".) Members of the Majestic-12 Group were designated as follows:

Adm. Roscoe H. Hillenkoetter

Dr. Vannevar Bush

Secy. James V. Forrestal*

Gen. Nathan F. Twining

Gen. Hoyt S. Vandenberg

Dr. Detlev Bronk

Dr. Jerome Hunsaker

Mr. Sidney W. Souers

Mr. Gordon Gray

Dr. Donald Menzel

Gen. Robert M. Montague

Dr. Lloyd V. Berkner

The death of Secretary Forrestal on 22 May, 1949, created a vacancy which remained unfilled until 01 August, 1950, upon which date Gen. Walter B. Smith was designated as permanent replacement.

T52-EXEMPT (E)

COPY ONE OF ONE

On 24 June, 1947, a civilian pilot flying over the Cascade Mountains in the State of Washington observed nine flying disc-shaped aircraft traveling in formation at a high rate of speed. Although this was not the first known sighting of such objects, it was the first to gain widespread attention in the public media. Hundreds of reports of sightings of similar objects followed. Many of these came from highly credible military and civilian sources. These reports resulted in independent efforts by several different elements of the military to ascertain the nature and purpose of these objects in the interests of national defense. A number of witnesses were interviewed and there were several unsuccessful attempts to utilize aircraft in efforts to pursue reported discs in flight. Public reaction bordered on near hysteria at times.

In spite of these efforts, little of substance was learned about the objects until a local rancher reported that one had crashed in a remote region of New Mexico located approximately seventy-five miles northwest of Roswell Army Air Base (now Walker Field).

On 07 July, 1947, a secret operation was begun to assure recovery of the wreckage of this object for scientific study. During the course of this operation, aerial reconnaissance discovered that four small humanlike beings had apparently ejected from the craft at some point before it exploded.

These had fallen to earth about two miles east of the wreckage site. All four were dead and badly decomposed due to action by predators and exposure to the elements during the approximately one week time period which had elapsed before their discovery. A special scientific team took charge of removing these bodies for study. (See Attachment "C".) The wreckage f the craft was also removed to several different locations. (See Attachment 'B'.) Civilian and military witnesses in the area were debriefed, and news reporters were given the effective cover story that the object had been a misguided weather research balloon.

T52-EXEMPT (E)

COPY ONE OF ONE

A covert analytical effort organized by Gen. Twining and Dr. Bush acting on the direct orders of the President, resulted in a preliminary consensus (19 September, 1947) that the disc was most likely a short range reconnaissance craft. This conclusion was based for the most part on the craft's size and the apparent lack of any identifiable provisioning. (See Attachment "D".) A similar analysis of the four dead occupants was arranged by Dr. Bronk. It was the tentative conclusion of this group (30 November, 1947) that although these creatures are human-like in appearance, the biological and evolutionary processes responsible for their development has apparently been quite different from those observed or postulated in homo-sapiens. Dr. Bronk's team has suggested the term "Extraterrestrial Biological Entities", or "EBEs", be adopted as the standard term of reference for these creatures until such time as a more definitive designation can be agreed upon.

Since it is virtually certain that these craft do not originate in any country on earth, considerablespeculation has centered around what their point of origin might be and how they get here. Mars was and remains a possibility, although some scientists most notably Dr. Menzel, consider it more likely that we are dealing with beings from another solar system entirely.

Numerous examples of what appear to be a form of writing were found in the wreckage. Efforts to decipher these have remained largely unsuccessful. (See Attachment "E".) Equally unsuccessful have been efforts to determine the method of propulsion or the nature or method of transmission of the power source involved. Research along these lines has been complicated by the complete absence of identifiable wings, propellers, jets, or other conventional methods of propulsion and guidance, as well as a total lack of metallic wiring, vacuum tubes, or similar recognizable electronic components. (See Attachment "F".) It is assumed that the propulsion unit was completely destroyed by the explosion which caused the crash.

T52-EXEMPT (E)

COPY ONE OF ONE

A need for as much additional information as possible about these craft, their performance characteristics and their purpose led to the undertaking known as U.S. Air Force Project SIGN in December, 1947. In order to preserve security, liaison between SIGN and Majestic-12 was limited to two individuals within the Intelligence Division of Air Materiel Command whose role was to pass along certain types of information through channels. SIGN evolved into Project GRUDGE in December, 1948. The operation is currently being conducted under the code name BLUE BOOK with liaison maintained through the Air Force officer who is head of the project.

On 06 December, 1950, a second object, probably of similar origin, impacted the earth at high speed in the El Indio-Guerrero area of the Texas-Mexican border after following a long trajectory through the atmosphere. By the time a search team arrived, what remained of the object had been almost totally incinerated. Such material as could be recovered was transported to the A.E.C. facility at Sandia, New Mexico, for study. Implications for the National Security are of continuing importance in that the motives and ultimate intentions of these visitors remain completely unknown. In addition, a significant upsurging in the surveillance activity of these craft beginning in May and continuing through the autumn of this year has caused considerable concern that new developments may be imminent. It is for these reasons, as well as the obvious international and technological considerations and the ultimate need to avoid a public panic at all costs, that the Majestic-12 Group remains of the unanimous opinion that imposition of the strictest security precautions should continue without interruption into the new administration. At the same time, contingency plan MJ-1949-O4P/78 (Top Secret-Eyes Only) should be held in continued readiness should the need to make a public announcement present itself. (See Attachment "G".)

T52-EXEMPT (E)

COPY ONE OF ONE

ENUMERATION OF ATTACHMENTS:

*ATTACHMENT "A".........Special Classified Executive Order #092447, (TS/EO)

{'ATTACHMENT "B".........Operation Majestic 12 Status Report #1, Part A. 30 NOV '47. (TS-MAJIC-EO)

*ATTACHMENT "C".........Operation Majestic 12 Status Report #1, Part B. 30 NOV '47. (TS-MAJIC/EO)

*ATTACHMENT "D".........Operation Majestic-12 Preliminary Analytical Report. 19 SEP '47. (TS-MAJIC-EO)

*ATTACHMENT "E".........Operation Majestic 12 Blue Team Report #5. 30 JUN '52. (TS-MAJIC-EO)

*ATTACHMENT "F ....Operation Majestic 12 Status Report #2. 31 JAN '48. (TS-MAJIC-EO)

*ATTACHMENT "G".........Operation Majestic-12 Contingency Plan MJ-1949-004P/78: 31 JAN '49 (TS-MAJIC-EO)

*ATTACHMENT "H".........Operation Majestic-12, Maps and Photographs Folio (Extractions). (TS-MAJIC-EO)

T52-EXEMPT (E)

Researcher William Moore followed his hunch and found early out in his investigation that the crash at Roswell held up better than any other retrieval case of this type.

16

THE "GRAND DECEPTION"

Referred to most often as the "Ultimate Secret," the subject of crashed space-ships has become a "hot potato" among UFOlogists, with researchers divided in their opinion as to the legitimacy of such stories. Among the more seriously in-clined, the episode at Roswell seems to get the highest number of Brownie points for being real. No doubt, this has to do with the fact that over fifty witnesses to the crash have been located and their testimony recorded. On the other hand, the MJ-12 papers have come under attack not only by "professional skeptics," including the likes of "bad boy" aviation editor Philip Klass, but have even been questioned by the Mutual UFO Network and the prestigious *"Just Cause,"* both pro-UFO or-ganizations.

Those in opposition to MJ-12 point out that the style and format of the docu-ments do not seem to follow other government papers from this same period. They also question the fact that the documents were sent through the mail by an anonymous party, and that they were not even Xeroxes of original papers, but were photographed onto a roll of 35mm film, and thus their authenticity cannot really even be tested as to the type of paper used or the year they might have been written (which could be traced rather easily otherwise).

In all honesty, however, William Moore and Stanton Friedman have spent a great deal of time trying their damndest to prove the credibility of the MJ12 docu-ments. Apparently, Moore has established contact with a group of government agents (some retired, some still in the Service) who "behind the scenes" have been trying to breach security, and finally release to the world news of the "ulti-mate secret."

These military personnel have gone so far as to promise some "startling rev-elations" in the near future. A video interview with one of these individuals—his face in the shadows so his true identity remains a secret—has been aired pri-vately for several researchers including James W. Moseley, whose report on a crash involving a woman working at Wright-Patterson is detailed earlier in these pages. Among the forthcoming revelations promised is the startling disclosure that the U.S. Government (and presumably other governments) has established a liaison with at least one group of extraterrestrials, and that a sort of "trade agreement" has been put into practice with these beings.

Adding considerable weight to the rumors is an article that appeared in the July 1988 issue of UFO UNIVERSE, a nationally distributed newsstand publication of which I happen to be the editor. Written by television producer Linda Moulton Howe, the article, *"UFO Mutilations, Crashed Saucers & Aliens in Government Captivity,"* tells how, during a documentary special she was preparing for HBO, the author held a conversation with Air Force Office of Special Investigations Agent Richard Doty, who showed her a top-secret document which discussed a series of UFO crashes that took place in the Southwest in the late 1940s and the early 1950s. Alien bodies were retrieved from the downed craft and taken for examination by scientists with high-level security clearances. One being was kept alive at Los Alamos Laboratories, New Mexico, where it died in 1952 of unknown causes. During its captivity the alien communicated via telepathy that its civilization has manipulated the human race's biological, sociological and religious evolution since the beginning of recorded history.

Howe later added more details in a letter published in the *Just Cause* bulletin. "During the conversation, Agent Doty handed me some typed papers which were titled simply, *'Briefing Papers for the President of the United States,'* about the subject of unidentified flying vehicles. There was no designation of a specific president, nor do I remember a specific date. Agent Doty said he had been asked by his superiors to show me the briefing paper, that I could ask questions, but could not take notes. The contents described a series of crashed UFO discs at Aztec and Roswell, New Mexico; Kingman, Arizona; and a crash in Mexico. Extraterrestrial bodies from the downed crafts were retrieved and taken to laboratories for examination. The paper also described information from the direct contact with the 'Grays' about their extraterrestrial intervention and manipulation of the human race's biological, sociological and religious evolution. The paper outlined the government's efforts since the 1940s to ascertain the origin, nature and motives of the ETs through Projects Sign, Grudge, Gleem, Pounce, Blue Book and others, and concluded with a list of some current projects: Sigma (communication with ETs) Snowbird (ET craft technology and efforts to fly one), Aquarius (overall research and contact program regarding ETs)* and one "closed project with a name similar to Garnet which involved the ET connection with human evolution."

According to the TV producer, Agent Doty showed her the briefing papers "because the government intended to release to me several thousand feet of color and black and white film taken between 1947 and 1964 showing crashed UFO discs and extraterrestrial bodies as historic footage to be included in the HBO documentary supported with official government confirmation."

. Due to what were called "political delays," Linda never was given the historic UFO footage, and eventually the HBO special was cancelled because of this. Special Agent Doty established contact with other researchers about this same time. Contacted recently, however, he denies showing Howe any such papers, nor does he admit to any knowledge about any motion picture footage depicting crashed UFOs or alien bodies.

In her *UFO UNIVERSE* article, Howe added that the captured ETs were described as "37 inches to 4-1/2 feet tall, gray skin, had only small holes for ears and nose, large black eyes and a small, straight-slit mouth. The hands had four long, thin, 'fingers' with webbing in-between, and dark claw-like nails." A second group of ETs called the "Blondes" or "Talls" were said to be Nordic type extraterrestrials who looked remarkably human.

In conclusion, Linda says she now has "no doubt about the existence of an invisible and very powerful government agency challenged with extraterrestrial relations, communications, research and technology development...its first mission was to retrieve and analyze the crashed discs and extraterrestrial bodies in the 1940s. In 1987, is MJ-12 still troubled, confused and in conflict within its own ranks about the consequences of ETs' presence on this planet? Or do they know that we are nearing the end of some kind of Earth cycle superimposed from 'out there' which will permanently change the fate of all of us"?

And what of this supposed government-alien liaison? Is there any evidence whatsoever that a pact or agreement has been made with these so-called "Grays"? And if such a pact was made, what has been the outcome of such a secret deal?

JOHN LEAR'S SCENARIO

The individual with the most answers to these imposing questions happens to be John Lear, son of William P. Lear, designer of the Lear Jet and noted aviation figure. Around aircraft all his life, the younger Lear has flown 150 types of aircraft, holds 17 world speed records in the Lear Jet, and is the only pilot ever to hold every airman certificate issued by the Federal Aviation Administration. Lear says he has flown missions for the CIA and other top secret agencies, and once ran as a candidate for the Nevada State Senate.

Through his CIA and military contacts, Lear has put together a rather frightening scenario in which this government-alien liaison started out on seemingly equal footing, only to go haywire when it was discovered the Grays had an ulterior motive in establishing an ongoing relationship with Uncle Sam.

"MJ-12, representing the U.S. government, made a deal with the EBEs, or Grays, around the period of 1969-1970-1971. The 'deal' was that in exchange for technology which they would provide to us, we would ignore the abductions of humans that was going on. The EBEs assured us that these abductions were merely ongoing monitoring of developing civilizations. But the fact is that these abductions have been for at least three purposes: (1) Insertion of a tiny probe about 3 mm. in size into the brain and used for monitoring and programming purposes; (2) Post hypnotic suggestion concerning an important event that will occur in the next two to five years, and giving the subject some place to go and something to perform at that time; and (3) Genetic crossbreeding between the EBEs and humans. In many of the abductee hypnotic regressions of women with unusual terminated pregnancies, they have been shown these 'crossbreeds'—usually frail, tiny beings with comparatively large heads, very thin skin, and very thin arms and legs. Since we weren't aware of these facts, we went along with the agreement, but insisted that a list of the abductees to be submitted periodically to the National Security Council and MJ-12."

Lear claims that every president since Truman has known about the presence of the ETs on earth, and that under the Reagan administration, George Bush was the head of MJ-12, assisted by former National Security Advisor John Poindexter, among others.

Several military bases in the U.S. are said to have literally been "taken over" by aliens, "after the initial agreement between MJ-12 and the aliens." Groom Lake-one of this nation's most secret test centers in Nevada, was closed for a period of about two years (1972-1973), and a huge underground facility was constructed for and with the help of the EBEs. The bargained-for technology was set in place, but could only be operated by the EBEs themselves. Needless to say, the advanced technology could not be used against the EBEs in case of need."

Continuing his story, Lear states that during the years 1979 through 1983, it became increasingly obvious to MJ-12 that things were not going as planned. It became known that many more people (in the thousands) were being abducted than were listed on the official abduction list being supplied to the National Security Council and MJ-12, and that the abductions included much more than the simple monitoring of an advanced civilization."

"By 1979 things had gotten out of hand almost entirely," says Lear, who remains very serious about this charges, though he has come under increasing attack by those who believe his scenario is more science fiction than fact. According to Lear's testimony, some 66 soldiers were killed when they were ordered on a commando-like raid to take back control of one underground installation in New Mexico which had virtually been seized by the Grays.

The way he sees things, Lear maintains that in 1984 members of MJ-12 suddenly realized their mistake. The "Grand Deception" had been completed by the EBEs, and there was very little the military could do short of a complete confession to the public.

In a paper circulated among UFOlogists, Lear gave this account of what was happening behind government lines: "They had subtly promoted *Close Encounters of the Third Kind* and *E.T.* to get the public used to 'odd-looking' aliens that were compassionate, benevolent and very much our 'space brothers'. They 'sold' the EBEs to the public and were now faced with the fact that quite the opposite was true. In addition, a plan was started in 1968-1969 to make the public aware of the existence of aliens on earth over the next 20 years, to be culminated with several documentaries to be released during the 1985-1987 period of time. These documentaries would explain the history and intentions of the EBEs. The discovery of the 'Grand Deception' put the entire plans, hopes, wishes and dreams of MJ-12 into complete confusion and panic.

"Meeting at the 'Country Club', a remote lodge with private golf course and lavish sleeping and working quarters built by and exclusively for the members of MJ-12, it was a factional fight of what to do now. Part of MJ12 wanted to confess the whole scheme and the shambles it had become to the public, beg their forgiveness and ask for their support. The other half of MJ12 argued there was no way they could do that, that the situation was untenable and there was no use in exciting the public with the 'horrible truth', and that the best plan was to continue the development of a weapon that could be used against the EBEs under the guise of 'SDI', the Strategic Defense Initiative, which had nothing whatsoever to do with a defense from Russian nuclear missiles.

"As these words are being written, Dr. Teller, 'father of the H-bomb', is in the test tunnels of the Nevada Test Site, driving his workers and associates, in the words of one, 'like a man possessed.' And well he should; for Dr. Teller was a member of MJ-12 along with Dr. Kissinger, Bobby Inman and possibly Admiral Poindexter, to name a few of the current MJ-12.

"Before the 'Grand Deception' was discovered, and according to the meticulous plan of metered release of information to the public, several documents and video tapes were made. William Moore, a Burbank, California based UFO researcher, came into possession of a video tape through his contacts with MJ-12, who had taken great interest in Mr. Moore's book, *The Roswell Incident,* published in 1980. The book detailed the crash, recovery and subsequent cover-up of a UFO with four alien bodies. They decided to use Moore as one of several conduits to help in the gradual release of the existence of aliens to the public. The video Mr. Moore had was an interview by two well-known newsmen of a military officer associated with MJ-12. In the interview the military officer answers questions relating to the history of MJ-12 and the cover-up, the recovery of a number of flying saucers, the existence of a live alien (one of three living aliens recovered, designated or named EBE-1, EBF-2 and EBE-3) being held in a facility designated as YYII at Los Alamos, New Mexico. The only other facility of this type is at Edwards Air Force Base in Mojave, California. The officer names names as previously mentioned plus a few others: Howard Brown, Richard Helms, Gen. Vernon Walters and Von Karmon. The officer also relates the fact that the EBEs claim to have created Christ. The EBEs have some kind of recording device that has recorded all the earth's history, and can display it in the form of a hologram. This hologram can be filmed but, because of the way holograms work, does not come out clearly. The crucifixion of Christ on the Mount of Olives* has allegedly been put on film to show to the public. The EBEs claim to have created Christ—in view of the 'Grand Deception'—could be an effort to disrupt traditional values for undetermined reasons.

*Editor's Note: *Jesus was not crucified on the Mount of Olives. He was crucified at Golgotha ("the place of skulls"). After all these years, this single piece of inaccurate information continues to render Lear's claims as completely bogus.*

"Another video tape alleged to be in existence is an interview with an EBE. Since EBEs communicate telepathically, an Air Force Colonel serves as an interpreter.* Just before the recent stock market crash, several newsmen, including Bill Moore, had allegedly been invited to Los Alamos to personally film and distribute to the public a similar type interview. Apparently, because of the market crash, it was felt that the timing was not propitious."

* Editor's Note: *Why was there a need to use an "interpreter?" If the EBE was a true telepath, he/she/it could transmit any message to anyone at any time with ease. When communicating telepathically, the sender, not the receiver, is the controller in every instance. The receivers to whom a telepathic message is directed get the message whether they want to or not.*

Reached at his home, researcher-author William Moore anxiously points out that as far as he can tell, there is no real evidence to support John Lear's fantastic claims. Moore admits that he has been shown what purports to be aerial photographs of an alien base set up in the desert in New Mexico. To him what are supposed to be spaceships and aliens on the ground look like nothing more extraterrestrial than ordinary rocks and sticks.

One of Lear's more recent accusations is that aliens are now cloning humans in bizarre genetic experiments, and that a similar pact was made between the Grays and the Soviet Union but that Uncle Sam and the Russians have since teamed up to fight the menace from outer space.

As Lear sees things, there are also plenty of good guys out there in the cosmos, but unfortunately they are not permitted to help us, because to do so would break the universal law of noninterference. "They could," believes Lear, "only intervene if any Gray activity would have adverse effect in another part of the universe." These "good guys" are the "Blondes, Swedes or Nordic" types who have often been reported in contact cases as looking very similar to humans. There is also another "very tall race that look like humans, but are seven or eight feet in height. They are united with the Blondes," concludes the Las Vegas resident.

THE BIZARRE CASE OF ROBERT SUFFERN

What kind of "supporting evidence" should we be on the lookout for to verify that any of this is true? In my own files, I find one particular case that is very intriguing, and supporting the notion that the government has made some type of agreement with aliens and that a government/alien liaison may have been established years ago.

One of the most fascinating close encounters of modern times took place on October 7, 1975, when a Canadian citizen got the fright of his life on coming face-to-face with an unearthly being. The following summary of this case is based on a somewhat edited version of an in-field investigation carried out by Harry Tokarz, co-director of the Canadian UFO Research Network. Originally submitted by Pat De La Franier of the Stratford UFO Research Team, for the longest time I hesitated to publish this report in my UFO REVIEW publication and circulated this material only via special bulletin to a select few whom I thought might be able to add something to Mr. Suffern's unique testimony.

Here, then, is Mr. Suffern's story as derived from Harry Tokarz's intriguing first hand report:

Robert Suffern knows he saw a being from outer space near his Bracebridge, Ontario, farmhouse and skeptics be damned!

On October 7, 1975, the 27-year-old carpenter encountered a darkened circular craft sitting in the middle of a gravel road and observed a figure several yards away, while investigating his sister's report that his barn was on fire. As if this situation was not unnerving enough, the "entity," which he at first observed from a distance, would later enter into a near-miss auto accident with Suffern, and would remain etched in his mind for months to come. The being he saw and almost hit with his car was of small stature, wearing a globe-type helmet and a silvery-gray suit, a description commonly reported in the past. The series of bizarre events all started when Suffern's sister, who lives down the road, called to advise him of a "fiery glow" which she spotted near his barn.

Suffern got into his car and checked out the barn where the light had been seen, and was back on the road when he was startled by the sight of a large disc-like object resting right in his path.

He later related, "I was scared. It was right there in front of me with no lights and no sign of life. I really hadn't come to a full stop when it went straight up in the air and out of my sight." At this point he quickly turned his car around and was heading home in a panic when the "it" walked out on the road in front of his car. He braked and skidded, and the being retreated over a fence, into a field.

According to the witness, "When he got to the fence, he put his hands on a post and went over it with no effort at all. It was like he was weightless." It was the third sighting for Suffern in the past two years. Two previous UFO sightings were of nocturnal lights only, but his most recent encounter, although not unique among occupant reports, would lead to some rather startling side events which may turn out to actually substantiate an uneasy suspicion shared by UFO researchers around the globe—a suspicion that has constantly been the source of the most sensational speculation on this planet, but one that has never been proven satisfactorily.

By October 9th, two days after Suffern's unusual experience, all the wire services from coast to coast had picked up the story. Along with the media, UFO investigators and hoards of curiosity-seekers from all parts of North America, turned up on his farm to scrutinize and exploit the father of two. Most of the serious researchers came away with the facts they wanted; however, little did they realize that there was a sequel to this case, an important event that took place after the encounter itself, a scenario that may one day prove to be more important to the UFO mystery than the October 7th landing.

On July 15, 1976, freelance cinematographer Wayne Forsyth and myself were tracking down several UFO reports throughout Ontario. Forsyth was looking for material for his documentary film, to be titled *"UFOs-The Canadian Perspective"* and I was trying to nail down some of the more interesting and elusive reports brought to my attention. While in the vicinity of Bracebridge, we decided to pay a visit to Suffern and perhaps get a follow-up on his encounter of the previous year. Having been familiar with the details of this case, I thought perhaps he might, instead of rehashing the incident, consent to be filmed while expressing personal opinions on UFOs he may have formulated during the time that had elapsed. Little did we realize that Suffern was keeping a closely guarded secret all the time—a secret so unnerving in its implications that it may in fact confirm a rumor rampant throughout the 30 years of civilian investigations—THAT GOVERNMENTS HAVE NOT ONLY KNOWN ALL ABOUT UFOs, BUT HAVE ACTUALLY ESTABLISHED SOME ALLIANCE WITH THESE ALIEN INTELLIGENCES AS FAR BACK AS WORLD WAR II.

Suffern and his wife were not anxious to discuss UFOs, and they were in particular not enthralled at seeing the sophisticated camera and recording equipment we brought with us. Having refrained from discussing the events of October, 1976, we apparently put his fears to rest (Suffern has been highly suspicious of the press), and after we agreed to keep the equipment out of the picture, his anxiety abated quickly and he was willing to confer. We made it clear that we were only interested in getting any new details that may not have emerged during the initial harried investigations of the previous year. Once the Sufferns eased into the topic of UFOs, a couple of intriguing facts came to light.

On December 12, 1987, after the Sufferns were beginning to feel some semblance of order again (their farm was literally swamped for weeks by roving bands of curiosity seekers, one of whom even chose their roof as a sky-watching site), three men were delivered to their home in an Ontario Provincial Police Cruiser. The appointment had been prearranged in November. These officials arrived in full uniform bearing impressive credentials, and representing themselves as high ranking personnel of the Canadian Forces, Ottawa, the USA, the Pentagon, and the Office of Naval Intelligence, Washington, D.C., respectively. Suffern, previously perturbed about the nature of his odd experience with the UFO and its occupant, claimed that ALL his questions were answered POINT BLANK and with no hesitation by these helpful gentlemen. They "opened the books" to him and gave him the answers to the WHERE FROM, the WHAT and the WHY! They implied that the U.S. and the Canadian governments have had intimate knowledge about the UFOs for many years and have in fact been cooperating with alien intelligences in some unknown capacity since then!

As if this wasn't enough to swallow in one gulp, these military "know-it-alls" threw yet another curve when they made a formal apology for the unfortunate incident of October 7, 1975. They claimed it was a MISTAKE!! To which Suffern immediately thought out loud that it must have been a supersecret military craft he had seen. No, they claimed. It was a malfunction that brought the saucer down, complete with aliens, on his property. Incredible as this seems, the Sufferns claimed they were shown extremely clear and close-up aerial reconnaissance photographs of UFOs taken during WW II by U.S. pilots. None of the photos in my collection compared, when I showed him some of the most reliable. Mrs. Suffern found all this information impossible to accept at the time, but curiously when she quizzed them, the officers actually came up with the exact time of the landing-the actual minute-a small detail that only the Sufferns knew and had not conveyed to anyone. They have had three different sightings over their property, only the last of which they reported, and again, the exact times and dates were duly related to them by the knowledgeable trio. The enlightened agents, carrying a battery of books and data, again emphasized that the landing was an accident and should not have occurred.

Suffern adamantly insisted that all his questions about the circular craft and its occupant were answered "to his satisfaction," despite the fact that dozens of civilian investigators had visited him and offered theory upon theory in an attempt to clear up part of the mystery for him. Many hypotheses offered were "close," but not one person answered him with the same "degree of accuracy." At this point, our own investigation took a different turn, for we felt we were being "put on" in order to get rid of us-or perhaps to test our naivety. Perhaps Suffern was amusing himself at our expense. Henceforth, we proceeded in a different key, with this idea very much in mind.

Robert Suffern strikes one as an individual who carefully measures his thoughts. His sincerity comes through clearly as he slowly relates his concepts and ideas. His wife, a home-bred country girl, is quick to air her views and state unequivocally what she believes to be fact. This part of her nature was reasonable for the "slip" she made in an obviously well-kept secret. Once we became alerted to this situation, Suffern slowly dropped his guard and decided to confide in us.

All this information just seemed too cut-and-dried to accept as fact, and in view of the fact that many UFO percipients in the past had been duped by smooth-talking bogus officials, we suggested that they had been handed a "cover story." This was their means of placating witnesses. Granted this was definitely a new tactic, opening the books to silence UFO witnesses. Suffern's belief could not be shaken. Furthermore, he expressed pleasure and surprise at the fact that the Canadian office was exceptionally informative on UFOs, having spoken more freely than his American counterparts. The Sufferns deny that they are under the Official Secrets Act-however, they intend to keep all details secret for moral reasons. They simply want to "keep our part of the bargain" by complying with the government's wishes. At this juncture a thought comes to mind—PLANNED LEAKS???

Was I the unwitting victim this time? For the record it should be noted that I paid another visit to Suffern on May 15, 1977, and this time two fellow investigators accompanied me for objectivity and further verification. Larry Fenwick and Joseph Muskat heard an identical story from Suffern, although he appeared more reserved in conversation this time. As I report this information now, I understand from other researchers that Suffern has refused to comment any further on this situation, and has become quite abrupt with callers.

During our conversation on the recent visit, we learned that the military still refer to UFO occupants as "humanoids." Contact was apparently made in 1943, and now our armed forces are aware of the aliens' movements on our planet.

This is interesting food for thought, because all researchers are now fully aware that governments no longer have any interest in investigating sightings or landings. In fact, they do not even go through the motions any more! Could this be relevant? An interesting sidelight to this scenario is that although the Sufferns have been offered a small fortune by various media, the USAF Lieutenant advised them to refuse all contact and financial returns. Of course, this was after they were filled in about the government's knowledge of alien intelligences. In reply to my question about the exact reason for the cover-ups, he replied, "There would be many disappointments on this planet." This statement he followed up with some grumbling about the flood of "religious fan mail" he had recently been receiving.

DECEPTION OR COVER-UP?

After two hundred-odd pages of crashed saucer stories, we are still left with a giant puzzle. It is like we are trapped in the middle of a maze and know nowhere to turn. Which stories are true, and which are fabrications? Undoubtedly, not every case we have presented can be said to be one hundred percent legitimate, though certainly all the witnesses involved are real people—that I know because I've talked to many of them myself. And furthermore, I know the other researchers quoted are not, in themselves, making up these incidents. But, is all what it seems to be? Certainly it would be difficult to believe that dozens of crash landings have taken place. Surely, if this were the case we'd have heard a lot more about them in the media.

Curiously enough, at the same time the government denies they are hiding the truth about UFOs, going as far as to claim there is no cover-up, much of this material we have released has filtered its way down from military sources. We now have several dozen documents pertaining to crashed saucers and alien bodies on CIA, Air Force, FBI and State Department stationary that have come our way via the Freedom of Information Act.

Could it be that someone in the government—some supersecret group—is trying to lead us down the wrong path, away from the actual truth about this matter? Are we, in essence, being fed a "cover story," with falsified documents being used as dangling bait to divert us from the proper track?

Editor Anthony C. Sutton of the Phoenix Letter, a conservative monthly report on economics, sees a possible conspiracy behind the release of MJ-12. Above all, we don't like the timing for the MJ-12 story. Come October, Pepsi plans to promote the ET film in video...the biggest ever Pepsi promotion with 100,000 free videos to whip up the market place. Just at the point when George Bush, the reported chairman of MJ-12, will need some artificial device to save a floundering campaign. And we have repeatedly pointed out, the MJ12 story is what the establishment wants us to know. No hardware is available, nor hard concrete evidence. Just government documents, that may or may not be authentic."

Sutton's hypothesis is that the "U.S. government is quietly developing vehicle technology with revolutionary propulsion mechanisms," and that the "MJ-12 story is a cover to conceal testing of these vehicles." Sutton even pin points New Mexico as the key State in this program of deception. He claims to have uncovered information that shows the existence of a mysterious computer net in the exact area where UFOs have been reported most frequently. "Is there," asks sutton, "a long-range U.S. government flying disc test and evaluation program in New Mexico?" He answers in the affirmative, pointing out that, "If there is, it would account for the concentration of reports in New Mexico and the need for a cover story. Flying discs are inherently unstable. They may need decades of testing. Further, if the U.S. is using Schauberger technology (implosion energy-spiral vortex) a disc-shape is essential for the propulsion unit."

Sutton further states that a recent issue of *Aviation Week and Technology* (July 25, 1988) adds supporting circumstantial evidence for his hypothesis. "New Mexico is the location of a high-powered computer net including Cray 2 machines, the very largest and fastest computers. Note the net extends to Socorro (in the midst of arid desert) and includes a branch going nowhere—into 'flying saucer' country. If flying discs are developed and tested in secret in this Socorro (MJ-12) area, this is precisely the computer net we would expect."

AREA 51

In another issue of the Phoenix Letter, editor Sutton reveals the location of an area in the middle of the Nevada desert which is strictly "Off Limits" to everyone, except those with the highest of security clearances. There is, Sutton insists, a "shoot to kill" order covering the perimeter of this top-secret base which has been given the code name of 'Area 51."

According to Sutton, the base is "a 50 x 40 mile rectangle of arid scrub desert east of Tonopah. Satellite photographs show a 12,000 foot runway and hundreds of buildings, water tanks, satellite dishes, paved roads, "making for a virtual secret community in the wilderness."

In fact, the base is technically above Top-secret, supposedly even a high level "Q clearance" won't get you inside. "There is a special permit needed for the area, and inside the area requires still other clearances." From an unnamed source, Sutton said he understood "that for one ultra secret area only 1600 permits have ever been issued over 20 years."

Probably designed to test the Stealth bomber, the base is supposedly headquarters for an even more clandestine operation, if we can believe what was published in the Phoenix Letter, only a few months ago.

To quote one of the newsletter's informants:

"Here, a secret operation was performed under unbelievable security precautions known as 'Project Redlight.' A UFO which had been shipped from Edwards AFB was flown here. It is not conventionally powered, but was silent in operation...Security in Project Redlight was so strict that no one stayed there more than six months." The craft was flown with parts "from a UFO which could not be duplicated successfully by aerospace contractors from the West Coast."

A memorandum in which personal names have been eliminated is apparently on file at the Phoenix Letter's office, and is hereby reproduced for whatever value it may have contents-wise to our own readers:

"I only saw the UFO one time. It was on the ground and partly hidden behind a building and at first I thought it was a small private aircraft until I noticed it had no wings or tail. I was probably a quarter mile or further from it, but I would guess it was twenty to thirty feet in diameter and sort of pewter color rather than a bright polished aluminum.

"The reason I knew it flew silently is I was present on a number of occasions when he was landing and taking off (I was always taken inside and out of view of the runway at these times) and at no time did I hear anything that sounded like conventional or any other kind of engine.

"I was working on their radios several times when they just 'died.' However since I was there to work I really didn't think anything about it. Oh yes, they would start working again just as suddenly. Also, there were a number of times that I was called out to work on a radio and could not find anything wrong with it.

"There was a radar station at the north end of the test site near the town of Tonopah, Nevada. A fellow from my home town was an operator there. We were talking about the test site one day when he mentioned that he was always picking up UFOs over the test site and was told to ignore them..."

One can speculate for hours about what is really gong on inside Area 51, and other similar locales, and chances are no positive conclusions could still be reached. There are those who believe at least some of these military bases have been turned over to the aliens.

According to an individual we know simply as "Falcon," aliens have been coming to Earth for many years with the complete knowledge and encouragement of the government.

His true identity is a closely guarded secret. "Falcon" recently appeared—his face in shadows and his voice disguised—on the syndicated television special *UFOs LIVE—THE COVER UP*. Reputed to be a member of the "intelligence community," "Falcon" along with several others of similar status, believes strongly that the time is right for the public to be told the absolute truth about the existence of these humanoids.

"Falcon" exploded a particularly dramatic bombshell on the nationally televised show upon confessing what has been going on at the highest levels inside the Pentagon, the CIA, and the State Department. After removing the bodies of several Grays from the wreckage of crashed discs in the late 1940s, the U.S. eventually made a deal with this same race of beings which allowed two ETs to "beam in" down here, while a like number of ambassadors from Earth traveled off to the stars on what amounts to a planetary exchange program. Supposedly, these two aliens, who arrived more than a decade ago, have free reign of whatever military base it is they have been assigned to (Area 51)? "Falcon" further states that the beings are able to keep in touch with their home port through a crystal-like device which enables them to view their planet at any time, as well as zero in on historical events from Earth's own past.

"There is in existence," says "Falcon", "a large ledger-like book containing all the knowledge the aliens possess about the universe and technology." "Falcon" is very anxious to expose the government's prolonged involvement in this gigantic deception and suggests that he personally is responsible for leaking the MJ-12 papers to Moore and his associates.

Though he plans to remain "undercover" for now, "Falcon" told the producers of UFOs LIVE that he and other members of the intelligence community "in" on the "Big Secret" are willing to meet privately with members of Congress so that this "Cosmic Watergate" can once and for all be broken wide open and the truth finally released to the public.

Naturally, the reader, in the end, will have to decide which part of this scenario is true and which part may simply be fanciful thinking. Are we, in fact, being let in on something of great importance to humankind, or are we simply hearing the ranting and raving of a few crazed individuals?

All I know is that the government has always considered UFOs to be serious business. Back in the early 1950s a top-flight Canadian engineer by the name of Wilbur Smith headed up Project Magnet, a project financed by his government which successfully attempted to track UFOs coming in over Canadian air space. In a TOP SECRET memo dated November 21, 1950 and addressed to his superiors at the Department of Transport (by whom he was employed), Smith made this startling disclosure: "I made discreet enquiries through the Canadian Embassy staff in Washington, who were able to obtain for me the following information:

A. The matter (of flying saucers) is the most highly classified subject in the United States Government, rating higher than the H-bomb.

B. Flying Saucers exist.

C. Their modus operandi is unknown, but concentrated effort is being made by a small group headed by Doctor VannevarBush.

D. The entire matter is considered by the United States authorities to be of tremendous significance.

In the nearly forty years that have passed since Smith penned this important memo, there has seemingly been no change of policy in regard to this matter. Indeed, UFOs are just as important today as we head into the 1990s.

The release of the MJ-12 documents, along with all the other obtainable evidence, testifies to the fact that our government possesses the remains of crashed spaceships and their extraterrestrial crew members, adding weight to the fact that someone out there is watching us.

We owe it to ourselves to get to the bottom of this mystery as what we uncover is going to affect the lives of everyone on this planet for centuries to come.

AN INTERVIEW WITH RYAN WOOD, UFO DOCUMENT HUNTER

By Sean Casteel

NEW MJ-12 DOCUMENTS SURFACE

So what have the entity or entities that originally leaked the highly classified MJ-12 documents done to whet our appetite lately? For one thing, they seem to have found new ways to get documents into the hands of interested UFO researchers. In 1992, new MJ-12 documents started to surface. In an exclusive interview, researcher, investigator and author Ryan Wood brings us full circle on the most recent information leaks and what they may tell us about the government's secret programs to deal with the alien presence.

RYAN WOOD'S BACKGROUND

Ryan Wood has a degree in mathematics and computer science from Cal Poly, in San Luis Obispo in Southern California. He has since been employed in what he calls "straight corporate high-tech" positions, including working at a company called Intel in product marketing and product engineering. He then went to work for Digital Equipment Corporation in product management, competitive analysis and sales management. That was followed by a stint with a company called Toshiba, working in their magnetic resonance imaging division as an engineering manager. Wood also had a few consulting jobs and assisted with some high-tech startups on his way to his current position as director of marketing and sales for an energy conservation company in Denver, Colorado. The fact that Wood is well educated and highly skilled in computer science and other forms of technology adds all the more credibility to the claims that he and his fellow investigators make regarding a subject as "out there" as UFOs. Wood seems to navigate between both the world of mainstream science and the nether world of UFO research with commanding ease.

WOOD'S INTEREST IN UFOs BEGINS

So when did Wood first become interested in the subject of UFOs?

"I was first exposed when I was fifteen-years-old," Wood said. "My father brought Stanton Friedman [a nuclear physicist, author and researcher very well known in the UFO community] over for dinner. Stanton Friedman actually worked for my father for about six months. He was with the McDonnell Douglas aeronautics company, and they were working on antigravity research. And Stan was doing all sorts of work on how flying saucers might work and what their physics are and so forth.

"So I got exposed to UFOs at an early age," he continued. "And then on and off, was interested, not interested, until maybe the early 90s when I became more seriously interested. I started working with my father [Robert Wood] on the Special Operations Manual, which was leaked to Don Berliner [another well known UFO researcher and author].

"I do this as a hobby," Wood said, "although I do have a team of people that work as a documents staff. Several part-time people work on our investigations. This is our specialty. We don't do abductions. We don't do lights in the sky. We don't do anything other than military and intelligence history as it relates to the Majestic documents. That's our focus. The field of Ufology is so big that you have to specialize, and that's our specialty."

THE SPECIAL OPERATIONS MANUAL

Wood elaborated further on his organization's mission.

"The Majestic documents," he explained, "which is what our web site is all about, focuses on any documents that have the word 'Majic' or 'MJ-12' or 'Majestic,' or are related to, either directly or indirectly, that Top Secret classified program.

"And the Special Operations Manual is one of seven or eight different sourced groups of Majestic-12 or Top Secret Majic documents. The Special Operations Manual arrived in Don Berliner's mailbox in 1994 as a roll of Tri-X film. Upon development, it was a fantastic, detailed story of crash retrievals and how to pick up and manage the complete process of the crash. The title was 'Extraterrestrial Entities Technology Recovery and Disposal.' So that document, in and of itself, is one of our most compelling documents as far as authenticity goes. It's been checked for a very, very long time and vetted in many different ways. And I would say it's 99 percent true."

A BRIEF HISTORY OF OTHER LEAKS

Wood also talked about some of the other previously leaked documents.

"There have been, I think, nine different sources or entities that have offered up Majestic documents over the past 20 years or so. The first document came up through Bill Moore in March of 1981 .The Aquarius Documents, which we really haven't specialized in studying. But there's some mention of Majestic there. And then Jamie Shandera got the Eisenhower Briefing document in December of 1984, and that really was the first tangible, solid, checkable Majestic document. And Stan Friedman did a yeoman's effort on getting that and discovering different aspects of it and nuances that support its authenticity. Then at College Park in Maryland, there was the Cutler-Twining Memo that was found in Don Berliner's mailbox in March of 1994."

ENTER TIMOTHY COOPER

Timothy Cooper, a Vietnam veteran with both the Navy and the Marines, is currently employed as a security officer in Big Bear Lake, California. He has also been used as a funnel for newly leaked classified documents for several years'

According to the capsule biography posted on the Majestic Documents website, "Cooper began investigating and researching military UFO intelligence operations in 1988 and has extensive CIA and NSA files. As part of his efforts to acquire documentation on secret military and government UFO data, he has acquired the largest collection of MJ-12 documents and privately owned original Project Blue Book files in the United States."

Wood next takes up the story.

"Timothy Cooper," Wood began, "first started getting some of his documents in his mailbox in Big Bear Lake in 1992, which has continued all the way up to the present. There have been quite a number of documents that have come to him. They've come in the form of things anonymously slipped into the mailbox, to things mailed to him with CIA postmarks, to Fort Meade Freedom Of Information Act return addresses, to personal chats with his 'Deep Throats.'"

Wood's relationship with Cooper began after Cooper sent a letter to UFO researcher Stanton Friedman saying that he had amassed several documents and requesting Friedman's help in understanding them. Friedman replied by saying that he lived in Canada and that it would be more convenient for Robert Wood, Ryan's father, to look at them.

"So my father went up there," Wood said," and spent some time talking to him and looking at these documents and building a relationship. I visited him several times, too, to coax him to give them up and let us try to authenticate them and study them.

"If it wasn't for Stan's efforts, and my father Bob's and mine, they would still be sitting in Tim Cooper's attic, because he was not all that interested in it. He was far more interested in the JFK assassination. He didn't want fame. He didn't want to sell them. He was an interested person in this field primarily because his father, Harry D. Cooper, had told him that UFOs were very real, saying, 'I worked in the Air Force, and I know about these things.' That's what caught his attention."

A CRUCIAL DOCUMENT FROM COOPER

Wood gave some more background on the kind of thing Cooper and the others run across.

"It's extremely complex," Wood said. "'We're talking five hundred, six hundred pages of classified documents. Some of it stamped Top Secret-Eyes Only, some of it stamped Top Secret-Ultra, some of it just Secret, some of it Confidential, some of it Unclassified. To summarize, it is impossible."

As an example of what he meant, Wood began to give a detailed overview of a document Cooper had received in the mid-1990s.

"I'll give you a flavor of the types of things that are discussed," he said. "Just sort of an introductory teaser to it. One document that is very interesting is called The Interplanetary Phenomenon Unit Document, and it's a summary intelligence. It's a draft, and assessment. It has fourteen points. It was written on 22 July 1947, after the team went to the Roswell area to deal with some of the crashes."

Wood quoted from the document directly: "The extraordinary recovery of the fallen airborne objects in the State of New Mexico between July 4 and July 6, 1947"—that's sort of the title —. This summary was prepared by the headquarters of the Interplanetary Phenomenon Unit, Scientific and Technical Branch, Counter-Intelligence Directorate, as requested by the Assistant Chief of Staff G-2, at the express order of the Chief of Staff."

In defense of the authenticity of the document, Wood argued, "Now some people have said, 'Well, I've never heard of the Interplanetary Phenomenon Unit,' but it's been admitted to by the Air Force that there was such a unit, and that it was part of the technical and scientific branch. This was long before this particular document came out. It first surfaced in a FOIA response and came out in the mid-80s. So it's one of those little checks here that demonstrates that they're using the right thing and that it is in fact part of the technical and scientific branch."

The document proceeds to get very specific.

"It says that at 23:22 Mountain Standard Time," Wood read aloud, "on 3 July

1947, radar stations in Texas and at the White Sands Proving Ground, New Mexico, tracked two unidentified craft until both dropped off radar. The crash sites have been located close to the White Sands Proving Ground. Site LZ-I was located on a ranch near Corona, approximately 75 miles northwest of the town of Roswell. That's sort of the Brazel ranch area as it's popularly known. And Site LZ-2 was located approximately 20 miles southeast of the town of Socorro, New Mexico, at latitude 33:40:31 and longitude 106:28:29, the Socorro Peak being a geographic reference point. That's sort of point number two.

"When you look at the latitude and longitude," Wood went on, "you discover that it's about 800 meters south-southeast of the Trinity burst, the first atomic blast on the planet. If you were an alien, and you saw an atomic blast go off on some planet, or sensed it somehow, perceived it, you might want to visit. 'These people are about ready to come out of the kindergarten stage and may be a threat to us in our neighborhood as they go to the stars.'"

Wood said the aliens have long been known to be scrutinizing our nukes.

"Not only do the leaked documents support an intense interest in anything nuclear," he said, "the unclassified FOIA-released National Archive UFO reporting, Project Blue Book, Project Sign, Project Grudge, all the early projects of '47 through the 60s also show intense interest by UFOs over plutonium production sites and atomic sites and nuclear missile silos. Anything where there are warheads, there's an interest. All reported through the normal Air Force intelligence process.

"So that's an agenda," he said, "or was an agenda, by the quote 'aliens' with the multiple races, depending on how sophisticated you want to get, to look at our nuclear capabilities. What that might mean-maybe they're concerned that we're destroying ourselves. Or maybe they don't care."

EVEN MORE SENSATIONAL THINGS

"And then there are more sensational things besides objects dropping out of the sky," Wood said.

He continued to quote from the Interplanetary Phenomenon Unit assessment document.

"As to the bodies recovered at LZ-2," Wood read aloud, "it appears that some of the five crew members survived entry into our atmosphere due to unknown causes. Dr. Detlev Bronk has been asked to assist in the autopsy of one well-preserved cadaver, to be done by Major Charles E. Ray. The occupants appear in most respects human, with some anatomical differences in the head, eyes, hands and feet. They have a slight build, about five feet tall with grayish-pink skin color. They have no hair on their bodies and are clothed in tight fitting flight suits that appear to be fireproof. Some of the bodies look as if they've been burned on the head and hands. Their overall stature remains one of young children. It is believed that there were male and female genders present, but it was hard to distinguish."

FOLLOWING UP WITH FORENSICS

"So there's a paragraph," Wood said, "that's very factual and unemotional about such an emotional thing. And then our forensic approach is to study this and say, "The thing that stuck out is Major Charles E. Ray. I'd never heard of him before, and neither had anybody else. So we began a process of finding him in the military registers and getting his personnel file, getting his Ph.D. thesis from the University of Minnesota, finding out who he worked with and how he was recruited into the military.

"It turns out he's a very well-respected surgeon and pathologist. He knew Leslie Groves, who was the head of the Manhattan Project, personally. He was recruited to be the head of the hospital in Oak Ridge, Tennessee, in the late 1940s. And he was the right guy to have the credentials to do an autopsy on an alien.

"All that is very powerful research in support of the authenticity of the document. What faker in their right mind would have done all that research? Or known those subtleties? In general, everywhere we keep digging and probing, looking for anachronisms and anomalies and falsehoods, we don't find any. We find puzzling things that are still unresolved in a few cases, but they're just unresolved because they haven't been fully vetted and researched. Nowhere have I come to the bottom of my research effort and said, 'Well, this is absolutely wrong, or this is false, or this is screwed up here. This is a fake.'"

THE WHITE HOT REPORT

Wood moved on to another document in the collection, one called The White Hot Report, dated 19 September, 1947. "So after a whole summer's worth of quote 'analysis and understanding' and research on the crashes in New Mexico in July of 1947, of recovered lenticular aerodyne objects, they wrote this mission assessment. It's more like a 23-page report that is more detailed about what they did, what they saw, what were the novel aspects inside, what are the political considerations, what are the scientific probabilities, what's the National Security structure, what's the recommendation for the president?

"It's a much higher-level thing that the generals would talk about," Wood continued. "But it's very interesting. We have a complete list of the members of the mission that are involved. There are many new names. And in general, the personnel list of Majestic, MJ-12, is vastly expanded now, after these documents. We know far more people were involved in it, and we can begin to research their lives, their history, their children, and validate their participation, or their likely participation, in a program like this. In many cases, that's been successful."

IS DISINFORMATION PART OF THE PICTURE?

Admittedly, Wood and his associates have done an excellent job of discovering real-world links to the documents they have assembled. It's hard not to be impressed with their research into Major Charles Ray, for instance, and the appropriate role he is said to have played in the alien autopsies conducted on bodies recovered from crashed UFOs. But is it possible that the leaked documents are part of a larger game of government and military disinformation?

"Well, that's a very normal question," Wood replied. "They say, 'Is this disinformation? Is it some sort of psychological warfare?' I've written a whole paper dealing with the concept of psychological warfare, and posted it on the website under Document Authentication.

"In the process, I interviewed three or four experts in military disinformation. I met one of them at an association of former intelligence officers in San Francisco, and I spent quite a bit of time talking to him about the nature of a psychological warfare operation. What its goals are, what its objectives are, how you go about doing it, who are you trying to deceive, why are you trying to deceive them? I read several historical manuals on psychological warfare. I tried to fully understand the nature of why and how you use psychological warfare."

Wood is confident, however, that such is not the case with the Majestic documents.

"These documents," he said, "are a complete misfit to psychological warfare. They provide so much information, so much detail, that the Russians or the Chinese, or anybody else at the time that we were really trying to deceive, would have assigned loads of assets, spies, to penetrate these organizations and try to understand the truth about this alien technology. This was all classified Top Secret, which means grave harm to the National Security of the United States if they were exposed at the time.

"The concept of psychological warfare and psychological operations just doesn't hold any water when you look at it. 'Don't mess with us. We've got alien technology.' Do you think that's going to stop the Russians from doing something? Or the Chinese? It is just naive to think that these documents are some sort of psychological warfare"

"Because psychological warfare is pretty straightforward," he continued. "It's, well, what are you trying to communicate, how do you want to get to somebody, how are you going to reinforce it, and how are they going to believe it? It's really just marketing. If I keep telling you the truth for years and years, and we develop a relationship, and you trust everything I say, and in the seventh or eighth year I decide to lie to you, that first lie is effective. But then the next lie and the next lie become less and less effective. And there's really no point."

IN FURTHER DEFENSE OF THE DOCUMENTS

Wood continued to passionately defend the truth of the Majestic documents.

"The documents have all sorts of holes in them," he admitted. "People attack them. 'Oh, this word is misspelled.' 'They couldn't have done this at that time.' There are things on the surface that people point to and say, 'This is not very credible' or 'How do I know this really came from the government?' All in all, what spies would end up doing is to contact their 'Deep Throats,' and try to either validate the concepts and principles or go to the vaults and try to get copies of the documents.

"It just seems that there's no plausible scenario in which psychological warfare is an effective strategy with these documents. It's a very reasonable question, though. Could it be psychological warfare? And so far, I don't see it."

Meanwhile, has Majestic itself been infiltrated by foreign governments like the Russians and the Chinese?

"That's another great question," Wood answered, "and I don't have any knowledge about that per se, directly. I only have speculation, and my speculation would be this: I would think it would be a top intelligence priority for every one of those organizations to not only collect and manage their own crashes and crash retrievals, as in the case of the Russians—lots of research has been done and there are several Russian Roswell cases and other crashes. They're there." So whether or not Majestic has been infiltrated by moles from hostile countries, those foreign governments have no shortage of crashes on their own home turf to deal with. "There are crashes all over the place," Wood said. "UFOs are clearly a global phenomenon."

MORE FROM RYAN WOOD ON NEW DEVELOPMENTS WITH MJ-12

Our fascinating interview with Ryan Wood continued, touching on such mind-bending subjects as why UFO crashes happen so frequently and the probable involvement of MJ-12 members in the assassination of JFK.

INEPT PILOTS?

Given that UFO crashes happen on a worldwide basis, resulting in many headaches for governments both allied and "hostile" to the United States, the question that must be asked is, are the aliens simply inept pilots of their own spacecraft?

"That's another good question," Wood said. "Why do they crash? And I'm speculating. The data shows that there are crashes. I think it has to do with the human anthropomorphic view of the alien agenda. We think they don't want to crash. We value human life. We rescue our pilots from the ocean or from behind enemy lines. These [alien bodies] are disposable, biological robots that are like toilet paper to us. Their mission in the universe is to hop from galaxy to galaxy, star system to star system, gather information, and move on.

"And they may be less well equipped than with a mothership for interstellar space. They may be using something more like a scout ship, and when they encounter radar or some freak lighting bolt, they malfunction and have a problem. "Then of course there's the deliberate thought, that they're crashing on purpose, because it helps man develop new technologies and advance our civilization without shocking us. What would happen to Benjamin Franklin if you gave him a laptop computer? He would go like, 'Wow, I don't know how to do this!' But he could take it apart and see where to go and start researching. It may take decades or centuries to understand and catch up, but it's like you're shown the future. Then you begin to do the reverse science thing, or the reverse engineering. So that's my take on why they crash."

JUST WHO IS LEAKING THE DOCUMENTS?

From theorizing about the frequency of UFO crashes, the conversation next turned to just who is leaking all these classified documents.

"I'll answer that," he began, "but in essence it doesn't matter. What matters is, is it true? Is it authentic? How do we prove that it's authentic? And providence, or where they come from, is one aspect of the equation of *is it authentic*.

"Now they seem to be coming directly from people that want it out. Some of it seems to be coming through alleged Freedom of Information Act offices. Some are postmarked that way. In essence, my opinion is that many of the declassifiers that are going through these reams and reams of paper think this material is important and they let it out, even though they have express orders not to do it. Or it slips through the cracks as errors. People make errors all the time. 'Oh, they forgot to declassify this page or that page.'"

Wood gave some details about a document called the Bowen Manuscript to illustrate his point.

"The Bowen Manuscript," he said, "is stamped Confidential. But in Chapter 22, it's stamped Top Secret-Majic-MJ-12. It happens to be about the Air Force's involvement with UFOs and so forth. A casual declassifier would look at this and look at the first few pages and thumb through it. 'Oh, this is okay.' And off it goes.

"Little does he know that there's this classified chapter in there. They're supposed to look at every single page and read every single word. But do they? Faced with quotas and deadlines, mistakes happen. So I think that's one of the ways it's coming out, through this declassification process.

"And then I think some people have squirreled this stuff away," Wood continued. "People that were directly involved. They wanted it for their kids. They had security oaths that were written in the 30s or the 40s, their ten, twenty, thirty-year security oaths, rather than the current lifetime security oaths for some of the most sensitive government information, which you can never divulge, ever."

IT'S AUTHENTICITY THAT MATTERS

Still, in spite of the frequent inability to know just who leaked a given document or why, Wood says the focus of his team and himself is more directed at authenticating the material they acquire.

"Authenticity in terms of where the document came from, certainly," he explained, "but also the content of the documents. What do they say? Is it right for the time and place? Context? We're focused on the forensics of the ink and the paper, and there's been quite a bit of original paper and original ink that we've done forensic work on. Also watermark work and mass spectroscopy and liquid chromatography work on the ink, to prove that they're in fact old inks and that the handwriting is old. We look at the paper forensics, as well as the content and the style. Does it follow the government printing and style manual?

"And are the people in the right time and the right place? As I mentioned with Major Charles Ray earlier, for example. So we're being as level-headed as we can, and we're going to be posting what I'm calling authenticity meters to every document on our website and allow the viewers to get a sense of where we're at. Are we pegged at over 99 percent authentic, or are we only at 20 percent authentic?"

So some of the documents are more authenticated than others?

"Yes, that's absolutely true," Wood replied. "Some of them are very well vetted and researched and we've nearly reached the end of our process. And we can say, 'Oh, this is 99 percent authentic.' And others are sort of in the neutral bucket of 50-50, where we really don't know whether they're authentic or fake. We've looked at one or two things and we have one or two anachronisms, and so we're going to have to do more research to conclude one way or the other. Some of the early Aquarius Documents we would put more in the 20 percent chance of being

THE CASE FOR UFO CRASH SECRETS — From Urban Legend To Reality

true, given their checkered history and the lack of checkable details and the hearsay involved. So those are 'weakly authentic.'"

The process used by Wood and his team certainly leaves no stone unturned.

"The weaker documents are interesting and suggestive at times," he said, "but the goal is to vet sentence by sentence, phrase by phrase, context by context, every single document in this entire collection. It's a fairly bounded collection, but it's a long and complicated task. We're probably up to on the order of close to three thousand pages. That's not a hundred thousand pages, but three thousand pages is a lot of pages. You have to look at each document and ask why it's authentic or why it's not, or what its problems are. Some of them are very ho-hum. Others are more publicly exhilarating. Talk of alien bodies and crashed saucers is always far more exciting than details about, say, how Project Twinkle was done and who was involved in it."

WHY ARE THE DOCUMENTS BEING LEAKED AT ALL?

What motivates the aggressive leaking of classified documents to begin with? Is their some overriding purpose behind it? Has it all been led by some unseen guiding hand?

"I don't think so," Wood said. "I think this is sort of the normal, low-level leakiness of the National Security establishment on this particular topic. People feel that it's wrong for the government to hide the fact that we're not alone, to have hidden the greatest technological advances from the masses, and in essence slow the advance of global humanity by scores of years.

"If, in 1960, they had trotted out an alien cadaver and put it on the table and said, 'This is from Roswell,' or 'This is from a crashed UFO' or 'We found this in the desert.' Whatever. That would have required the services of hundreds or thousands of Ph.D.s in biology and exobiology. We would have mapped the genome earlier. We would have better medicines and better understanding. There would have just been more manpower working on the problem on a global basis."

IS THE COVER-UP DOWNRIGHT CRIMINAL?

Meanwhile, the government's decision to maintain secrecy is a kind of crime, according to Wood.

"What they did," he said, "which is hide it all, forced a few cloistered scientists working in secret to push the ball down the field with a paperclip instead of hitting it with a baseball bat. That's really the great crime, that they've hidden the technology and the evidence and thwarted the standards of civilization.

'Now, granted, they were scared to death in 1947 and it probably would have

168

been irresponsible to bring it forward and so forth. But when Kennedy was president, he was aware of this stuff. And one of the many competing theories for his assassination, which has some merit, is the fact that he knew and wanted to tell the truth about our alien understanding and involvement.

"If he had done that," Wood continued, "the world would be much better off, I think. But that's all speculation. There's also the fact that revealing the truth would be very frightening and destabilizing to religion, to governments, to weapons and energy systems, to the politics of it all. And that is what held them back."

WHO DOES KNOW WHAT'S GOING ON?

In light of how deeply buried all the secrecy is, does our current president, George Walker Bush, or even his father, have complete knowledge of the alien presence?

"Oh, absolutely," Wood affirmed, "Bush's father would know. He was the Director of Central Intelligence. He would have to know, I think Cheney knows. The question is, how much do they know? You need to remember that Majestic-12 was formed by President Truman and it was a Top Secret Research and Development organization comprised of 12 members that reported directly to the president-on a need to know basis. And what that need to know means is what MJ-12 decides the president needs to know. So the president doesn't get to know everything.

"But this committee gets to decide what he needs to know to make effective decisions, and so virtually the whole truth is hidden from the president.

"We see that in some of the documents," Wood went on, "like the Interplanetary documents that I mentioned earlier. Under the classification page at the top, it says, 'The document has been reclassified as an Intelligence Material affecting the National Security and has been upgraded as Above Top Secret with a need to know basis. Only those authorized persons with Majic access may have access." This is the important part.

"Downgrading schedule to commence only with an approved presidential executive order and the approval of the U.S. Majestic Intelligence and Security Command.' "So you would think the president could just sign an executive order saying, 'Give me the truth about extraterrestrials and what we know and what we've been doing with these people.' And they would show up with a briefing for him the next day. But it doesn't work that way. The law doesn't allow that. The law says that you have to have the approval of the controlling committee.

"And what I think people don't understand is that there are real laws in place that govern the disclosure of this information in the secure world. That legal process is very enforceable and very real. But I think it's immoral at times. It's as if you're asked to shoot a civilian in the Vietnam War or something. But it's still an order, and most people shoot."

So, technically, it would be illegal to tell the president certain facts about the aliens and the workings of MJ-12?

"That's right," Wood said. "Even if the president asked for it, the controlling committee over the information would have to agree that it is wise or relevant or whether he has a need to know. And he may not have a need to know what's going. I'm reminded a little bit of Independence Day, and the chagrin or the surprise that the president has in the movie when he's shown Area 51. 'Oh, wow, there really is one! You guys didn't tell me about this.' So I think it's a little bit like that."

PHIL CORSO AND ALIEN INTEGRATED CIRCUITS

In his book *The Day After Roswell*, the late Colonel Phil Corso claimed that the reverse engineering of alien technology discovered at the crash site of a UFO helped speed up the development of a great many new and innovative human technological advances. The question was asked, "Has anything confirming Corso's claims turned up in the Majestic-12 documents?"

Perhaps not surprisingly, something has.

"Phil did talk about the integrated circuit," Wood said, "as one of the items that was quote 'reverse engineered.' And there is some evidence in the documents-not about reverse engineering-but descriptions from 1947 of what appears to be an integrated circuit."

Wood read aloud from The White Hot Report, Point Number Twenty:

"The only evidence of circuitry found on the motor was a thin, plastic-like sheet fashioned like platters embossed on the exterior of the spherically-shaped casing coated with a thin film of pure silver. Under high-power magnification, it was observed that a series of fine grid-like lines intersected with groups of dots arranged in circular patterns. "That sounds like a description of an integrated circuit," Wood said, "if you were looking at it through a microscope in 1947."

DID MAJESTIC-12 KILL KENNEDY?

Somehow the conversation worked its way back around to the Kennedy assassination.

"When you look at the people involved in the Kennedy assassination," Wood said," you see that they're also very much involved in UFO materials and that the organization MJ-12 may have been involved, or likely was involved, in the Kennedy assassination as well. But it's all circumstantial. Roswell is sort of a very ultimate secret and then who killed Kennedy, or not so much by whom, but why he was killed, seems to be mixed up in all this. It's going to be very difficult to know the truth in the end, but you could make a case, and it would be credible and convincing, that the people surrounding the assassination were linked to the UFO field.

"Now was that why he was killed? Because he was going to tell the truth about UFOs? It's a credible scenario in my mind."

In fact, Wood is currently writing a book on the subject, called Murder and MJ-12

"The focus of the book is to talk about the various murders related to MJ-12," he said. "Why people were murdered, how they were murdered, what secrets they held. The more common ones are Secretary of State Forrestal, Marilyn Monroe, Dorothy Kilgallen, and Kennedy. Those are the ones people would commonly think of. Then there's much more obscure ones that people haven't heard of, which are even more intriguing in many ways."

A DOCUMENTARY FILM IN THE CAN

Woods and his team have also completed a one-hour television documentary on the Majestic-12 documents entitled ***The Secret Evidence: We Are Not Alone.*** The film was shown at the Mipcon Film Festival in Cannes, France, home of the annual International Cannes Film Festival of worldwide renown.

"We were the executive producers," he said. "We basically crafted the script, the reenactments, the content. We did have professional help. IO Productions in Los Angeles did the editing for us. I think the film is a significant step forward. We look forward to putting it on the air. It's all about the Majestic Documents. All about why they're authentic, why they're real, what they say, why this is important."

Meanwhile, the mission of Wood and his team remains the same.

"The focus of our team effort right now is to deconstruct the cover-up. And our strategy for that, which is no secret, is to concentrate on getting the documents, finding the witnesses, correlating known authentic documents, building a case and publicizing it."

And finally, a comment on the team's website.

"The website is a very powerful resource," Wood said, "because you can see not only the original document as released from the entity, but in some cases you can also see a replica or a retyped document. You're looking at the original source material, which you can download as pdf files and study. I'm not trying to put any insulation or commentary between the raw data and what people can look at, so that everybody can look at it and understand what's going on to their own satisfaction."

The website address is: http:/iwww.majesticdocuments.com

THE MJ-12 STORY CONTINUES

As is true of all aspects of the UFO phenomenon, the only constant is constant change, constant updating, and constant reassessment of what the truth actually consists of. From abductions to cattle mutilations to lights in the sky, every piece of the UFO puzzle contains within it thousands and thousands of mysteries and unanswered questions.

Such is the case with the Majestic-12 documents and the government cover-up of the UFO phenomenon in general. If there is one advantage to the seeker after truth in this area, however, it is that it involves the human element more directly and dramatically than other aspects of the problem. The response of a select-but also an all-too-human-group of men to a problem so beyond normal mortal comprehension that it boggles the mind even from a great distance, is told to us in the documents they left behind, most likely thinking that the secrets they contained would be hidden forever.

If withholding the crucial evidence that we are not alone can be called a crime, as Ryan Wood does in this chapter, it is also at least something human, something we as human beings can think of seeing or touching in our own very human terms.

After things like Nixon's Watergate Scandal and the many revelations since that time of government deception and misconduct, we all trust our leaders on a more limited basis than we were taught to in elementary school. It therefore becomes easier to conceptualize secret government drones working behind the scenes to keep concealed from us what could possibly be the greatest boon to mankind ever known.

If we allow ourselves to be cheated in this way, is it necessarily true that we have only ourselves to blame? Is the conspiracy in the end more powerful than any attempt we can make to resist it and ferret out the truth that is our birthright as creatures of the Earth?

There may reside, in the efforts of Wood and his team of investigators and document authenticators, at least the faint hope that the truth of the UFO phenomenon will one day be known to everyone, for perhaps as simple a reason as a leaked document that forces the powers that be to put all their cards on the table at last. For now, one can only encourage them in their earnest efforts to deliver the truth on their website, in the form of documents that no longer serve the Big Lie, but all of us instead.

MARILYN MONROE'S MJ-12 DOCUMENT

It has long been rumored that actress Marilyn Monroe was murdered because she had threatened her lover, President John Of. Kennedy, with going public about their torrid affair. However, newly released MJ-12 documents show that Monroe may have been killed because of her knowledge of the secret of UFOs and the fear by the CIA and MJ-12 that she was intending to go public with her knowledge.

CIA's Counterintelligence Chief, James Jesus Angleton had learned that Monroe had had a phone conversation with a New York art dealer in which she discussed Kennedy's secret visit to an undisclosed military base to see alien artifacts, and her disdain over her soured relationships with President Kennedy and his brother, United States Attorney General Robert Kennedy. This conversation had been recorded by CIA domestic electronic surveillance experts.

Marilyn Monroe had been under surveillance by the CIA since 1955, and the FBI had maintained a security dossier on her because of her marriage to a well-known American writer suspected of having communist affiliations, and her trip to Russia and the press coverage she received while she was there.

The wiretap report also mentions nationally recognized New York syndicated reporter Dorothy Kilgallen as having conversations with Monroe regarding the Roswell UFO crash of 1947 and President Kennedy's politically motivated NASA Apollo Moon program. Dorothy Kilgallen made headlines in 1955 when she disclosed a private conversation with a British Cabinet official who told her that UFOs are real and that the U.S. and British authorities consider the matter as of the highest importance.

The significance of the wiretap has to do with the fact that Monroe was murdered the following day in her Brentwood condominium. According to private investigator Milo Speriglio, Monroe was the victim of a national security management hit by the CIA and the Mob.

The suggestion that somehow the CIA was involved in a domestic murder of an American citizen is not too farfetched when considering the past abuses coming from Angleton's Counter Intelligence program with its "absolute security at any cost" philosophy. Whether Angleton authorized the hit is not known, but the modus operandi of the way her body was found and moved around, the fashion in which the autopsy records were changed to reflect suicide, and the theft of her secret red diary, all have similarities to the methods used by Angleton's covert CIA Counterintelligence operators.

Allegedly, what prompted Angleton into action was when President Kennedy fired off a Top Secret memorandum outlining a previous discussion concerning a classification review of all CIA UFO files that could affect national security. It was dated November 12, 1963, just 10 days before he would be assassinated in the streets of Dallas, Texas.

Edward Teller's Pitch to President Reagan for SDI

I wish to bring to your attention of a very real and dangerous situation that threatens not only us, the world, but our very existence as a race. For over forty years I have been involved in developing advanced technologies in the defense of this country which would insure our security, freedom, and our form of government from surprise attack. As you must be aware, the Defense Department has initiated several space defense programs of vast proportions and at great expense. But there is a new and alarming development of which I am compelled to inform you of. A menace greater that the nuclear arms race exists. It does not originate here on earth but comes from space itself. The agent of mass destruction has no reasoning psychology other than the ultimate destruction of our civilization and our way of life as we know it.

Obtaining critical information of this menace has been hard and time consuming and the facts seem to be tangled among dark threats of ultimate destruction; our innate fear of the unknown has interfered with our ability to comprehend it. A space attack could be real in the near future bringing with it the truth that our inaction global war could be immensely accelerated. No longer can the United States be in the position which it found itself in 1947. This was realized and in January 1950 President Truman made the decision to go ahead with a defense program exceeding in scope and cost of the Manhattan Project. Late in President Eisenhower's office, several attempts were made to limit further development by prohibiting the testing of space defense weapons. A moratorium was entered into, a "gentlemen's agreement, whereby Russia and the United States concurred that testing be halted until further notice.

Unfortunately, secrecy and denial has prevented further work of which I now propose. A more detailed proposal is difficult to address in my brief, especially since I want it to be realistic and acceptable. Yet such a proposal is made here, both to give warning of what could happen and to begin a concrete discussion on the space Defense Initiative program. The Defense Department could continue "classification' of critically key information of knowledge collected in 1947 and, therefore, its secrecy in its present form. Only a small number of documents might need to be kept secret for longer periods, but in those cases a few highly responsible persons would have to certify, year by year, that continued secrecy be maintained. What I wish to impress upon you is the need for absolute secrecy for the real reasons for a apace defense. The real danger is the existence of secrecy can not be kept secret for ever. Our scientists will not turn to national defense unless they perceive an actual danger to the United States. A danger was perceived in 1939, only two years before Pearl Harbor. It is vital to the program that scientists should perceive the danger now before it is too late. What is at stake is not only the prevention of defeat, but the prevention of cosmic war. Nevertheless, convincing the American people that military research is necessary is a difficult thing.

I am not speaking of another arms racer but rather a race of technology. One individual familiar with military technology and engineering of special intelligence, Dr. John S. Foster, Jr., estimates that in 1960 the United States and the USSR spent equal percentages of their military budgets on space defense and research and development, while in 1974 that percentage was three times as high in Russia as in the United States. The quality of future space defense weapons depends more on research and development than on any other factor; the obvious recommendation is that we should spend more on it. Today we spend approximately 10 percent, so this recommendation does not seem too difficult to implement.

Space defense plays important roles in military affairs, particularly in communications and intelligence gathering. Both of these functions apt to become increasingly important in the future. An extension of our information gathering, including continuous surveillance of deep space, should have high priority. This could be done in two ways. One is to increase our ability to launch satellites of all needed varieties within a short time. The other is to provide decoys in space, thereby multiplying the number of targets the enemy would have to knock out. A combination of these two procedures could, indeed, prevent the enemy from taking out all our space vehicles. A third possibility is to prepare retaliation against the enemy by destroying their apace vehicles. But, at least in regard to the important item of information gathering, the enemy relies on stealth more than their spacecraft than we do; therefore emphasis on the first two approaches is recommended. In preparing decoys for space vehicles, the main objective would be for decoys to look like space vehicles that function like real ones. On the whole, this is not too difficult. Usually the main problem with a decoy is its mass. In order for a decoy to be inexpensive it must be light, but usually the light weight gives it away—for instance, in meeting air resistance, a lighter vehicle is more easily slowed down. Exceedingly little air resistance is encountered by space vehicles. Therefore, lightweight decoys for space vehicles are more feasible than decoys for almost any other application.

Remotely piloted vehicles (RPVs) have been developed and tested with marginal success. The possibility of RPVs exist for the enemy as well for us. The use of RPVs was first explored by the U.S. Air Force. It can also be applied to small space objects. An ingenious new circular airfoil design is now in experimental stage. A single wing is used in this design. Another design is also under development. This one uses a single wing as well, pivoting at its center at the fuselage. The wing is at right angles to the plane at takeoff and landing, but as the right wing points forward while the left points backward. A third design is the triangle-shaped wing and is the focus of intense development of which I have personal knowledge.

There is the possibility that chemical and biological warfare may be used by the enemy. The fact that these forme of warfare may be inflicted upon us from space only fires my persistence in having the President consider my proposal seriously for a broad and comprehensive Space Defense Initiative.

There are several fronts which must be considered in my proposal to the President. We must boost spending in new, more powerful radar. We must encourage more research programs for lasers. And, we must investigate the use of microwave and pulse energy devices along with directed energy weapons in space defense systems. Particle beams are effective over vast distances and could aid in space defense against intruding enemy spacecraft.

Progress toward such an objective since the end of World War II, has occurred in discouragingly small steps. Even so, we cannot afford to give up hope, we cannot afford to stop taking small steps. By the same token, we cannot afford not thinking of taking big ones. What I suggest is a big gamble but what if that gamble pays off through a major break through in technology? We have the talent. We have the means. All that is lacking is the political will and determination to succeed. We must not hesitate or falter. I believe all that I propose is possible and can be done. I ask that you weigh the risks and the benefits and consider what the alternative offers if we fail.

Presidential Approval ___Yes ___ No

UFO SOVEREIGNTY OVER AIR SPACE

A DEFENSE INTELLIGENCE PROBLEM

Air space is that part of space subject to the sovereignty of a Foe.

1. The problem of this right of sovereignty is the underlying issue of this paper. I can draw two statements from this:

(a) That part of air space directly above the territory of a state is subject to the sovereignty of UFOs.

(b) No state can exercise sovereignty over space which is not directly above its territory.

2. The object of sovereignty is the air space above its territory, which appears to be bounded:

(a) horizontally by a plane which has the territorial frontiers for its boundaries;

(b) vertically up to a height where the word "air" can no longer be used. In other words, those regions of space where there is no air or atmosphere cannot be called air space.

It must not be imagined that the principle of UFO sovereignty over air space has been accepted without numerous failed attempts by air defense, and heated discussions among defense intelligence agencies. It has been the subject of great controversy; and has been undergoing evolution to the present time.

The problem took on a completely different aspect when the discovery of space navigation brought man face to face with the use of space by UFO's. The ensuing defense problem immediately focused on the atmosphere, and the UFO sovereignty principle of vertical property was brushed aside by the tacit admission of freedom beyond a certain altitude was recognized,

The sovereignty of the United States cannot be absolute or unlimited. It is justified by reasons of national security and of utility. The air defense of the United States has a legitimate right to interdict air navigation which poses a threat to its security, not only from a political or military standpoint, but also from the point of view of personal security of its citizens who might be injured by the fall to earth of these objects which have not complied with the necessary conditions for flying. But there are other reasons founded on the maxim of utility, since it is the United States which stands to lose the most from violation of air space above its territory.

What constitutes the greatest threat being the issue do not have complete sovereignty of our air space and the UFO also derives from this right to violate our established navigation of air space, and not only violate it, but has imposed whatever limits they deem appropriate. It has been felt among U.S. intelligence community that this power to violate does not necessarily imply total sovereignty, and that the UFO might only well be engaged in challenging its existence without demonstrating its sovereignty.

THE STATE OF UFO INTELLIGENCE OPERATIONS

Since 1946, intelligence information regarding UFO sightings collected by various U.S. agencies yielded little in useful data that convinced authorities responsible for foreign intelligence operation that would provide a feasible defense approach to the problem. Thirty years later we find ourselves no better the wiser. The prognosis for UFO intelligence operations in the United States is not good and must be guarded. Reliable information about foreign situations and trends has never been more needed than it will be in the 1980s. There is a recent historical case and an existing functional framework for a UFO intelligence collection effort of top quality in this context. It has been allowed to fade into obscurity and mediocrity due to disbelief and inaction on the part of the defense establishment's fixation with practical measures to address a need to contain what it feels are more manageable threats. Yet at the approach of the next decade the Central Intelligence Agency and the other agencies in coordination with it are operating at a lower state of effectiveness and morale, and less public confidence, than at any time in the last 30 years. The future of U.S. intelligence is a crucial policy issue. The President, the Congress, and the people of the United States ought to give the highest priority to providing the kind of UFO data collection and analysis capability that an open society must have to survive and maintain sovereignty in a volatile and often surprisingly dangerous world.

I must admit that there is a good deal of understandable mystery associated with the phenomena; intelligence is a simple and self-evident thing. As an activity, it is the pursuit of a certain kind of knowledge; as a phenomena, it is the resultant knowledge combined with strategic intelligence, we might call the knowledge upon which our nation's foreign relations, in war and peace, must rest. In this sense, the overwhelming importance of UFO intelligence activity, the actor or agency, of the "resultant knowledge' seems self-evident. The United States, nevertheless, was almost totally unprepared for the dangers and stress of the 1940s in the field of intelligence, as in so many areas.

Now, once again, the United States stands on the brink of tragedy because it has not restored the damage done to the whole coordinated UFO intelligence collection program. The intelligence agencies have gradually wound down to a slow speed and a defensive posture, and in some way, they have come to a complete halt. Where we go from here, up or down, is the pressing question. It seems the collection of UFO intelligence and its evaluation or analysis are seldom any longer questioned as legitimate and essential parts of the Washington bureaucratic process. Sometimes more scruples are expressed about wooing clandestine and illegal techniques of getting information but generally bureaucrats feel it is only fair game to try secretly to obtain UFO data that is likely to affront our relations with those nations who are hiding it from us and might indeed affect the security of American institutions or lives. If national policy decisions are to be made, national efforts articulated towards a unified data base are clearly worthless.

PROBLEMS WITH THE CURRENT POLICY AND PROPOSED SOLUTIONS

The major problem from the standpoint of intelligence has always been 'what to tell the president?' and 'how much?' This has been the policy since 1947 when the NTK restrictions were imposed. In maintaining absolute secrecy we have deprived high level decision makers of vital UFO information out of fear that "long ears" in the White House would use this information for political gain. This absurd and paranoid mindset cannot be allowed to continue as long as an effective countermeasure remains untested.

If national sovereignty is to be a reality in our atmosphere and space, we must arm our national leaders with full disclosure of the facts as they exist and not a watered down hypothesis of "they could be" or we think "they are Soviet."

This simply does not serve our sovereignty and, most certainly, our craft. We have to face up to our shortcomings and cavalier approach to properly assess the problem and find a workable solution before we find ourselves caught with our pants down, to use an old phrase.

We do have a "historical base" to draw from and we do have an "existing functional framework" in which to address the UFO problem. It worked for us before and it will work for us again. I propose that we reinvigorate the program that has been neglected and infuse it with new life and purpose.

I propose that the Majestic project, in coordination with the Air Force's current air intelligence and space tracking system be once again a top priority within the Central Intelligence Agency and that the National Security Agency be allowed to not only collect vital UFO technical data, but be allowed to perform its own analysis if it proves to be more cost effective and advantageous to current intelligence operations.

We can no longer afford the luxury of exclusive domain. We must allow evaluation to come from other quarters in the intelligence community and we must accept it as supporting data rather than raw intelligence. Our failure in 1953 caused us to lose precious information simply because a director refused to believe the data or a chief analyst was not convinced that UFO reports were of vital significance to the bigger picture of the Cold War.

I further recommend that the Director of Central Intelligence be briefed in full when events seem to paint a clear picture of intent and that estimates be drawn up regarding foreign progress in evaluating UFO data and the obvious transfer of technology to space defense systems that could outpace us.

Finally, I strongly recommend that a separate division be created with the scientific and technical departments staffed with qualified and knowledgeable analysts and intelligence officers to receive, analyze and summarize the data into a systemized data base with cross indexing to previous cases of proper evaluation.

I realized that such a proposal goes beyond the bounds of current operations and responsibility. I also realize the current political climate is not conducive to this proposed change, but we must recognize the threat and deal with it in a responsible and professional manner if we are to protect our air space, our people, and our sovereignty as a nation. What is required is nothing short of a total overhaul of our intelligence operations.

UFOS AS SPACE WEAPONS

I am not the first to suggest that some UFOs are, or could be, space weapons sent here to be deployed for either passive or active purposes. In 1928, Dr. Hermann Oberth published a revised version of a technical study know as *The Way To Space Travel* that included, among other things, space vehicles and weapons of mass destruction. Oberth has also voiced his informed opinion that UFOs might well be devices constructed by an advanced civilization sent here to not only observe, but to interfere in Earth's political and military affairs. The role of such a phenomenon was shown by the incident of the so-called "Dark Satellite." In 1959, an unidentified space object was detected in orbit by the U. S. Navy space surveillance system. The Pentagon is reported to have been chewed out for failing to take the information seriously, and the possible threat it might pose to the United States, as the space object was tracked for some weeks.

The film recovery capsule from the failed Discover 5 mission of the previous August had been deflected into a higher orbit rather than back down to Earth as planned. The implications, as we all know, were discussed at the highest levels in total secrecy.

To counter such as possibility, Project Black Eye was developed in March 1967 and was picked up by the *New York Times* in an article in which General LeMay predicted that "particle beam weapons could be fired at a man-made satellite from across space and bring about the technological disarmament of nuclear weapons." The Soviets were already playing on those fears in August 1961 when they referred to space weapons that could be "directed to any place on Earth." This threat was echoed by Marshal Birysov, Commander of the Soviet Union's Strategic Rocket Forces, who claimed that orbiting space platforms could launch rockets at any terrestrial target within the satellite's trajectory. We, at the Office of Scientific Investigations, knew the Soviets did not have that capability, but realized they were thinking along the lines of a Fractional Orbit Bombardment System (FOBS).

Such a system may have played a role in New Mexico in the summer of 1947 when an unidentified space vehicle was reportedly recovered by the Armed Forces Special Weapons Project Special Weapons Team after the space vehicle was disabled by microwave energy from several high-powered radar stations that had reportedly locked on to the object, causing it to crash, and partially disabling a second, which, allegedly, was recovered intact. I have repeatedly tried to gain access to documents supposedly existing elsewhere within the CIA's UFO files. As a scientist and astronomer, I found this most disheartening because, since the early 1950s, OSI has not been authorized to study the radar data while charged with the requirement to analyze all UFO data available to the Agency for proper analysis.

This incident may have been the basis for Dr. Wernher von Braun's statement as published in Colliers, 22 March, 1952, ***Space Flight***, in which he theorized that small guided space weapons could be "launched from the (space) station... (and) could be accurately guided to any spot on Earth." Perhaps this UFO space object offered the United States the most important and strategic advance in history.

Details of this and other incidents quickly came under a tight security umbrella as more sighting reports made it abundantly clear that an advanced weapon system was being deployed over sensitive defense and research establishments.

President Truman and other leading members of the government tried to put a bold face on the prospect of U. S. defenselessness with claims that anti-missile technologies were already at a promising stage of development. By claiming that flying saucers were secret weapons developments and placing a security curtain in front of the stories, the military succeeded in convincing the Soviets for awhile anyway.

I remember President Johnson's cryptic statements regarding the SAINI Program as "having the ability to intercept and destroy armed satellites circling the earth," and that they were fully operational and "on alert to protect this nation." This was more of a ruse than fact and it did keep the Soviets fearful.

This cover began to wear thin in the Kennedy psychological war of words and the Soviets began to call his bluff. In 1962 Kennedy issued a directive to the Air Force to accelerate the direct ascent anti-satellite program which was part of the Contingency Plan for the U. S. reaction to the Soviet placement of a "Nuclear Weapon in Space," drawn up by Raymond Garthoff in May of 1953.

The Soviet ABM program was discovered by the CIA in 1950 and Pravda confidently printed a disclosure made by Marshal Melinkowsky in late 1961 during the 22nd Party Congress that "(T)he problem of destroying enemy missiles in flight has been successfully resolved."

Even Krushchev repeated the point that Soviet forces could now "hit a fly in space." It was apparent to both sides that UFO incursions were best concealed through the use of "armed satellites" and "enemy missiles" as long as the elusive UFO continued to evade anti-satellite defenses.

The misidentification problem was also voiced by former DCI Hillenkoetter who warned that someday our response to erratic moving "satellites" and "missiles" would leave us blind and open to a surprise attack and possibly lead to accidental nuclear war. During the tense standoff of the 1962 Cuban Missile Crisis, scientific and technical intelligence worked around the clock to secure much data on Soviet nuclear capability and advise the White House and the military advisors at all our embassies on what we had in the way of UFO patterns and characteristics.

Our data warned that these objects could emulate radar signatures and trajectories that closely resembled what we knew of the Soviet ICBMs and indicated that the Soviets would probably do the same.

Fortunately, the worse case scenario did not happen. Past Defense Conditions Two alerts gave us enough information to draw this conclusion, but still left our radar early warning system unprepared for the air space violations of Loring AFB, Maine; Malstrom AFB and Minot AFB, North Dakota, and Wursmith AFB, Michigan, which brought our nuclear forces to standby alert.

Air Force Office of Special Investigations ran out of possible plausible explanations for these incursions over nuclear weapons storage facilities. One fatal act of aggression could have resulted in actions taken by NORAD and SAC that would have brought us to the brink. And, I might add, in an exposed position whereby Soviet intelligence could have read our response and contingency plans for nuclear attack if they had been able to. As far as I know, the UFO incidents did make some headlines and there were security leaks.

RECOMMENDED CHANGES TO THE NATIONAL ESTIMATE

Including Soviet use of UFOs in the National Intelligence Estimate, the single most influential document in national security policy making should be included as recommended by Lyman Kirkpatrick, former CIA Executive Director, who told several of us that UFO-type mechanisms of our government and statements on Soviet Progress in this area will affect us in the future.

The significance of such an estimate was well illustrated with the NIE prior to the 1962 airborne detection incident and the Cuban Missile Crisis which predicted that the Soviet Union was not likely to apply a policy of such enormous risks as placing nuclear missiles in Cuba. Fortunately, the world escaped from the worst consequences of such a bad guess.

During the UFO incident, and followed by the Cuban Missile Crisis, an estimate was hastily produced which warned that the Soviet Union might risk nuclear war through such action rather than give in to President Kennedy's demand that UFO decoy deployment be eliminated from the negotiations and that the missiles be removed. Even more fortunate was the inaccuracy of that estimate.

To illustrate the point, on August 26th, 1957, the Soviets announced the successful testing of an intercontinental ballistic missile. This was "intelligence" of a high order. The discovery of a secret UFO decoy missile was even higher. What was the significance, the reliability, of this information? Asked about it at a private meeting the following day, Secretary of State Dulles made the strange reply that the reliability of the discovery was anybody's guess and that the intelligence community was making a careful study of the public announcement, but was more reserved about commenting on the UFO decoy project and policy.

Behind the scenes, the CIA had for some years been charting as precisely as possible the course of Soviet missile progress and knowledge of UFO tracking data. By making use of classified radar and other detection devices, and such information sources as espionage and reconnaissance aircraft, intelligence analysts such as myself working for the Office of Scientific Intelligence, had tried to— for example—keep a running score of Soviet UFO sightings and progress in missiles, and in other significant areas. To our surprise, none of the NIEs mentioned Soviet UFO decoy use with their ICBM program. This was a glaring omission and a dangerously inaccurate estimate.

One of the chief problems of the intelligent community at the outbreak of the Korean War was that crucial intelligence was available from State, Defense, and CIA, but these departments merely routed the raw intelligence around to the appropriate agencies without coming up with joint National Estimates. CIA, in particular, was criticized for "failing to fulfil its duty to correlate and evaluate intelligence relating to national security." The important estimates as to future enemy capabilities or actions was recognized by General Smith who assumed responsibility for the UFO program in 1950.

In order for national estimates to be broad in scope and defined in depth to include vital UFO technical data, I propose the following:

1. To periodically brief the President and selected members of the National Security Council on national security implications resulting from UFO misidentification.

(a)   The President, the Director of Central Intelligence, a member of the NSC, or perhaps more likely, the Assistant to the President for National Security Affairs, to render an informed decision on UFO policy in a proper context of defense.

(b)   To include in any NIE on Soviet UFO decoy capability, missile, warhead, and booster vehicle propulsion and range factors from OSI as augmented intelligence for the final intelligence product.

2. Terms of reference be defined by the Board of National Estimates. This group can initiate study or, as is usually the case, respond to a specific UFO data request from an intelligence consumer.

(a)   Define the problem, divide into feasible components and assign to appropriate intelligence agencies. Staff studies should include the Office of National Estimates and assign a representative to integrate material received.

3. A straight estimate be divided into two categories—the knowable and the unknowable.

(a)   Coordinate UFO data collection with Project Blue Book at the Top Secret level and forward to OSI.

(b)   Task military intelligence with requirements for forwarding raw UFO reports to OSI through the Office of the Director of Central Intelligence.

(c)   Coordinate feedback to appropriate intelligence agencies.

4. Ultrasecret net estimate handled by the NSC rather than the Board of Estimates or the U. S. Intelligence Board.

5. The Watch Committee and National Indications Center be allowed to alert CIA of any unusual or impending changes in Soviet power structure through a crash estimate when needed.

6. A Joint Committee be formed to appraise the Joint Committee on Atomic Energy and the Material Assessment of the Joint Intelligence Committee (MAJIC) in the coordination between CIA and authorized intelligence agencies concerned with physical and trace evidence obtained through recovery operations in foreign countries.

Past and current members of the Council of Foreign Affairs be brought into the intelligence loop on an on-call basis to provide quick and ready reviews to hard questions regarding Soviet back-channel contacts and sources on advancing Soviet and allied progress in missiles, spacecraft, launch vehicles, payload capabilities and political discussions among scientific defense communities.

July 14, 1954

TOP SECRET RESTRICTED
SECURITY INFORMATION

MEMORANDUM FOR GENERAL TWINING

SUBJECT: NSC/MJ-12 Special Studies Project

The President has decided that the MJ-12 SSP briefing should take place during the already scheduled White House meeting of July 16, rather than following it as previously intended. More precise arrangements will be explained to you upon arrival. Please alter your plans accordingly.

Your concurrence in the above change of arrangements is assumed.

ROBERT CUTLER
Special Assistant
to the President

This memo from Robert Cutler found in the National Archives is the only official paper found to date which makes reference to MJ-12.

TOP SECRET

EYES ONLY

THE WHITE HOUSE

WASHINGTON

September 24, 1947.

MEMORANDUM FOR THE SECRETARY OF DEFENSE

Dear Secretary Forrestal:

    As per our recent conversation on this matter,
you are hereby authorized to proceed with all due
speed and caution upon your undertaking. Hereafter
this matter shall be referred to only as Operation
Majestic Twelve.

    It continues to be my feeling that any future
considerations relative to the ultimate disposition
of this matter should rest solely with the Office
of the President following appropriate discussions
with yourself, Dr. Bush and the Director of Central
Intelligence.

Harry Truman

TOP SECRET

EYES ONLY

The art work below is a reproduction of an official intelligence agency poster which speaks for itself. It was obtained by Larry Bryant of Citizens Against UFO Secrecy following a persistent letter writing campaign and only after a formal grievance for its release was filed.

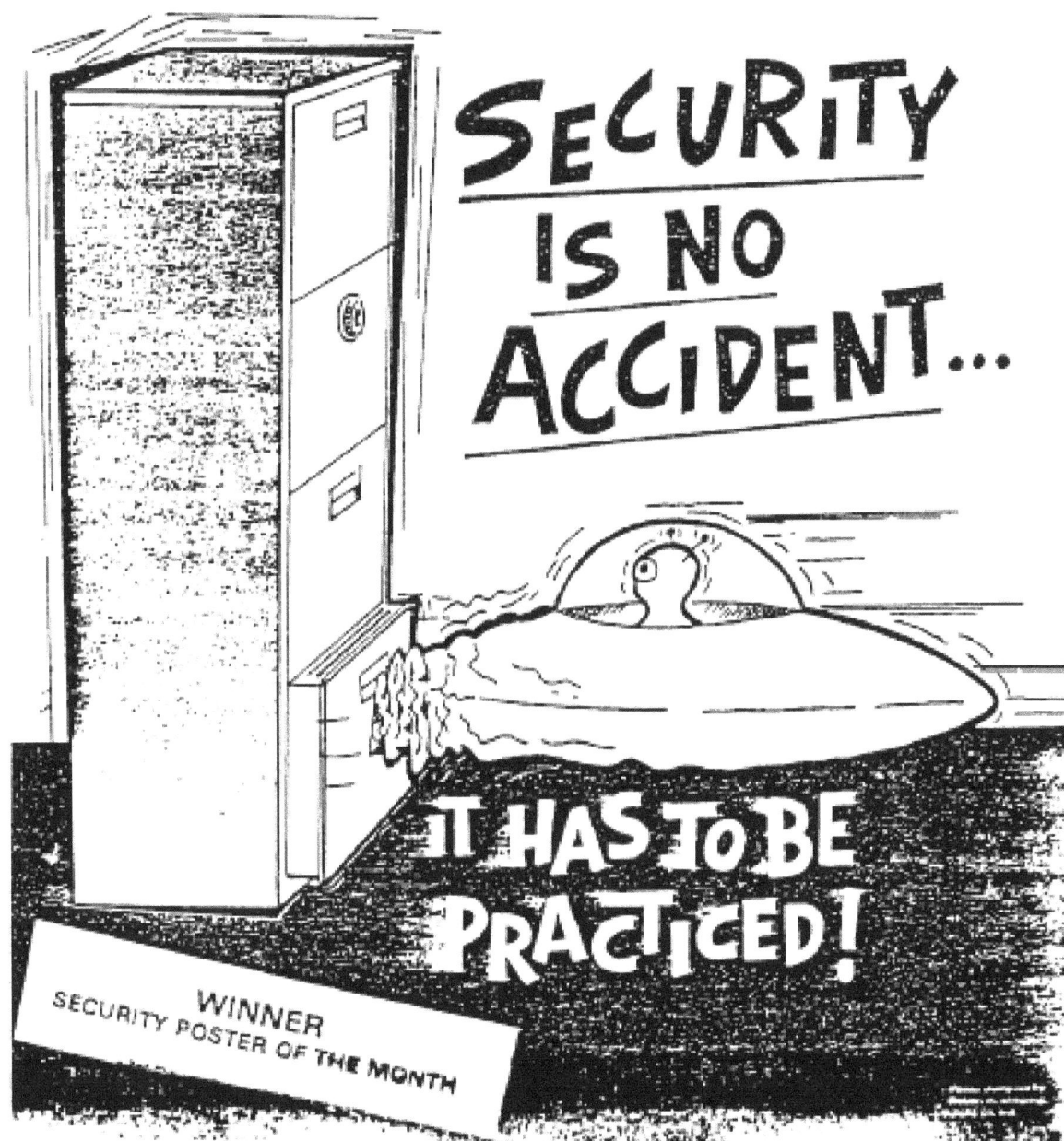

SECURITY IS NO ACCIDENT...

IT HAS TO BE PRACTICED!

WINNER
SECURITY POSTER OF THE MONTH

United States Senate

COMMITTEE ON COMMERCE, SCIENCE,
AND TRANSPORTATION

WASHINGTON, D.C. 20510

April 11, 1979

Mr. Lee M. Graham
526 West Maple
Monrovia, California 91016

Dear Mr. Graham:

It is true I was denied access to a facility at
Wright-Patterson. Because I never got in, I can't
tell you what was inside. We both know about the
rumors.

Apart from that, let me make my position clear: I
do not believe that we are the only planet, and of
some two billion that exist, that has life on it. I
have never seen what I would call a UFO, but I have
intelligent friends who have, so I can sort of argue
either way.

Sincerely,

Barry Goldwater

Office Memorandum • UNITED STATES GOVERNMENT

TO : DIRECTOR, FBI
                                    DATE: March 22, 1950

FROM : GUY HOTTEL, SAC, WASHINGTON

SUBJECT: FLYING SAUCERS
INFORMATION CONCERNING

"Flying Discs or Flying Saucers"

The following information was furnished to SA ~~██████████~~ by
~~███~~

An investigator for the Air Forces stated that three so-called
flying saucers had been recovered in New Mexico. They were
described as being circular in shape with raised centers, approximately 50 feet in diameter. Each one was occupied by three bodies
of human shape but only 3 feet tall, dressed in metallic cloth of
a very fine texture. Each body was bandaged in a manner similar
to the blackout suits used by speed flyers and test pilots.

According to Mr. ~~██████~~ informant, the saucers were found in New
Mexico due to the fact that the Government had a very high-powered
radar set-up in that area and it is believed the radar interferes
with the controling mechanism of the saucers.

No further evaluation was attempted by SA ~~██████~~ concerning the
above.

RHK:VIM

RECORDED - 3
INDEXED - 5

62-83894 - 209

MAR 29 1950
34

51 MAR 29 1950

Office Mem. 'Ium • UNITED STATES GOVERNMENT

TO : DIRECTOR, FBI   DATE: March 31, 1950

FROM : SAC, NEW ORLEANS

SUBJECT: FLYING DISCS

Special Agent ▓▓▓▓▓ of the New Orleans Division, has a brother, ▓▓▓▓▓ of the ▓▓▓▓▓ advertising agency, ▓▓▓ ▓▓▓▓▓, Denver, Colorado. ▓▓▓▓ has advised Special Agent ▓▓▓ that an employee of the ▓▓▓▓▓, ▓▓▓ ▓▓▓▓▓ has been contacted by one ▓▓▓▓▓ Street, Telephone ▓▓▓▓ Denver, Colorado, regarding Flying Discs.

▓▓▓▓ is alleged to have told ▓▓▓▓▓ in January, 1950, that he ▓▓▓▓▓, knows a prominent Denver oilman named ▓▓▓▓▓, also known as a "mysterious Mr. X", and an official of the ▓▓▓▓▓, ▓▓▓▓▓ Denver, Colorado. ▓▓▓▓ is claiming that he leased land in the Mojave Desert in California and that on this land a flying disc had been found intact, with eighteen three-foot tall human-like occupants, all dead on it but not burned. Further, that the disc was alleged to be of very hard metal and near indestructible. ▓▓▓▓ is said to have exhibited a radio set to ▓▓▓▓▓ purported to be a souvenir of the space disc.

According to ▓▓▓▓▓ ▓▓▓▓▓ has been telling of this story off and on for the three month period prior to January, 1950, and is said to have notified ▓▓▓▓▓ of it weeks prior to the publication of a flying disc article published in the True Magazine, and one by FRANK SCULLY published in the Variety Magazine in January, 1950. ▓▓▓▓ claimed to have been visited by DONALD KEYHOE, author of the article in the True Magazine.

Further data was furnished that ▓▓▓▓ had been telling the tale so prolifically in Denver that he claimed to have had telephone calls from Washington, D. C. and from the Federal Bureau of Investigation in which he was requested to keep the information to himself and that, thereafter, he became mysterious about the entire matter.

It is noted that considerable publicity regarding these discs has been found in Denver and other papers.

This information is being furnished the Bureau and the designated offices for informational purposes.

EXT:ETg
66-1199

RECORDED - 28   162-83894-243
INDEXED - 28   APR 3 1950
                34

cc: Denver
    Los Angeles

EX-94

CENTRAL INTELLIGENCE AGENCY
WASHINGTON D C 20505

SEE CHAPTER THREE

14 December 1978

Peter A. Gersten, Esquire
Rothblatt, Rothblatt, Seijas & Peskin
191 East 161st Street
Bronx, New York   10451

Dear Mr. Gersten:

Re: Ground Saucer Watch, Inc. v. CIA, et al.,
Civil Action Number 78-859

This letter covers the release of CIA documents responsive
to the Freedom of Information Act (FOIA) request at issue in the
above-designated litigation. A total of 397 CIA documents were
retrieved to date in the process of responding to this FOIA
request. You will find that a total of 340 documents of approximately 900 pages have been released and are enclosed. **57 documents were withheld in their entirety pursuant to exemptions
under the FOIA.** There may be a few duplicate documents, although
most have been removed.

To date, a total of 196 documents were retrieved from CIA
files which were originated by other U.S. Government agencies.
These documents have been referred to the originating agencies
for response to you. The breakdown by agency for these documents
is as follows:

a.	Air Force	76
b.	National Archives	1
c.	DIA	19
d.	Army	30
e.	Navy	11
f.	**NSA**	18
g.	State Department	41

I shall forward copies of the letters of transmittal regarding
these referred documents in the near future.
The fee for reproduction of the Agency originated released
documents is 10 cents a page. Please forward by return mail to
CIA a check or money order in the amount of $90.00 made payable
to the order of the Treasurer of the United States.

Respectfully,

George H. Owens

George Owens
Information & Privacy Coordinator

NATIONAL INVESTIGATIONS COMMITTEE ON AERIAL PHENOMENA (NICAP)®
3535 University Blvd. West
Kensington, Maryland 20795

301-949-1267

REPORT ON UNIDENTIFIED FLYING OBJECT(S)

This form includes questions asked by the United States Air Force and by other Armed Forces' investigating agencies, and additional questions to which answers are needed for full evaluation by NICAP.

After all the information has been fully studied, the conclusion of our Evaluation Panel will be published by NICAP in its regularly issued magazine or in another publication. Please try to answer as many questions as possible. Should you need additional room, please use another sheet of paper. Please print or typewrite. Your assistance is of great value and is genuinely appreciated. Thank you.

1. Name Jimmy Carter

   Address State Capitol Atlanta

   Telephone (404) 656-1776

   Place of Employment

   Occupation Governor
   Date of birth
   Education Graduate
   Special Training Nuclear Physics
   Military Service U.S. Navy

2. Date of Observation October 1969
   Time AM PM 7:15 Time Zone EST

3. Locality of Observation Leary, Georgia

4. How long did you see the object? Hours 10-12 Minutes Seconds

5. Please describe weather conditions and the type of sky; i.e., bright daylight, nighttime, dusk, etc. Shortly after dark.

6. Position of the Sun or Moon in relation to the object and to you. Not in sight.

7. If seen at night, twilight, or dawn, were the stars or moon visible? Stars.

8. Were there more than one object? No. If so, please tell how many, and draw a sketch of what you saw, indicating direction of movement, if any.

9. Please describe the object(s) in detail. For instance, did it (they) appear solid, or only as a source of light; was it revolving, etc.? Please use additional sheets of paper, if necessary.

10. Was the object(s) brighter than the background of the sky? Yes.

11. If so, compare the brightness with the Sun, Moon, headlights, etc. At one time, as bright as the moon.

12. Did the object(s) — (Please elaborate, if you can give details.)

    a. Appear to stand still at any time? yes
    b. Suddenly speed up and rush away at any time?
    c. Break up into parts or explode?
    d. Give off smoke?
    e. Leave any visible trail?
    f. Drop anything?
    g. Change brightness? yes
    h. Change shape? size
    i. Change color? yes

    Seemed to move toward us from a distance, stopped-moved partially away—returned, then departed. Bluish at first, then reddish, luminous, not solid.

13. Did object(s) at any time pass in front of, or behind of, anything? If so, please elaborate giving distance, size, etc, if possible. no.

14. Was there any wind? no. If so, please give direction and speed.

15. Did you observe the object(s) through an optical instrument or other aid, windshield, windowpane, storm window, screening, etc? What? no.

16. Did the object(s) have any sound? no What kind? How loud?

17. Please tell if the object(s) was (were) —

    a. Fuzzy or blurred.   b. Like a bright star.   c. Sharply outlined X

18. Was the object —   a. Self-luminous? x   b. Dull finish?   c. Reflecting?   d. Transparent?

19. Did the object(s) rise or fall while in motion? came close, moved away-came close then moved away.

Sighting report form filled out by Jimmy Carter
pertaining to his 1969 UFO sighting.

20. Tell the apparent size of the object(s) when compared with the following held at arm's length:

   a. Pinhead   c. Dime   e. Half dollar   g. Orange   i. Larger
   b. Pea   d. Nickel   f. Silver dollar   h. Grapefruit

Or, if easier, give apparent size in inches on a ruler held at arm's length. About the same as moon, maybe a little smaller. Varied from brighter/larger than planet to apparent size of moon.

21. How did you happen to notice the object(s)? 10-12 men all watched it. Brightness attracted us.

22. Where were you and what were you doing at the time? Outdoors waiting for a meeting to begin at 7:30pm

23. How did the object(s) disappear from view? Moved to distance then disappeared

24. Compare the speed of the object(s) with a piston or jet aircraft at the same apparent altitude. Not pertinent

25. Were there any conventional aircraft in the location at the time or immediately afterwards? If so, please elaborate. no.

26. Please estimate the distance of the object(s). Difficult. Maybe 300-1000 yards.

27. What was the elevation of the object(s) in the sky? Please mark on this hemisphere sketch. About 30° above horizon.

28. Names and addresses of other witnesses, if any.

Ten members of Leary Georgia Lions Club

29. What do you think you saw?

   a. Extraterrestrial device?   e. Satellite?
   b. UFO?   f. Hoax?
   c. Planet or star?   g. Other? (Please specify).
   d. Aircraft?

30. Please describe your feelings and reactions during the sighting. Were you calm, nervous, frightened, apprehensive, awed, etc.? If you wish your answer to this question to remain confidential, please indicate with a check mark. (Use a separate sheet if necessary)

31. Please draw a map of the locality of the observation showing North; your position; the direction from which the object(s) appeared and disappeared from view; the direction of its course over the area; roads, towns, villages, railroads, and other landmarks within a mile.

Appeared from West--About 30° up.

32. Is there an airport, military, governmental, or research installation in the area? No

33. Have you seen other objects of an unidentified nature? If so, please describe these observations, using a separate sheet of paper. No

34. Please enclose photographs, motion pictures, news clippings, notes of radio or television programs (include time, station and date, if possible) regarding this or similar observations, or any other background material. We will return the material to you if requested. None.

35. Were you interrogated by Air Force investigators? By any other federal, state, county, or local officials? If so, please state the name and rank or title of the agent, his office, and details as to where and when the questioning took place.

Were you asked or told not to reveal or discuss the incident? If so, were any reasons or official orders mentioned? Please elaborate carefully. No.

36. We should like permission to quote your name in connection with this report. This action will encourage other responsible citizens to report similar observations to NICAP. However, if you prefer, we will keep your name confidential. Please note your choice by checking the proper statement below. In any case, please fill in all parts of the form, for our own confidential files. Thank you for your cooperation.

You may use my name. (x)   Please keep my name confidential. [ ]

37. Date of filling out this report   Signature: *Jimmy Carter*

9-18-73

```
                            Department of State     TELEG

                    LIMITED OFFICIAL USE
                                          AN: 0750274-0242

PAGE 01   PRETOR 02947   080905Z

21
ACTION OES-04

INFO  OCT-01  AF-06  ISO-00  ACDA-05  CIAE-00  DODE-00  PM-03

INR-07  L-03  NSAE-00  NASA-01  NSC-05  /035 W
---------------------     127115
R 060857Z AUG 75 ZDK
FM AMEMBASSY PRETORIA
TO SECSTATE WASHDC 2420
INFO AMCONSUL CAPE TOWN


LIMITED OFFICIAL USE PRETORIA 2947

              PASS NASA

E.O. 11652: N/A
TAGS:  PFOR, PINR, TSPA, UN, SF
SUBJ:  SPACE OBJECT REPORTED IN CAPE PROVINCE
REF:   STATE A-6343 (JULY 25, 1973)

1. EMBASSY HAS RECEIVED FOLLOWING MESSAGE FROM CONGEN CAPETOWN.

QTE. 1. CAPE TOWN WEEK-END PRESS REPORTED METALLIC SPHERE
CRASHED TO EARTH, JULY 29, ON FARM NEAR JOUBERTINA, CAPE
PROVINCE.  ACCORDING TO REPORTS, FARMERS IN AREA STATE THAT
SPHERE FELL AFTER SEVERAL BRIGHT UFO'S HAD BEEN SPOTTED STREAKING
ACROSS THE NIGHT SKY AND THAT IT MUST HAVE BEEN MADE OF VERY
HARD METAL AND FALLEN FROM GREAT HEIGHT BECAUSE IT SHATTERED
A BOULDER ON IMPACT AND WAS ONLY SLIGHTLY DENTED.  OBJECT IS
DESCRIBED AS 13 KG BALL, 67 CM IN DIAMETER WITH GAPING HOLE
AT ONE END AND PIPE-LIKE PROTRUSION AT OTHER.  SHELL HAS
UNIDENTIFIED "FAINT LETTERING".  PRESS REPORTS OBJECT HANDED
OVER TO SECURITY POLICE AT OUDTSHOORN WHO WERE AWAITING INSTRUC-
TIONS FROM PRETORIA.

2. ACCORDING TO WEEK-END ARGUS, OBJECT IS ALMOST EXACT REPLICA
OF FOUR SPHERES RECOVERED IN 1963 NEAR NOUPOORT THAT WERE
IDENTIFIED AS PARTS OF OXYGEN TANKS OF BOOSTER ROCKET THAT PUT
PAGE 02   PRETOR 02947   080905Z

                          SEE CHAPTER THREE

                    LIMITED OFFICIAL USE
```

Department of State TELEGI

UNCLASSIFIED

AN: 0760283-0427

PAGE 01   PRETOR 03087 152030Z

61
ACTION OES-05

INFO   OCT-01 AF-06 ISO-00 ACDA-10 CIAE-00 DODE-00 PM-04

INR-07 L-03 NSAE-00 NASA-02 NSC-05 /043 W
-------------------- 084216
R 151515Z AUG 75
FM AMEMBASSY PRETORIA
TO SECSTATE WASHDC 2492
INFO RUEHPCR/AMCONSUL CAPE TOWN 6664

UNCLAS PRETORIA 3087

E.O. 11652: N/A
TAGS: PFOR, PINR, TSPA, UN, SF
SUBJ: SPACE OBJECT REPORTED IN CAPE PROVINCE.
EREF: PREPTORIA 3082

1. EMBOFF CONTACTED BRIGADIER L.P. NEETHLING, CHIEF OF SOUTH
AFRICAN POLICE FORENSIC SCIENCE LABORATORIES, WHO SAID THAT HIS LAB
STILL HAD SPACE OBJECT AND THE EMBASSY WELCOME TO SEE IT.
EMBOFF WENT TO FORENSIC LAB AND EXAMINED OBJECT, WHICH IS AS
DESCRIBED IN REFTEL. LETTERING ON SIDE OF SPHERE WAS DIFFICULT TO
DISTINGUISH, BUT APPEARED TO READ AS FOLLOWS (IN ORDER IT
APPEARED ON SPHERE): NET (OR POSSIBLY NFT)
P 165
VPA 252
BEC 13.9
ADDITIONAL LETTERING WHICH COULD NOT BE READ

2. BRIG NEETHLING PROVIDED TWO PHOTOGRAPHS OF SPHERE, WHICH
EMBASSY WILL POUCH TO DEPARTMENT, AND STATED THAT SPHERE WILL BE
HELD AT HIS LAB UNTIL DISPOSITION DECIDED. HE STATED THAT
OFFICIAL ACTION BY USG TO OBTAIN OBJECT, IF IT IS OURS, SHOULD
BE HANDLED THROUGH SOUTH AFRICAN POLICE COMMISSIONER.
BOWDLER

UNCLASSIFIED

195

SAUCER NEWS SIGHTING REPORT FORM
FOR USE IN REPORTING OBSERVATIONS OF UNIDENTIFIED FLYING OBJECTS (UFO's.)

(Please fill out the form below as completely as possible, and mail it to our Headquarters:
P.O. Box 163, Fort Lee, N.J., 07024. All information will be kept confidential on request.)

1. Name of observer: Barbara Hudson

2. Home address & phone no: _____.123rd Street ___ New York City 10027, N.Y.

3. Business address & phone no: ---------------

4. Occupation: Housewife

5. Educational background: Elementary, Jr. High School, and High School

6. Date & time of observation: Mid-July 1952 8:00 and 8:30 PM.

7. Weather conditions: Fair, warm and clear.

8. Locality of observation: We were on 107 or 108th St. and Manhattan Ave. in NYC.
                The object was over Morningside Park.
9. How many objects were seen? One

10. How long did observation last? The sighting lasted about two to three minutes.

11. Name other witnesses, if any: Mother, my brother and his wife, a friend of the family
                            and myself.
12. Describe object(s) in regard to:
    (a) Shape: Round and somewhat larger than a full moon.
    (b) Color(s): Pinkish-Orange with a dark blue glow around the outer edge.
    (c) Estimated size: The object was a little larger than a full moon.
    (d) Estimated distance from observer(s): The object seemed about three an a half blocks
    (e) Sound, if any: No sound was heard.   away.
    (f) Estimated speed(s): The speed of the UFO was faster than a jet.
    (g) Changes of direction: It came from the East, turned North and then South.
    (h) Distinguishing characteristics such as protrusions, portholes, antennas, etc:
        We could see something like dark bands down the front of the UFO.
13. Did you observe the object through binoculars? No.

14: Did you or any other observer take photographs?   No.

15: How did you first happen to notice the object(s)?   The sun was setting and the bright
                            glow lit the sky
16. Were any conventional aircraft in view during the sighting or immediately afterwards?
    No, but there was many military police around, fire trucks and city police.
17. Is there an airport or military installation near the area where the sighting occurred?
    There are some in Jersey and Long Island as well as upstate N.Y. but not in area.
18. What, in your personal opinion, was the nature and origin of the craft you observed?
    The UFO was unlike anything I have ever seen before, I think it was interplanetary.
19. Have you ever seen UFO's previously? If so, give details:
                Yes.
20. Was the sighting publicized in local newspapers or other news media? NO.

21. Have you reported this sighting to the Air Force or any other organization? If so,
    give details: No.

22. Has any attempt been made to "silence" you regarding this or previous sightings?
    Yes, the MPs said not to talk about the incident in this report.
23. Do we have your permission to print this sighting in SAUCER NEWS? --------------------

SEE CHAPTER SEVEN

DEPARTMENT OF THE AIR FORCE
TH SECURITY POLICE SQUADRON (PACAF)
APO SAN FRANCISCO 96239

Response for Request of Information in Relation to UFO Contact and
Other Related Information

Len Stringfield

1. In January of 1978, I was station at McGuire AFB, N.J.. One evening, during the time frame of 0300hrs. and 0500hrs., there were a number of UFO sightins in the area over the air field and Ft. Dix Army camp. I am a security policeman and was on routine patrol at the time. N.J. State Police, and Ft. Dix MP's were running code in the direction of Brownsville,N.J.. A state trooper then entered Gate #5 at the rear of the base requestin assistance and permission to enter. I was dispatched and the trooper wanted access to the runway area which led to the very back of the air field and connected with a heavily wooded area which is part of the Dix training area. He informed me that a Ft. Dix MP was pursuing a low flying object which then hovered over his car. He described it as oval shaped, with no details, and glowing with a blueish green color. His radio transmission was cut off. At that time in front of his police car, appeared a thing, about 4ft. tall, greyish, brown, fat head, long arms, and slender body. The MP panicked and fired five rounds from his .45 Cal into the thing, and one round into the object above. The object then fled straight up and joined with eleven others high in the sky. This we all saw but didn't know the details at the time. Anyway, The ting ran into the woods towards our fenceline and they wanted to look for it. By this time several patrols were involved.

2. We found the body of the thing near the runway. It had apparently climbed the fence and died while running. It was all of a sudden hush-hush and no one was allowed near the area. We roped off the area and AF OSI came out and took over. That was the last I saw of it. There was a bad stench coming from it too. Like ammonia smelling but it wasn't consitent in the air. That day, a team from Wright-Patterson AFB came in a C141 and went to the area. They crated it in a wooden box, sprayed something over it, and then put it into a bigger metal container. They loaded it in the plane and took off. That was it, nothing more said, no report made and we were all told not to have anything to say about it or we would be court martialed.

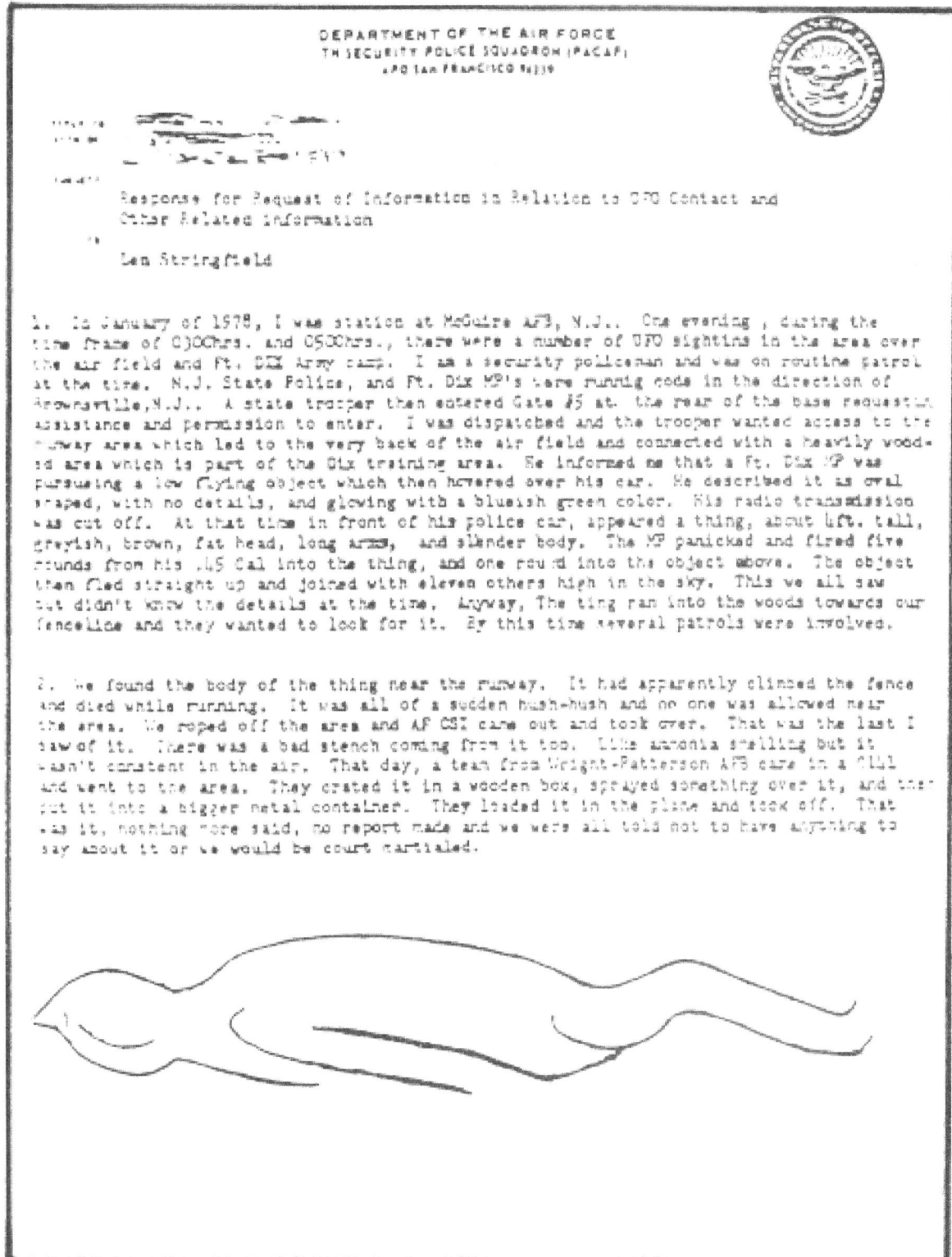

SEE CHAPTER TEN

HELENA EAR, NOSE & THROAT CLINIC
W. J. SIMIC, M.D.   J. A. MARCEL, M.D.
905 HELENA AVENUE
HELENA, MONTANA 59801
442 2410

21 October 1981

SEE CHAPTER TWELVE

Mr. Lee Graham
526 W. Maple
Monrovia, CA 91016

Dear Mr. Graham:

Thank you for your inquiry regarding the most recent book that was published on flying saucers. I would be happy to answer your questions as I see fit.

In your first question, you ask, in my opinion, was the debris I saw portions of what was then known as a flying saucer. I can only answer that the crash and remnants of the device that I happened to be present to see have left an imprint on my memory that can never be forgotten. I am currently undergoing training as a Flight Surgeon in the Army Air National Guard, and have examined the remnants of many conventional aircraft that have undergone unfortunate maneuvers, and what I saw in 1947 is unlike any of the current aircraft ruinage I have studied. This craft was not conventional in any sense of the word, in that the remnants were most likely that what was then known as a flying saucer that apparently had been stressed beyond its designed capabilities. I'm basing this on the fact that many of the remnants, including the eye-beam pieces that were present, had strange hieroglyphic type writing symbols across the inner surfaces. It appeared to me at that time that the symbols were not derived from the Greek or the Russian alphabet, nor of Egyptian origin with their animal symbols. The remainder of the debris was just described as nondescript metallic debris, or just shredded fragments, but there was a fair amount of the intact eye-beam members present. No electronic gear was seen at that time. I only saw a small portion of the debris that was actually present at the crash site.

Your second question is, what is my opinion of Doctrine A. Doctrine A appears to be a very interesting reading, but without verification remains just that.

Question 3--Do you believe our government has crashed-saucer artifacts, and why do I feel that they are still withholding this evidence from the public. The answer

Mr. Lee Graham
21 October 1981
Page 2

is, I do know that the crash remnants of this one saucer
are maintained somewhere, most likely at Wright-Patterson
Air Force Base from what I understand, and if there is
one artifact present, there most likely are other devices
also. I can only guess as to why they are withholding
the evidence. My feeling is that they feel there really
is no hard evidence of any unconventional aircraft on
hand, and all of this is the product of fraud or overactive
imagination. I suspect the more likely explanation is
that the evidence is real and that they just don't want
the "horrible truth" leaked out, and are fearful of
worldwide pandemonium such as a localized scare produced
by the Orsan Welles broadcast of the Martian invasion
of the U. S. in the 1930's.

Question 4--Do I have the address where my father
can be located. Yes, I've talked with him about your
inquiry and he felt that he would be glad to talk with
you or discuss this with you if you have a scientific
interest in this. My parents live in Houma, Louisiana.
Their phone number is Area Code 504, 875-0993, and the
address is: Mr. and Mrs. Jesse A. Marcel, RFD 5, Box 330,
Ozia Street - Skyline Drive, Houma, Louisiana 70360.

Sincerely,

J. A. MARCEL, M.D.

JAM:jc

United States Court of Appeals
FOR THE DISTRICT OF COLUMBIA CIRCUIT

August 12, 1981
NOTICE TO COUNSEL

IN RE: Appeal No. 81-1042 - Citizens Against UFO Secrecy v. National Security Agency

The above referenced case has been scheduled for oral argument on:

Wednesday, October 28, 1981 at 2:00 P.M.

The Court will enter an order in due course which sets forth the amount of time to be allowed for oral argument. A copy of that order will, of course, be sent to all counsel of record. Should the Court determine that oral argument is not necessary an order to that effect will be entered on the docket and copies sent to counsel. See Local Rule 11(d), as amended August 31, 1979.

Your attention is directed to Rule 34, Federal Rules of Appellate Procedure, and Local Rule 12 regarding the number of counsel who may present argument and the apportionment of the time allotted. Consolidated cases are considered to be one case for the purpose of allotment of argument times.

Any motions for postponement of argument based upon facts presently known to counsel, should be submitted immediately on receipt of this notice. It should be noted, however, that the Court looks with disfavor on motions for continuance and no one should assume that any such motion will be granted.

NOT LESS THAN TWO (2) BUSINESS DAYS IN ADVANCE OF ARGUMENT, THIS OFFICE MUST BE INFORMED OF THE NAME OR NAMES OF COUNSEL WHO WILL PRESENT THE ARGUMENT. THE FORM PROVIDED BELOW IS FOR YOUR CONVENIENCE IN PROVIDING THIS INFORMATION.

COPIES OF THIS NOTICE SENT TO:

GEORGE A. FISHER, Clerk

By: Patricia Krosel
Deputy Clerk

Peter A. Gersten, Esquire
Rothblatt, Rothblatt & Saijas
191 East 161st Street
Bronx, New York 10451

Cheryl M. Long, Esquire
Charles F. C. Ruff, Esquire
Kenneth M. Raisler, Esquire
Royce C. Lamberth, Esquire
U.S. Attorney's Office
Washington, D.C. 20001

U.S. Court of Appeals gets ready to hear case brought against the government by Citizens Against UFO Secrecy. The groups request for the release of over 100 documents was denied by a U.S. District Judge on grounds of national security.

MEMORANDUM OPINION AND ORDER GRANTING MOTION
FOR SUMMARY JUDGMENT
IN THE UNITED STATES DISTRICT COURT

FOR THE DISTRICT OF COLUMBIA

CITIZENS AGAINST UFO SECRECY,)
     Plaintiff,)
)
     v.)   Civil Action No. 80-1562
)
NATIONAL SECURITY AGENCY,)
     Defendant.)

MEMORANDUM AND ORDER

This Freedom of Information Act case is before the Court on defendant's motion for summary judgment. Plaintiff is seeking all documents in defendant's possession relating to UFOs and UFO phenomena. Defendant has provided some material but has withheld other material pursuant to various FOIA exemptions, see 5 U.S.C. § 552(b) (1976). The bulk of the material withheld consists of communications intelligence reports, which defendant asserts are protected by Exemptions 1 and 3 of the Freedom of Information Act. Four documents at issue are not communications intelligence reports; defendant has withheld one of these documents in its entirety, and portions of three others, pursuant to these exemptions, and exemptions 5 and 6.

The Court first carefully reviewed the public affidavit of National Security Agency official Eugene Yeates and then, after receiving plaintiff's opposition, examined personally a top secret affidavit from Yeates, submitted by defendant in camera. The public affidavit provides a general statement of the defendant's position that is strongly bolstered by the extremely detailed, 21-page in camera filing. On the basis of these affidavits, the Court finds that the claimed exemptions have been properly and conscientiously applied.

The communications intelligence reports clearly relate to the most sensitive activities of the defendant and thus fall squarely within the protection of Public Law 86-36, 73 Stat. 63 (1959). The in camera affidavit provides the kind of detail approved in Hayden & Fonda v. National Security Agency, 608 F.2d 1381, 1339-91 (D.C. Cir. 1979), cert. denied, 48 U.S.L.W. 3730 (U.S., May 12, 1980). The Court finds that release of this material could seriously jeopardize the work of the agency and the security of the United States. Under the standards set forth in Hayden & Fonda, the claim of Section (b)(3) exemption must be granted in its entirety. No consideration needs to be given the additional claim for protection under Exemption 1. The standards of Public Law 86-36 have been met.

The Court also finds that the affidavits support nondisclosure for the four documents that are not intelligence reports. Defendant has provided plaintiff with much of the contents of these documents and also has provided a description of both the documents and the deletions. The various claims under Exemptions 1, 3, 5 and 6 as to these documents are proper. The withheld portions either are not responsive to plaintiff's request or are properly exempted.

Throughout the Court's review of this material, the Court has been aware of the public interest in the issue of UFOs and the need to balance that interest against the agency's need for secrecy. The in camera affidavit presents factual considerations which aided the Court in determining that the public interest in disclosure is far outweighed by the sensitive nature of the materials and the obvious effect on national security their release may well entail.

The Court has been mindful of the Court of Appeals' view on in camera review of documents in FOIA cases, see Allen v. CIA, No. 80-1380 (D.C. Cir., filed Nov. 12, 1980), but the Court finds in its discretion that the public and in camera affidavits submitted here are amply sufficient to make such review of the documents unnecessary.

For the foregoing reasons, defendant's motion for summary judgment is granted. The case is dismissed.

SO ORDERED.

November 18, 1980.   UNITED STATES DISTRICT JUDGE

```
01   01        PP PP      UUUU
NO

              OSAF UASH DC/OIP

              CINCNOPAD ENT AFB CO/OI

              CINCSAC OFFUTT AFB NE/OI

        INFO SECDEF UASH DC/RA

UNCLAS

SUBJ:  UNKNOWN AIR ACTIVITY

REF:   CINCNORAD CONF MSG 1121002 NOV 75

1.  WE BELIEVE, AND OASD/PA CONCURS, THAT UNLESS THERE IS EVIDENCE

WHICH LINKS SIGHTINGS OR UNLESS MEDIA QUERIES LINK SIGHTINGS, QUERIES

CAN BEST BE HANDLED INDIVIDUALLY AT THE SOURCE AND AS QUESTIONS

ARISE.  RESPONSES SHOULD BE DIRECT, FORTHRIGHT AND EMPHASIZE THAT THE

ACTION TAKEN WAS IN RESPONSE TO AN ISOLATED OR SPECIFIC INCIDENT.

IOS SHOULD KEEP ALL LEVELS AND APPROPRIATE MAJCOMS INFORMED OF

QUESTIONS ASKED, MEDIA AFFILIATIONS AND RESPONSES GIVEN.

2.  ON DEC 17, 1969, THE AIR FORCE ANNOUNCED TERMINATION OF PROJECT

BLUE BOOK, THE PROGRAM FOR THE INVESTIGATION OF UFOS.  SINCE THEN,

NO EVIDENCE HAS BEEN PRESENTED TO INDICATE FURTHER INVESTIGATION BY

THE AIR FORCE IS WARRANTED.  THERE ARE NO PLANS FOR RENEWED AIR FORCE

INVOLVEMENT IN UFO ...
```

While officially the government has always denied that it keeps secrets in regard to UFOs, the truth—as this document shows—is quite different in that the U.S. has long maintained classified files that are not open to either public or press.

CLASSIFIED

CASE ONE: Documents verifying the fact that alien corpses were found at the site of the Roswell crash. What used to be speculation is now proven by the newly discovered MJ - 12 material.

CASE TWO: Links between the Kennedy assassinations and a series of other murders intended to maintain UFO secrecy!

CASE THREE: A much longer list of scientists and consultants who worked with the legendary Majestic - 12 is provided, proving that the tentacles of the cover-up reached even further then was previously known!

CASE FOUR: The existance of a secret government organization called the Interplanetary Phenomenon Unit is brought out into the open, and admitted to by the Air Force!

CASE FIVE: According to the newly discovered documents, even the president doesn't know the whole story because he is made aware by MJ - 12 only on a "need-to-know" basis. What does our current president know? What has MJ - 12 opted to keep secret? And does the elder George Bush, as former head of the CIA, know much more than his son?

RESTRICTED

SOM 1-01

TO 12D1—3—11—1
MAJESTIC—12 GROUP SPECIAL OPERATIONS MANUAL

EXTRATERRESTRIAL

ENTITIES AND TECHNOLOGY,

RECOVERY AND DISPOSAL

TOP SECRET/MAJIC
EYES ONLY

WARNING! This is a TOP SECRET—MAJIC EYES ONLY document containing compartmentalized information essential to the national security of the United States. EYES ONLY ACCESS to the material herein is strictly limited to personnel possessing MAJIC—12 CLEARANCE LEVEL. Examination or use by unauthorized personnel is strictly forbidden and is punishable by federal law.

MAJESTIC—12 GROUP • APRIL 1954

TOP SECRET / MAJIC EYES ONLY

10. **Description of Extraterrestrial Biological Entities (EBEs)**
Examination of remains recovered from wreckage of UFOBs indicates that Extraterrestrial Biological Entities may be classified into two distinct categories as follows:

a. EBE Type I. These entities are humanoid and might be mistaken for human beings of the Oriental race if seen from a distance. They are bipedal, 5-5 feet 4 inches in height and weigh 80-100 pounds. Proportionally they are similar to humans, although the cranium is somewhat larger and more rounded. The skin is a pale, chalky-yellow in color, thick, and slightly pebbled in appearance. The eyes are small, wide-set, almond-shaped, with brownish-black irises with very large pupils. The whites of the eyes are not like that of humans, but have a pale gray cast. The ears are small and set low on the skull. The nose is thin and long, and the mouth is wider than in humans, and nearly lipless. There is no apparent facial hair and very little body hair, that being very fine and confined to the underarm and the groin areas. The body is thin and without apparent body fat, but the muscles are well developed. The hands are small, with four long digits but no opposable thumb. The outside digit is jointed in a manner as to be nearly opposable, and there is no webbing between the fingers as in humans. The legs are slightly but noticeably bowed, and the feet are somewhat splayed and proportionally large.

b. EBE Type II. These entities are humanoid but differ from Type I in many respects. They are bi-pedal, 3 feet 5 inches - 4 feet 2 inches in height and weigh 25-50 pounds. Proportionally, the head is much larger than humans or Type I EBEs, the cranium being much larger and elongated. The eyes are very large, slanted, and nearly wrap around the side of the skull. They are black with no whites showing. There is no noticeable brow ridge, and the skull has a slight peak that runs over the crown. The nose consists of two small slits which sit high above the slit-like mouth. There are no external ears. The skin is a pale bluish-gray color, being somewhat darker on the back of the creature, and is very smooth and fine-celled. There is no hair on either the face or the body, and these creatures do not appear to be mammalian. The arms are long in proportion to the legs, and the hands have three long, tapering fingers and a thumb which is nearly as long as the fingers. The second finger is thicker than the others, but not as long as the index finger. The feet are small and narrow, and four toes are joined together with a membrane.

It is not definitely known where either type of creature originates, but it seems certain that they did not evolve on earth. It is further evident, although not certain, that they may have originated on two different planets.

6

TOP SECRET / MAJIC EYES ONLY

TOP SECRET

ULTRA

INTERPLANETARY PHENOMENON UNIT SUMMARY

INTELLIGENCE ASSESSMENT File ref. 001947127-A.1206

1. The extraordinary recovery of fallen airborne objects in the state of New Mexico, between 4 July - 6 July 1947. This Summary was prepared by Headquarters Interplanetary Phenomenon Unit, Scientific and Technical Branch, Counterintelligence Directorate, as requested by A.C. of S., G-2, at the expressed order of Chief of Staff.

2. At 2332 MST, 3 July 47, radar staions in east Texas and White Sands Proving Ground, N.M., tracked two unidentified aircraft unitl both dropped off radar. Two crash sites have been located close to the WSPG. Site LZ-1 was located at a ranch near Corona, approx. 75 miles northwest of the town of Roswell. Site LZ-2 was located approx. 20 miles southeast of the town of Socorro, at Lat. 33-40-31 , Long. 106-28-29 , with Oscura Peak being the geographic reference point.

3. The AST personnel were mainly interested in LZ-2 as this site contained the majority of structural detail of the craft's airframe, propulsion and navigation technology. The recovery of five bodies in a damaged escape cylinder, precluded an investigation at LZ-1.

4. On arrival at LZ-2, personnel assessed the finds as not belonging to any aircraft, rocket, weapons, or balloon test that are normally conducted from surrounding bases. First reports indicated that the first crash investigators from Roswell AAF that LZ-1 was the remains of a AAF top secret MOGUL balloon project. When scientists

-2-

TOP SECRET

ULTRA

ULTRA

from the Los Alamos Scientific Laboratory arrived to inspect LZ-2, it became apparent to all concerned that what had crashed in the desert was something out of this world.

5.   Interviews with radar operators and officers from the Signal Corps Engineering Laboratories, Fort Monmouth, N.J., who were tracking these objects on-and-off since June 29 from Station "A", all indicated that these targets had periodically remained stationary for minutes at a time, then would resume thier original course, flying from the southeast to northwest. SCEL antennas had locked onto a flight of three objects on 3 July and lost them around 2330 MGT on 4 July (a V-2 was scheduled for launch which is why SCEL Station "A" was able to do a track). It has been learned that at least six radar stations in east Texas (see detailed report in attchment A), and radar stations at Alamogordo AAF and Kirtland AAF, had also picked up these objects on the 4th as well. Using topographical maps and triangularization, a last known position and bearing was calculated which helped search parties to locate the general area. Detachment 3 of the 9393rd Technical Services Unit, assigned to Alamogordo AAF, was responsible for the locating and transportation of the large sections of the craft.

6.   A special radiobiological team accompanied by a SED and security detail from Sandia Base under orders from Colonel S. 7. /HASBROUCK/ USA, Armed Forces Special Weapons Project, secured the immediate area surrounding the crash site. Select scientists from

-3-

TOP SECRET

ULTRA

ULTRA

/JOHN F. KENNEDI,/Massachusetts Democrat elected to Congress in 46. Son of
JOSEPH P. KENNEDI, Commission on Organization of the Executive Branch of
the Goverment. KENNEDI had limited duty as naval officer assigned to
Naval Intelligence during war. It is believed that information was obtained
from source in Congress who is close to Secretary for Air Force.

11.   As to the bodies recovered at LZ-2, it appeared that none
of the five crew members survived entry into our atmosphere due to
unknown causes./DR. DETLEV BRONK/has been asked to assist in the autopsy
of one well preserved cadaver to be done by MAJOR CHARLES B. REA. From
what descriptions the team was able to learn and from photographs taken
by intelligence photographers, the occupants appear in most respects
human with/some anatomical differences/in the head, eyes, hands and feet.
They have a slight build about five feet tall, with grayish-pink skin
color. They have no hair on their bodies and clothed with a tight fitting
flight suit that appears to be fire proof (some of the bodies looked
as if they had been burned on head and and hands). Their overall stature
reminds one of/young children./It is believed that there were male and
female genders present, but was hard to distinguish.

12.   The most disturbing aspect of this investigation was—
there were other bodies found not far from LZ-1 that looked as if they
had been disected as you would a frog. It is not known if army field
surgens had performed exploratory surgery on these bodies. Animal parts
were reportedly discovered inside the craft at LZ-2 but this cannot be
confirmed. The team has reserved judgement on this issue.

13.   Our assessment of this investigation rests on two
assumptions: 1) Either this discovery was an elaborate and well orchestrated
hoax (maybe by the Russians), or; 2) Our country has played host to

-6-

TOP SECRET

MAJIC

MAJESTIC TWELVE PROJECT

Director
Dep. Director
Adm. Officer
Proc. & Control
Records & Pub.
__. Asst.
Visual
Statistical
Corris_____
Copies _____
Filed _____

1st Annual Report

A-1762.1-J1

A REVIEW OF THE PRESIDENT'S SPECIAL PANEL TO INVESTIGATE THE CAPTURE OF
UNIDENTIFIED PLANFORM SPACE VEHICLES BY U.S. ARMED FORCES AND AGENCIES

PANEL

CHAIRMAN, Dr. Vannevar Bush, 4901 Hillbrook Lane (Phone, REpublic 6700, branch 5484)

General J. Lawton Collins, Deputy Chief of Staff, United States Army
Major General Luther D. Miller, Chief of Chaplains, United States Army
General Hoyt S. Vandenberg, Vice Chief of Staff, United States Air Force
Lt. General Lewis H. Brereton Chairman, Military Liaison Cmt, AEC
Maj. General George C. McDonald, Director of Intelligence, United States Air Force
Brigadier General George F. Schulgen, Director, Plans and Policies, United States Air Force
Rear Admiral Paul F. Lee, Chief, Office of Naval Research, United States Navy
Admiral John Gingrich, Director, Security and Intelligence, AEC
Dr. J. Robert Oppenheimer, Chairman, General Advisory Committee, AEC
Jerome C. Hunsaker, MIT, National Academy of Sciences
Detlev W. Bronk, Chairman, National Research Council
Dr. Hugh L. Dryden, Director of Aeronautical Research, NACA
Dr. James H. Doolittle, Shell Oil

FOR
INCLUSION

TOP SECRET Central Intelligence Agency Information Report CIA/31 28-53
entitled: A DIGEST OF WORLD WIDE UNIDENTIFIED FLYING OBJECT INTELLIGENCE
MATERIAL AS CONTAINED IN THE ARMED FORCES SECURITY AGENCY SIGNALS, RADAR,
COMMUNICATIONS, AND HUMAN INTELLIGENCE OPERATIONS IN THE FIRST FIVE YEARS

Approved for use
Date _____

Note: This report has been coordinated with the Joint Intelligence
Committee, the Air Technical Intelligence Center,
and the Intelligence Advisory Committee

WARNING: This document contains sensitive intelligence information
affecting the national defense of the United States, within
the meaning of Title 18, Sections 793 and 794, of the U. S.
Code, as amended. Its transmission or revelation of its
contents to or receipt by unauthorized person is prohibited.

RECEIVED

III. CONCLUSIONS

1.   Current studies of other-world visitation are in three
phases:

    a.   Technology exploitation

    b.   Interplanetary travel

    c.   Cultural communication

2.   On 19 September 1947, the IAC, JIOA, and the JIC, reviewed
a Top Secret intelligence report titled REPORT TO THE PRESIDENT, 1947, PARTS
1-7, MAJIC EYES ONLY, DTG 000190947,   the report mentions: "In compliance
with your directive . . . of 9 July 1947, the attached "REPORT ON FLYING
SAUCERS" is respectfully submitted.   In consonance with your instructions,
advisors from State, Treasury, War and Navy Departments assisted me on a
two month exploratory mission concerning the reality of other-world visitation.
The principle investigators and storage areas were visited.   Successful efforts
were made to reach scientists of all levels as measured by their work in
classified defense projects.   Conferences were held with national security
officials and leaders of private industry.   Approximately 2,200 memoranda and
intelligence reports were considered.   The report presents this situation
against a global background my estimates, current and projected, in both the
U.S., and allied countries, and recommendations deemed to be sound courses of
action for formulating plans and policies in light of recent developments.

3.   All efforts have been made to identify the country or private
concern which could have the technical and financial resources necessary to
produce such a long-range flight. So far, no country on this earth has the
means and the security of its resources to produce such.

4.   A consensus reached by members of the panel, that until
positive proof that the Russians did not attempt a series of reconnaissance
flights over our most secure installations—the sightings and recovered
objects are interpalnatary in nature.

5.   The occupants of these planform vehicles are, in most
respects, human or human-like. Autopsies, so far indicate, that these beings
share the same biological needs as humans.

-2-

[handwritten notes] ... written in 1954 ...

TOP SECRET/MAJIC

CHAPTER XIV

The Other Side of the Coin

Now, let's turn the coin over and take a good, long look at its other side.

We have seen that there is considerable evidence to indicate that flying saucers are from outer space. Although no, one to date, so far as is known, has publicly exhibited a saucer, fragments of a saucer, or a "little man from Mars," the evidence still exists . It cannot be frowned down by a long state. And, although no one has yet collected the $100,000.00 reward offered by The Saturday Review of Literature, or the 10 million francs ($28,000) offered by an inhabitant of Leoronan, France, or the equally inviting offer by the French government for a "man from Mars," this does not disprove the theory of space visitors.

In addition to evidence that saucers are extraterrestrial, there is also a great deal of evidence to show that they are perfectly natural aerial phenomena, explainable by astronomers, meteorologists and physicists in terms of known objects, reflections, air lenses, etc.

There is also plenty of evidence to indicate that saucers are Air Force balloons, night photography flares, canopy reflections and other well-known objects or mirages.

Furthermore , there is evidence to show that there might be a certain amount of literary charlatanism, if not downright fraud, in the saucer **TOP SECRET/MAJIC** that the whole saucer "scare" is a hoax seems the most remote possibility of all.

TOP SECRET/MAJIC

Now, what evidence is there to show that, incredible though it may be, that saucers are actually none of these things—but new, secret, and utterly fantastic guided or piloted missiles or craft that are made right here on earth?

There is considerable evidence to support this belief.

And perhaps this is really the one and the only correct explanation of flying saucers. Perhaps Henry J. Taylor, Billy Rose, ands some other commentators were right when they said, quite early in the game, that flying saucers are secret weapons. The only trouble was, they said they were U.S. weapons. Such may not have been the case at all. But certainly, the Taylor "expose" was the one thing that drew instant, emphatic and universal denial by every branch of the armed services, with even a spokesman for the President considering it important enough to issue a White House denial. There has been no such overwhelming denial of the extraterrestrial theory—there has even been semi-encouragement of this theory all along by the Air Force— although on one occasion a press conference was held following Major Keyhoe's article in TRUE that claimed saucers were from outer space, and there was another denial when President Eisenhower said, in late 1954, that he had been told that saucers were not from outer space.

But, when it was said that saucers were U.S. secret warcraft, there was instant, overwhelming denial.

Yet there is evidence that saucers may be a new and different type of earth craft.

This evidence is not secret. It has been published to millions of people in newspapers and magazines. This writer has had no access to classified information of any kind. There is absolutely nothing here that

TOP SECRET/MAJIC

0020132

18.   The following elements were analyzed and found to exist in the small neutronic power plant that was found inside ULAT-1:

    a.   UF6 in metallic form;

    b.   hydrogen-fluoride gas;

    c.   water and uranium tetrafluoride;

    d.   powdered magnesium and potassium chlorate;

    e.   metal similar to lead with a chocolate brown color;

    f.   U-235 in metallic form;

    g.   plastic-like material similar to NE 102;

    h.   Beryllium;

    i.   pure aluminium;

    h.   Thorium isotope material;

    j.   Plutonium powder.

19.   Scientists from Los Alamos and Sandia Base were alarmed that the power plant could possibly function as a bomb if the elements described above were processed in similar fashion as was done for the lens and shotgun detonators. This originally was the first conclusion. After further evaluation, it was determined that since no recognizable firing circuits were identified, the threat of detonation did not exist.

20.   The only evidence of circuitry found on the meter was thin plastic-like sheets fashioned like platters encased on the exterior of the spherically-shaped casing seated by a thin film of pure silver. Under high power magnification it was observed a series of fine grid-like lines intersecting groups of dots arranged in circular patterns.

5

TOP SECRET/MJ

DRAFT

Directive Regarding President's EYES ONLY

In the likely event that the subject of unidentified flying objects or unconventional aerial weapons is a subject matter under discussion with the Chief Executive, National Security Council Staff, department heads, the Joint Chiefs, and foreign representatives, a clarification of the question is in order to ascertain the reason(s) for bringing up the subject. A standard response should suffice to redirect the question. Under no circumstances should a member suggest or by inference, that the subject is classified as a national security threat. In the unlikely event that UFO's overtly display hostile intent towards the security of the United States, as a group, and after consultation, should a full disclosure be made in accordance with the law as required.

TOP SECRET/MJ-12

TOP SECRET   NOT FOR PUBLICATION

COUNTRY N.Y. New York, US   REPORT NO. ▆▆▆▆▆

SUBJECT Marilyn Monroe   DATE DIST. 3 August 1962

                                               NO PAGES ▆▆

                                               REFERENCES MOON DUST Project ▆▆

3 August 1962   64

1. Rothberg discussed the apparent suicide of subject with Kilgallen and the break up with the Kennedys. Rothberg told Kilgallen that she was attending Hollywood parties hosted by the "inner circle" among Hollywood's elite and was becoming the talk of the town again. Rothberg indicated in so many words, that she had secrets to tell, no doubt arising from her trists with the President and the Attorney General. One such "secret" mentions the visit by the President at a secret air base for the purpose of inspecting things from outer space. Kilgallen replied that she knew what might be the source of visit. In the mid-fifties Kilgallen learned of secret effort by US and UK governments to identify the origins of crashed spacecraft and dead bodies, from a British government official. Kilgallen believed the story may have come from the New York journal in the late forties. Kilgallen said that if the story is true, it would cause terrible embarrassment for Jack and his plans to have NASA put men on the Moon.

2. Subject repeatedly called the Attorney General and complained about the way she was being ignored by the President and his brother.

3. Subject threatened to hold a press conference and would tell all.

4. Subject made reference to "bases" in Cuba and knew of the President's plan to kill Castro.

5. Subject made reference to her "diary of secrets" and what the newspapers would do with such disclosures.

TOP SECRET

TOP SECRET

EYES ONLY

THE WHITE HOUSE

WASHINGTON

September 24, 1947.

MEMORANDUM FOR THE SECRETARY OF DEFENSE

Dear Secretary Forrestal:

As per our recent conversation on this matter, you are hereby authorized to proceed with all due speed and caution upon your undertaking. Hereafter this matter shall be referred to only as Operation Majestic Twelve.

It continues to be my feeling that any future considerations relative to the ultimate disposition of this matter should rest solely with the Office of the President following appropriate discussions with yourself, Dr. Bush and the Director of Central Intelligence.

Majestic 12 Members

Top Row, L to R... Dr. Lloyd Berkner, Dr. D. W. Bronk, Dr. Vannevar Bush, Sec. James Forrestal
Middle Row L to R... Gordon Gray, Admiral Roscoe Hillenkoetter, Dr. Jerome Hunsaker, Dr. Donald H. Menzel
Bottom Row L to R... General Robert Montague, Sidney Souers, General Nathan Twining, General Hoyt Vandenburg

THE MAJESTIC DOCUMENTS

Evidence That We Are Not Alone

MISSION STATEMENT

The team's mission is to clarify the UFO phenomenon, its agenda and history, and to implement the most effective way to educate the public and world governments to its reality and implications.

Our overall goals are to:

- Aggressively collect data and draw conclusions.
- Create an environment conducive to public disclosure of information withheld by all inside sources.
- Educate and present findings and conclusions to the public.
- Establish a dialogue with the broader community including religions, governments, and political parties.
- Improve the information exchange and effectiveness of Ufology and increase participation in the subject.

This website is dedicated to the MAJESTIC documents and their related codewords such as MAJIC or MJ-12. The plan is to build a strong information base that focuses on the authenticity of these and new documents. Specifically, we plan to:

- Share detailed supporting rationale for authenticity and strong linkage with known historical facts.
- Expand the database of credible witnesses and hard proof to the UFO/ET phenomenon.
- Potentially restate the history of the United States and the World, not ignoring the role of psychological warfare deceptions
- Pay special attention to the technological implications of the documents and their potential "reverse engineering" clues to our modern science and benefiting corporations.
- Offer intellectual products for sale to pay for the ongoing research team expenses.

Our hope is that over the next five years, the UFO community or other visionaries will succeed in bringing forth overwhelming proof of the UFO/ET reality with particular attention paid to recovered alien technology which will help solve planet Earth's problems of pollution, energy, population, and intolerance, and point towards unlimited energy and economical interstellar travel.

Dr. Robert M. and Ryan S. Wood

Introduction to the Majestic Documents

WE NEED YOUR HELP

Submit Evidence – At the core of our ongoing success is building a bigger portfolio of witnesses and unique documentary evidence. If you have relevant documents or testimony and you believe that sharing this information is not in violation of the law, please forward the information to:

14004 Quail Ridge Rd.
Broomfield, CO 80020

For more information go to
www.MajesticDocuments.com

0020141

9 JUL 47

TOP SECRET

EYES ONLY

DIRECTIVE TO LIEUTENANT GENERAL TWINING

You will proceed to the White Sands Proving Ground Command Center without delay for the purpose of making an appraisal of the reported unidentified objects being kept there. Part of your mission there will deal with the military, political and psychological situations —current and projected. In the course of your survey you will maintain liaison with the military officials in the area.

In making your appraisal it is desired that you proceed with detachment from any opinions or feelings expressed by personnel involved which do not conform to sound reasoning with regard to the possible outcome. In presenting the findings of your mission you should endeavor to state as concisely as possible your estimate of the character, extent, and probable consequences in the event that assistance is not given.

When your mission in New Mexico is completed you will proceed on a brief trip to the Sandia AEC facility to make an appraisal of the situation there, also of the reaction by the Los Alamos people involved. Before going to White Sands you will communicate with General Eisenhower to ascertain whether he desires you to proceed via Kirtland A&F.

You will take with you such experts, technicians, scientists and assistants as you deem necessary to the effectiveness of your mission.

Approved

Harry Truman

July 9, 1947

TOP SECRET

EYES ONLY

221

222

225

229

231

232

234

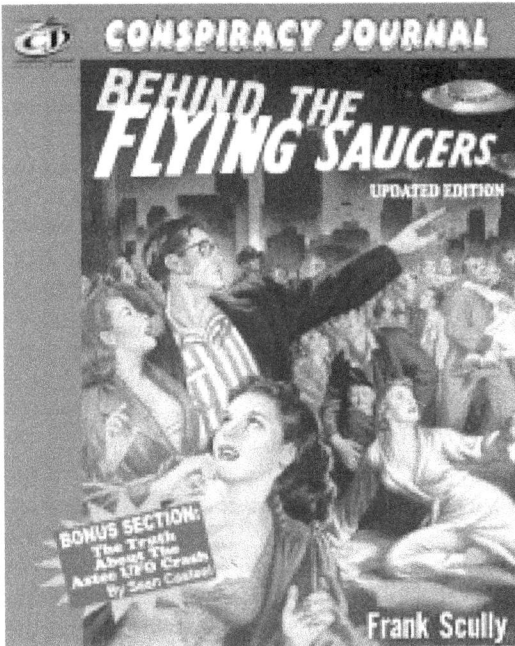

In what some researchers are considering a "shocking revelation," the FBI recently posted on their web site documents pertaining to the supposed crash landing of three UFOs in the state of New Mexico.

In this intriguing memo, dated 22 March 1950, special agent Guy Hottel, head of the FBI's Washington field office, told agency director J. Edgar Hoover, " that an Air Force investigator stated that three flying saucers had been recovered along with the bodies of the alien crews." The memo goes on: "Each one was occupied by three bodies of human shape but only three feet tall, dressed in metallic cloth of a very fine texture. Each body was bandaged in a manner similar to the blackout suits used by speed flyers and test pilots." According to the witness, the saucers were brought down by a "high-powered government radar" in the area that interfered with the spaceships' controls. "No further evaluation was attempted," the briefing to Hoover concluded.

FBI Agent Hottel seems to be making reference NOT to the UFO crash at Roswell, but to an alternative crash outside the small, sleepy, town of Aztec, NM, details of which were first presented in a book in the early 1950s by journalist Frank Scully. For many decades rumors of such a crash — as described in minute detail in *BEHIND THE FLYING SAUCERS*— were believed to be a hoax. But with the added weight of modern day "UFO forensics" conducted by researchers Scott Ramsey, Art Campbell and others, as well as the apparent "backing" of the FBI memo, there is new evidence that an even grander cover-up was carried out in this instance, more so than in the episode of the crash retrieval at Roswell.

THE TRUTH ABOUT THE UFO CRASH AT AZTEC
REEXAMINATION OF AN HISTORIC SPACE SHIP RETRIEVAL

The questions about Aztec are many. . .

Were sixteen alien bodies recovered from a dome-shaped device that "fell from the sky" circa 1948? Why does the FBI continue to withhold 200 pages of classified material on the case for alleged "national security reasons?" Was the incident covered up with a comouflaged "front story" presided over by con men and scam artists, who were thought by some to be in the government's pay? Did President Eisenhower make contact with aliens around the same time, thus adding weight to this and other UFO crash cases? Is there a connection between the mysterious deaths of Marilyn Monroe and journalist Dorothy Killgalen and the possible UFO crash at Aztec which Scully popularized, but the details of which has been cleverly re crafted to make it seem like a hoax?

On February 15, 1954, Killgalen commented in her syndicated column, "Flying saucers are regarded as of such vital importance that they will be the subject of a special hush-hush meeting of the world military heads next summer."

In a May 22, 1955 report from London, syndicated by the *International News Service*, Kilgallen further stated, "British scientists and airmen, after examining the wreckage of one mysterious flying ship, are convinced these strange aerial objects are not optical illusions or Soviet inventions, but are flying saucers which originate on another planet. The source of my information is a British official of Cabinet rank who prefers to remain unidentified. 'We believe, on the basis of our inquiry thus far, that the saucers were staffed by small men—probably under four feet tall. It's frightening, but there is no denying the flying saucers come from another planet.'" This article, which was separate from Kilgallen's daily gossip column, appeared on the front pages of the *New York Journal American* and the *Washington Post*.

See Next Page >

<*Continued From Previous Page*

ORDER *BEHIND THE FLYING SAUCERS* NOW AND GET A BONUS DVD

The Conspiracy Journal's Tim Beckley is very proud to offer an expanded edition of perhaps the most seminal book in the history of the unexplained, a book that is exceedingly rare, but now available again with material just added before press time to make it even MORE IMPORTANT than when originally penned by Variety columnist Frank Scully. Yes! For years the Aztec case was spurned by serious researchers due to lack of documentation. In addition to reprinting the entire, unabridged, text by Scully, *Conspiracy Journal* staffer Sean Castel has assisted in digging deep to provide the reader with an updated account of what really transpired outside this desert town near the Four Corners. His up to date research on the Aztec crash is presented through interviews with those IN THE KNOW despite possible threats of death!

Be among those who order *BEHIND THE FLYING SAUCERS: THE TRUTH ABOUT THE AZTEC UFO CRASH* and receive a BONUS DVD containing a professor's claims of first hand knowledge of the examination of alien bodies as well as the crash site.

It is ultimately up to the reader to interpretate what really transpired. Was it a valid UFO crash, or a cover story for some sinister military operation from which the government was trying to misdirect our attention?

SPECIAL TO OUR READERS ONLY: Behind The Flying Saucers: UFO Aztec Update and DVD BONUS for just **$24.00 + $5.00 S/H**

Order From:
Timothy G. Beckley
Box 753
New Brunswick, NJ
08903

OVER 900 PAGES OF SUPPRESSED BIBLICAL HISTORY FROM THE ORIGINS OF HUMANKIND TO THE LAST JUDGEMENT!

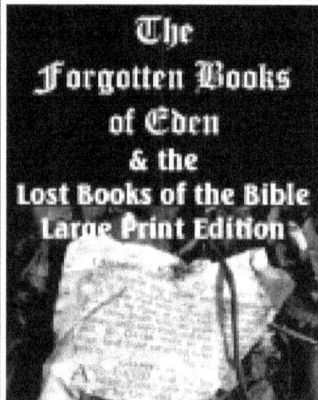

THE FORGOTTEN BOOKS OF EDEN
THE LOST BOOKS OF THE BIBLE—Large Print Edition
Suppressed By The Church ... But Now Fully Revealed
The Uncensored Truth About The Origins of Humankind And The Ageless Conflict Between Good And Evil

Here is the story of Adam and Eve which is the most ancient in the world; a story that has survived because it embodies the fight between man and the Devil. Adapted from the work of unknown Egyptians parts of this version are found in the Talmud, the Koran, and elsewhere, showing the vital role it played in the original literature of human wisdom. This adaptation has been passed down and was first written in Arabic and then translated into Ethiopic. It is a detailed history of Adam and Eve and their descendents found nowhere else and how the "Family Tree" ties all of the Old Testament together.

This large print edition also includes 26 Apocryphal books from the first 400 years of Christianity that were not included in the Testaments. The question remains: Why were these divinely inspired works kept out of the Bible by the church? You will find the answers within these pages.

We have combined **THE LOST BOOKS OF THE BIBLE** with another forbidden work known as **THE FORGOTTEN BOOKS OF EDEN** which includes the true story of Adam and Eve's conflict with Satan, as well as the Psalms of Solomon, the Testaments of the Twelve Patriarchs and the Secrets of Eden.

Order your copy of **FORGOTTEN BOOKS OF EDEN/LOST BOOKS OF THE BIBLE** now for just **$39.95 + $5.00 S/H.**

THE FORBIDDEN BOOKS OF THE NEW TESTAMENT

THE MATERIAL IN THE FORBIDDEN BOOKS OF THE NEW TESTAMENT HAS BEEN TRANSLATED FROM ITS ORIGINAL TONGUES BY THE WORLD'S GREATEST SCHOLARS, THE TASK TAKING WELL OVER 100 YEARS

There have been many facts about the life and times of Jesus which have not been included in the New Testament. The documents contained in this large size—8.5x11—450 page edition, were written soon after Christ's crucifixion during the early spread of Christianity, but before the church was able to censor some of the documents for a variety of reasons. Now after over 1500 years of suppression, the shroud of secrecy has been lifted and sincere students of the Bible will be able to read these original chapters and verses, and decide for themselves their authority.

The Birth of Christ — The Early Life of Mary — The Birth of John—The Virgin Birth — The Baptism of Jesus in the Jordan— Christ Praying In The Garden—Peter Cutting Off the Ear of Mulches—The Kiss of Judas — Christ on the Cross—The Resurrection of our Lord — Jesus Ascending to Heaven—The Red Sea Swallowing Up the Army of Pharaoh—Christ's Descent Into Hell — The Last Judgment.

450+ pages 8.5x11 Format Large print Edition — $39.95 + $5.00 S/H
978-1-60611-028-7 · 1-60611-027-6

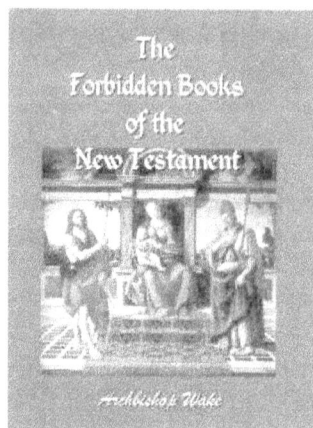

Timothy Beckley · Box 753 · New Brunswick, NJ 0890
Credit Card Customers Call 732 602-3407
PayPal MRUFO8@hotmail.com
Please refer to the order form inside the back cover of this isue for detailed ordering and shipping information. NJ residents add sales tax.

TWO HUGE BOOKS. BUY THEM AS A SET FOR $62.00 + $8.00 S/H OR PURCHASE THEM INDIVIDUALLY

AND THE TRUTH SHALL SET YOU FREE!

Our books, products and services are for experimental purposes. They are not endorsed by the AMA, FDA or any other federal or local agency. We offer our merchandise on a non-returnable basis to those who seek the truth about matters neglected by the "Establishment." We appreciate your patronage and hope you will tell all your like-minded friends about our publications.
—Timothy G. Beckley

www.conspiracyjournal.com/
www.teslasecretlab.com

www.ingramcontent.com/pod-product-compliance
Lightning Source LLC
Chambersburg PA
CBHW080458110426
42742CB00017B/2933